1992

Business to Business Direct Marketing

Proven Direct Response Methods to Generate More Leads and Sales

BUSINESS TO BUSINESS DIRECT MARKETING

Proven Direct Response Methods
to Generate More Leads
and Sales

Robert W. Bly

NTC Business Books
a division of *NTC Publishing Group*

Library of Congress Cataloging-in-Publication Data

Bly, Robert W.
     Business-to-business direct marketing: proven direct
response methods to generate more leads and sales /
Robert W. Bly.
       p. cm.
   ISBN 0-8442-3472-9
   1. Industrial marketing.   I. Title.
   HF5415. 1263.B58   1992
   658.8'4—dc20   91–44519
                                       CIP

Published by NTC Business Books, a division of NTC Publishing Group,
4255 West Touhy Avenue, Lincolnwood (Chicago), Illinois 60646-1975, U.S.A.
© 1993 by NTC Publishing Group. All rights reserved. No part of this book may
be reproduced, stored in a retrieval system, or transmitted in any form or by
any means, electronic, mechanical, photocopying, recording or otherwise,
without the prior permission of NTC Publishing Group.
Manufactured in the United States of America.

2 3 4 5 6 7 8 9 BC 9 8 7 6 5 4 3 2 1

This book is dedicated to everyone who
markets products and services to business and industry,
and not to consumers.

We are second-class citizens no longer.

Contents

Part Two
Business-to-Business Direct Marketing Tasks

Foreword

If you sell to business, industry, or professionals, I believe you can boost sales 20 percent, 50 percent, 100 percent or more by applying what this book teaches in the first two chapters alone!

And that's whether you're a small business owner, agency copywriter, advertising director for a large manufacturer, or head of marketing for an industrial distributorship like myself.

Written by a highly successful independent business-to-business copywriter and consultant, whose clients include prestigious banks, manufacturers, service companies, and computer software firms, this book is filled with practical how-to advice, samples, and helpful checklists on direct mail, catalogs, card decks, press releases, presentations, feature articles, and more.

Bob Bly begins by contrasting the radical differences between consumer and business-to-business direct marketing and describing how to make the latter most effective. You'd consult dozens of books and experts to amass his *hundreds* of easy to apply, time-tested tips. Like the ideal mailing size for testing, when and when not to emphasize features and benefits equally, approximate response rates to expect from "hard" and "soft" offers, ways of appealing to multiple target audiences in one piece, and clever ways of ending each page of a sales letter to "force" the reader to the next.

Bob's main premise is that every marketing communication you use or create should be direct response oriented. General advertising alone, with its emphasis on building image and creating awareness (although both worthy goals), isn't effective in generating immediate response and therefore wastes money.

And when you think about it, how often have you been moved to buy a product, service, or even stock in a company after reading a full page advertisement touting its number of years in business, annual sales, or state-of-the-art pollution control facility in Nepal? Ah! But when dove-tailed with proven direct response techniques, asserts Bob, general advertising becomes a powerful synergistic medium.

The techniques include using benefit-oriented headlines; appealing to the reader's self interest; addressing anticipated objections; writing in an informal style; targeting your audience; and using toll-free telephone numbers, free booklet offers, coupons, and business reply cards. Bob explains them all in detail.

"I'm already familiar with some of those techniques," you say. Perhaps, but Bob's explanation is rich in example and packed with alternative approaches you may not know. And as he does throughout the book, Bob includes advice from other business-to-business direct response experts to support and supplement his own.

Plus, he shows you how to successfully apply direct response techniques to marketing communications that traditionally haven't used them.

You'll learn how to intrigue editors with irresistible press releases. How to reap thousands of dollars worth of free advertising using feature articles. How to elicit inquiries from speeches, seminars, even simple presentations. How to turn mundane sales brochures into potent response-grabbing magnets. And much more.

Business-to-Business Direct Marketing is an enjoyable, concisely written guide by an experienced practitioner. You can read this book chapter by chapter or skip around without losing the flavor. Whatever, you'll come to trust its advice and consult it often.

What makes me so certain?

In the mid '80s after reading a glowing review of Bob Bly's *The Copywriter's Handbook* in *Business Marketing* magazine, I bought it. As a newcomer to business-to-business copywriting, it gave me the clear guidance and practical advice I was seeking.

In 1986 I received a catalog from New York University listing Bob Bly's business-to-business copywriting course (which he no longer teaches). I was so impressed with his book that I signed up for his course, although it meant traveling six hours by bus to New York and back one day a week for 13 weeks.

I learned more from the course than any other I had taken in both undergraduate and graduate studies. In person, he's as dynamic and straightforward as he is in print.

Since then I've continued my association with Bob and have learned loads more about business-to-business direct marketing.

You will, too, by buying this book.

Tony Peterson
Vice President of Marketing
Atlantic Fasteners
West Springfield, MA

Preface

There are dozens of books on direct marketing, direct mail, and direct response advertising. But *Business-to-Business Direct Marketing* is unique: It is the only book that tells *business-to-business* marketers—industrial firms, high-tech manufacturers, service companies, and others who sell to business and industry rather than consumers—how to apply proven direct marketing methods to get better results from *all* their marketing communications, including ads, mailings, brochures, and public relations.

The days when entrepreneurs and executives were content with advertising and PR programs that "built image" or "created awareness" are over. In the 1990s and beyond, clients in the advertising business, whether they own their own firms, work for a medium-size company, or handle marketing for divisions of large corporations, demand a tangible result from their advertising—a qualified, measurable, direct response that can be converted into sales. In short, the kind of response that only direct marketing, not general advertising, can produce.

Business-to-Business Direct Marketing is based on two simple but powerful premises. First, that *every* marketing document or activity, and not just ads or direct mail, should be a direct marketing vehicle that "asks for the order" or at least for some immediate, tangible response (and does not merely "communicate a message").

The second premise is that, while there are some similarities, many of the techniques and strategies of business-to-business marketing are fundamentally *different* from consumer marketing—hence, the need for a book that speaks directly to the special needs of the business-to-business marketer.

This book presents a collection of simple but highly effective marketing techniques you can use to immediately achieve a dramatic increase in the response rates of your current marketing communications programs.

I know they work, because I've used every one of them for my own businesses or those of my clients.

If you think there are certain facets of business-to-business direct marketing I've left out of *Business-to-Business Direct Marketing,* you're right. The book is by no means intended as a comprehensive encyclopedia covering all aspects of business-to-business direct marketing.

Rather, I cover only the things I do well and know to be effective through repeated testing. For me to write about anything else would be giving you theory. And you don't want theory; you want ideas, strategies, and techniques that work—and that *don't* cost you a fortune to implement. Well, here they are.

Remember, no single practitioner in this field can do *everything* well or use every technique ever invented; as a result, every practitioner has developed his or her own "bag of tricks." In this book, you get mine.

A word about the audience: This book is for you if you are a business-to-business marketer, period, regardless of whether direct marketing is a primary marketing communications tool for you, a secondary marketing communications tool, or just something you've become interested in and want to know more about.

If you're like most people reading this book, you probably work for a business-to-business, high-tech, or industrial firm and are looking to use direct marketing techniques to generate sales leads and inquiries.

You don't consider yourself in the "mail order" business, as traditional direct marketers do. Rather, you see direct marketing as an increasingly cost-effective, result-getting supplement or alternative to conventional "image" and "awareness" communications methods.

As consultant Donald Libey writes in his special report, *The Rebirth of Direct Marketing,* "Today's relevant direct marketing organization is not a direct marketing company in the classic sense of the term; rather, it is an organization that *employs* direct marketing techniques as a part of its totality of multiple-channel sales and marketing."

Some of you, however, *are* "mail-order marketers" in that you sell products *directly* to the business or professional buyer from your mailings, catalogs, ads, or other promotions. I've designed the book to include a wealth of response-boosting tips and techniques directly applicable to your needs, as well.

I do have one favor to ask. If you've developed a business-to-business marketing technique or strategy that's especially effective, or recently created an ad or mailing that was a real winner, please send it to me so I can share it with readers of the next edition of this book. You will receive full credit, of course. Write or call:

Bob Bly
22 E. Quackenbush Avenue
Dumont, NJ 07628
(201) 385-1220

Acknowledgments

I'm indebted to Donald Libey, Dr. Jeffrey Lant, Dr. Andrew Linick, Ed McLean, Milt Pierce, Dave Kanegis, Ken Morris, Steve Roberts, Wayne Roberts, Lee Roman, Bob Jurick, Steve Isaac, Sig Rosenblum, David Yale, Jerry Buchanan, Ed Werz, Joan Harris, Mitch Hisiger, Don Hauptman, Howard Shenson, Herman Holtz, Jeff Davidson, Pete Silver, Ray Jutkins, Herschell Gordon Lewis, Dan Kennedy, Dottie Walters, Russ von Hoelscher, Mark Nolan, Robert Serling, Galen Stilson, Mike Pavlish, Richard Armstrong, Joe Barnes, and the other authorities on direct marketing mentioned throughout this book. I'm proud to call most of them friends as well as colleagues, and their earlier efforts pointed the way.

Thanks also to my clients, some of the smartest businesspeople and savviest marketers I've ever met. Working with them has given me a priceless education on how to promote and sell business-to-business products and services more effectively.

There are many other people I've come in contact with over the years who have helped me refine the tested marketing methods presented in this book. I won't name them all here. But they know who they are. Thanks, folks!

Thanks also to Anne Knudsen and Karen Shaw, my editors at NTC, for having faith in me and in this book.

And of course, the greatest thanks to my wife, Amy Sprecher Bly, my total partner in everything and the love of my life.

Part One

Fundamentals of Effective Business-to-Business Direct Marketing

1

Is Business-to-Business Really Different from Consumer Marketing?

This book is written solely for the business-to-business marketer—the company, agency, or individual who markets products and services to business, professionals, and industry rather than to consumers. The obvious first question that arises when discussing business-to-business marketing is, "Is business-to-business really different from consumer marketing, or are they pretty much the same?"

If they are different, then it makes sense for you to seek out books, seminars, conferences, periodicals, consulting services, ad agencies, and other information resources that specifically deal with business-to-business as opposed to consumer marketing. On the other hand, if they're pretty much the same, you don't need specialized information, specialized consultants, specialized ad agencies, specialized seminars, specialized books, or any other resources specializing in business-to-business marketing.

If there are no significant differences between consumer and business marketing, you should be able to read books and articles on consumer marketing, then apply what they teach you to solving business-to-business marketing problems. And a consumer ad agency or copywriter should be able to do just as good a job on your business-to-business ad campaign as an agency or writer specializing in business-to-business.

Before we deal with this issue, however, we must first define precisely what we mean by *business-to-business, consumer, direct marketing,* and so on.

A short glossary of marketing terms

Advertising refers to promotional messages that are paid for by a sponsor (the advertiser) and carried in print or broadcast media. These include newspaper ads, magazine ads, trade journal ads, Yellow Pages ads, directory ads, radio commercials, TV commercials, and billboards.

Business-to-business marketing is designed to sell products or services to business, industry, or professionals rather than consumers. Ads that appear in trade journals are a prime example of business-to-business marketing. So are industrial catalogs.

People often think of business-to-business advertising as "technical" advertising, but not all business-to-business products are technical. A catalog selling paper clips, envelopes, and other office supplies to business offices is business-to-business, but hardly technical.

Consumer marketing is designed to sell products or services to individual consumers, families, and households. Examples include most of the TV commercials, radio commercials, and newspaper ads you see, hear, and read every day.

Joe Lane, a specialist in business-to-business marketing, defines consumer advertising as "simple thoughts for simple folks." But that's an overstatement. While it's true that most consumer advertising deals with simple products—soap, detergent, beer, hamburgers—not all of it does. Brochures written to describe cars, VCRs, and stereo systems, for example, often get quite technical in their discussion of features and functions.

Direct mail is unsolicited advertising or promotional material (that is, material the recipient has not requested) sent to an individual or company through the mail. A four-page sales letter asking you to subscribe to *Time* or *Newsweek* is an example of direct mail. So's that big package Publishers' Clearing House sends you every now and then.

Direct marketing is any type of marketing that seeks some sort of reply from the reader, typically by phone, mail, or fax. Direct marketing print materials usually have response coupons or reply cards you can use to request more information or order the product.

Direct marketing TV and radio commercials typically use toll-free 800 numbers (and nowadays, 900 numbers as well). Lester Wunderman, chairman of Wunderman, Ricotta & Klein, a New York City ad agency, came up with the term *direct marketing* in 1961.

Direct response and **direct marketing** mean the same thing. Direct response seeks an immediate action on the part of the reader. This could be to call a toll-free number, visit a showroom, try a product, mail a reply card, or see a demonstration.

As you will see, one of the basic premises of this book is that virtually all business-to-business marketing communications can be made more powerful, effective, and profitable by converting them from conventional communications to direct-response communications.

High-tech advertising promotes software, computer hardware, electronics, and other technology products. Most of it is aimed at business buyers; some of it is designed to appeal to consumers. So *high-tech* marketing is not necessarily *business-to-business* marketing, although most high-tech advertising is probably business-to-business.

General advertising, also known as **image advertising,** doesn't seek an immediate response, but instead aims at building an image or creating an awareness of a product or a company over an extended period of time.

Examples include TV commercials for consumer products such as fast foods (McDonald's, Wendy's, Burger King), soft drinks (Coke, Pepsi), and wine coolers (Calvin Cooler, Bartles & Jaymes). The institutional or corporate advertising that appears in *Forbes* and *Fortune* is another example of the genre.

Industrial marketing refers to marketing used to advertise and promote products and services aimed primarily at engineers and other buyers working in traditional U.S. "smokestack" industries such as chemical processing, pulp and paper, construction, mining, food processing, oil and gas, water and wastewater treatment, and so forth.

All industrial advertising is business-to-business advertising, but there's a lot of business-to-business advertising that isn't industrial (for example, firms promoting accounting, legal, and other professional services are business-to-business but not industrial). In 1983, the leading trade magazine in the field of business-to-business marketing changed its name from *Industrial Marketing* to *Business Marketing*. Some people use the two terms interchangeably, but this is inaccurate.

Junk mail is a popular term for direct mail and is often used in a derogatory sense. Many professionals who work in direct marketing consider the term a put-down of their industry and take great offense whenever the words "junk mail" are used. In fact, whenever a major media story on the direct mail industry refers to direct mail as "junk mail," numerous direct marketers protest by writing letters-to-the-editors to both the offending newspaper and the direct mail trade magazines.

Everyone else knows and uses this familiar term all the time. I suspect the average citizen doesn't have much of an idea of what direct marketing or direct response is—nor do they care.

Mail order is the selling of products through the mail. In mail-order selling, the buyer typically purchases the product directly from an ad, mailing, or catalog without visiting a store or seeing a salesperson. The product is then shipped by mail or UPS; again, with no "middle man" involved.

Marketing refers to the activities required to get a customer to give you money in exchange for your product or service. Although many people (including me) commit the language sin of using the terms *advertising* and *marketing* interchangeably, they are not the same. Marketing consists of four key components: the product, the price, distribution, and promotion. Advertising is only one small part of promotion. (Other parts of promotion include trade shows, direct mail, catalogs, sales brochures, and publicity.)

The seven key differences between business-to-business marketing and consumer marketing

So . . . are business-to-business and consumer marketing fundamentally the same, or fundamentally different? There are two basic schools of thought.

The first says, "Business-to-business and consumer advertising are fundamentally the same. After all, executives and engineers are still human beings, and they don't stop being human when they step into the office. So the basic consumer advertising techniques of cleverness, humor, entertainment, color, good graphics, design, and so forth will still appeal to them."

People of this school think that all consumer advertising techniques apply equally to business-to-business, that business-to-business advertising shouldn't be handled any differently than consumer advertising, and that the surest way to create an exciting, effective, interest-grabbing business ad is to make it look and read like a consumer ad.

If you're doing an industrial ad for widgets, for example, and want to include some specifications, these people will likely object on the basis that specifications are boring. What they do not realize, of course, is that what bores *them* does not necessarily bore a design engineer specifying widgets for a new plant.

The second school says, "Business-to-business marketing is fundamentally different from consumer advertising. For businesspeople, buying is a part of their job responsibility, and they treat it very seriously. Also, as professionals, most businesspeople are highly knowledgeable as buyers, and therefore simplistic (and simple-minded) consumer appeals do not work. You must communicate with business buyers using language that reflects their level of sophistication and technical knowledge. Copy should be factual and present sufficient detail about the product or service to enable the business buyer to make an informed, intelligent buying decision."

There is ample evidence to support this position. For example, a survey published in *Mainly Marketing,* a newsletter covering the high-tech marketing industry, showed that when creating ads for technical products, advertising agencies stressed features that *buyers* of such products considered unimportant, and they also omitted information that was vital. The ad agencies felt the high-tech ads should always stress the benefit of how the product saved time and money. But engineers and purchasing agents said product specifications and limitations were more important to them.

What's *my* position on the topic of business versus consumer advertising? I fall somewhere in the middle, but lean more toward the school that says business and consumer advertising are different. Having worked primarily in business-to-business marketing since 1979, here is my conclusion: *While there are some similarities between business-to-business and consumer marketing, the two are fundamentally different and require a different approach.*

Depending on which school you belong to, at this point you're either nodding your head in agreement—or vehemently rejecting my premise. Let me identify what I consider to be the seven key differences between business-to-business and consumer marketing. You can then judge for yourself whether you agree with them.

Key difference #1: The business buyer wants to buy.

Most consumer marketing offers people products they might enjoy but don't really need. These include luxury automobiles, wide-screen and high-definition TVs, compact disc players, VCRs, $90 sneakers with built-in air pumps, designer fragrances, brand-name jeans, wine coolers, fast foods, and premium and gourmet ice creams in exotic flavors. If we buy these items, we do so for pleasure, status, or enjoyment, and not because they are essential to our day-to-day activity. For example, you could easily survive without all of the items on my list. These are luxuries—not necessities.

As a result, powerful persuasion and massive advertising budgets are needed to motivate consumers to buy these items. The consumer is indeed being "sold" on something he or she doesn't really need and may never have thought of acquiring before reading the ad or viewing the commercial.

But in business-to-business marketing, the situation is different, because *the business buyer wants to—and has to—buy*. Indeed, all business enterprises must routinely buy products and services that help them stay profitable, competitive, and successful or that are needed for the day-to-day operation of the business. The proof of this is the existence of purchasing agents: employees whose sole function is to purchase things on behalf of the company.

Not all business-to-business products are necessities. But in most cases, the business buyer needs to acquire either your product, your competitor's product, or some other type of product to address a specific need or solve a particular problem. For example, if you operate a business office and want the ability to send or receive faxes, you must either buy my fax, my competitor's fax, rent a fax, or use a public fax service. But whatever you do, you're going to have to spend money on a fax product or service to solve your problem.

Even if you say, "I'm going to resist modern technology and not use a fax," you still need to buy a product or service to get documents to your clients and customers quickly. This might be an express-delivery service, messenger service, or a flock of trained carrier pigeons. But the point is, you have to buy *something* to satisfy the need for fast document delivery.

The microcomputer is another example. Consumers don't really need personal computers, so it's a tough sell. Early computer ads proclaimed the personal computer could do marvelous things like store all your recipes on a computer disk. But people were perfectly happy storing recipes the old-fashioned way on index cards, so sales didn't boom.

Businesses, on the other hand, weren't interested in computers *per se* (indeed, the thought of learning to use a personal computer has terrified many a brave entrepreneur and executive), but they definitely *did* want to get documents typed faster, manipulate customer lists more efficiently, produce better-looking reports and proposals, and automate inventory and accounting—all of which could be done with the personal computer. So, *business* became the primary target market for the personal computer, because the business buyers needed to find a better way to increase office productivity.

What does all this mean to the business-to-business marketer? Simply that it's often not necessary to resort to the far-out creative approaches and entertainment-oriented techniques consumer marketers use to engage the consumer's attention. Remember, the consumer isn't looking to buy, but business prospects are. So the marketing approach can be more direct.

If the business buyer is looking to solve a problem, you can often create a successful ad or mailing just by identifying the problem in your headline. Example: "HOW TO CUT HEATING AND COOLING COSTS BY 50%" was used to appeal to building owners who were spending too much money to heat and cool their buildings. If the business buyer is looking for a specific product or service, you can often get their attention just by identifying the product or service in the headline. As one expert explains, "If I were writing an ad for stokers, and I could only have one word in the headline, I would make it the word 'STOKERS' in large, all-caps, 72-point type!" Wouldn't this gain your attention if you were in the market for a stoker?

The bottom line of difference #1 is this: Because the business buyer is looking to buy, business-to-business marketing can and should be more direct and to the point. Don't be afraid to talk about your product and what it can do for the buyer. That's what he or she wants to find out more about.

Key difference #2: The business buyer is sophisticated.

Business-to-business marketing is usually aimed at a fairly sophisticated audience. With the growing illiteracy rate in America, there's always a question when writing to consumers of how well educated prospects are, how well they can read, or even whether they can read at all. That's why consumer marketing strives to be simplistic and frequently aims at the lowest common denominator. But it's fairly safe to assume that your average middle manager, engineer, systems analyst, or corporate executive has a college degree or at least some higher education and can read at a decent level. Therefore, business-to-business copy should be clear and concise but not simplistic.

The business buyer is often fairly sophisticated when it comes to the product or service you are trying to sell them. They typically have a high interest level in, and understanding of, the product—or at least, of the problem the product is designed to solve. In fact, a great difficulty for those of us who create business-to-business advertising is that our reader usually knows more about the product and its use than we ever will. This is a major difference between business-to-business and consumer copywriting.

A copywriter working on a promotion for a record club doesn't have to stretch her imagination far to get inside the mind of a target prospect for this promotion, because she probably is one. Most of us, after all, have bought records, read record club ads, and thought about joining a record club at one time or another. On the other hand, when I'm hired to write a brochure selling networking equipment to telecommunications managers, I have to do a lot of work to get inside the mind of my target prospect, because I've never been a telecommunications manager.

In fact, most business-to-business marketers have not worked as doctors, chemical engineers, lawyers, accountants, systems analysts, traffic managers, or held any of the other positions of the people they are writing to. Therefore, they don't have the same intimate knowledge of the buyer's likes, dislikes, concerns, and prejudices that the consumer copywriter usually has.

Your business-to-business prospect typically has years of training and experience in his or her field. Therefore, they often know much more about the subject you're writing about than you do. That doesn't mean they have superior knowledge about the specific product. But they probably know a lot about that generic type of product, or at least about the issues or problems it addresses.

For example, I may, at this point, know more about implantable spinal bone growth stimulators than doctors reading my copy, because my client is the leader in this field. But I do not know *nearly* as much about spine surgery as the orthopedic surgeons reading my client's mailings. So I always have to work much harder than the consumer copywriter to be accurate and not make technical errors that would destroy the credibility of my copy. The realization that your prospect probably knows more than you do makes us business-to-business marketers a bit more humble than our consumer counterparts.

The business prospect does not respond well to sloganeering or oversimplification. We've got to communicate with them on a peer-to-peer level—to gain their trust, establish credibility, and prove that we are knowledgeable enough about their situation to be of real help to them. This means the business-to-business marketer must do a tremendous amount of research and digging into the market, the product, and its application. Just writing an ad "off the top of your head" seldom produces an effective promotion.

Key difference #3: The business buyer will read a lot of copy.

The other day I was giving an in-house seminar in copywriting for the staff of a company that produces conferences and seminars. One of the students asked me, "Do business buyers read, or are they like consumers in that they won't read a lot of copy and will look only at the pictures and headlines?"

"It's really a paradox," I responded. "On the one hand, it's true that business prospects are *readers*. For most executives, managers, and professionals employed in the business world, a significant part of their job consists of reading printed material—not only reports, letters, and memos, but also proposals, product literature, and other information concerning products and services they need to acquire to perform their job function. So the business buyer *does* read, in fact *must* read, and is *accustomed* to reading . . . something that isn't necessarily true about all segments of the general public.

"On the other hand, today's business executive is *tremendously* busy: more time-pressured, with too much to read and not enough time to read it, than ever before. So, although your message may indeed be beneficial or useful, often they won't get to it simply because there are too many things in their in-baskets competing for their attention."

My seminar attendee then asked, "How does that affect copy length, then? You've said one of the key differences between business-to-business and consumer is that business readers will read a lot of copy. But if they're pressed for time, shouldn't copy be as concise as possible?" This question has a three-part answer.

First, yes, business-to-business copy should be as concise as possible.

But this doesn't mean copy should be short; rather, it means copy should tell the complete story in the *fewest possible words.* So being concise does not necessarily mean limiting the text to a few superficial paragraphs. It means getting to the point and not wasting the reader's time by saying in three paragraphs what could be said in one sentence.

Second, business readers *will* read a substantial amount of copy, but only if it's interesting and relevant. The more interesting or relevant, the more they'll read. If you send me a four-page letter on managing my staff, I may not read it, because I only have one employee, and so management is not a critical issue in my business. But if you send me a four-page letter on "How to Get Rich Selling Books and Tapes by Mail," I'll read every word (if it's interesting, useful, and well-written) because I'm fascinated by the topic.

Third, although business buyers will ultimately read many words in the process of making a purchase decision, all of these words are not necessarily contained in a single document. When selling a piece of capital equipment, for example, you will have many contacts with the prospect, most of which involve some written marketing document: an ad, a brochure, a proposal, a letter. While each may be brief, in total they add up to many thousands of words. So business buyers do read a lot of copy, but not necessarily at one sitting.

As a result, we business-to-business marketers can't, like some of our consumer counterparts, always adopt the attitude that "shorter is better." You can sell a pair of jeans or a perfume with a slogan and a sexy picture; this approach won't work with a programmable controller. Therefore, a question we wrestle with when creating any marketing communication is, "How long should the copy be? How much information should I include?" I offer the following formula: *The copy should contain enough information—no more, no less—to convince the greatest number of qualified prospects to take the next step in the buying process.*

The product, audience, and purpose of the promotion are the three factors that ultimately determine this length.

First, consider the product. With some products—software, for example—there's an overwhelming amount of information that could be conveyed. You could literally write a book about most software products. (The proof is that many major PC software products in fact have several books written about them!) So the challenge becomes one of selectivity: How can we select the most essential sales points to include in our ad or brochure, and what can we safely leave out? With other products and services, the opposite is true. A service like office cleaning, for example, may be so simple that you're hard-pressed to find enough things to say about it to create a meaningful, interesting brochure. This makes it easier to be brief, but more difficult to be interesting.

The second factor determining copy length is the audience: Different audiences have different levels of interest in—and different concerns about—your product or service. Let's take telephone systems as an example. The telecommunications manager is interested in the details of how your telephone system operates, so a brochure aimed at this audience would contain a lot of detail and could run six to eight pages or longer. But let's say you were selling the same telephone system to small business owners, not corporate telecommunications managers. These entrepreneurs have no technical background in telecommunications. And they don't have the time—or the inclination—to learn a lot about phone systems. Their main concerns are *features* (Does it handle three-way calling and give them the other functions they want?), *benefits* (How much money will it save them?), *performance* (Will it provide quality, trouble-free performance?), and *support* (Is your company reputable, and will you be there if they need service?). So a brochure aimed at them will just hit the high points and skip the details.

The third factor determining copy length is purpose. Let's say you are writing a letter to promote a testing device costing $349. If your letter is merely seeking an *inquiry*—that is, you want the prospect to mail a reply card to request a brochure, or to call and speak to a salesperson—then you don't have to go into complete detail about the device, because your brochure or salesperson can do that. You only have to say enough about the device and its special advantages to get the prospect interested in finding out more about it. So your copy can be brief and leave the details to the follow-up presentation.

On the other hand, suppose you didn't have a sales force and wanted your letter to generate mail orders for your $349 testing meter. Now your mailing package has to give complete details, because there *is* no follow-up from a sales force. Your mailing must not only tell the buyer about the benefits, specifications, functions, and features, but it must also answer any questions or objectives they have, as well as explain precisely how to or-der. So the *purpose* of your promotion also affects copy length.

The key point? The business buyer *will* read copy—if it's interesting, relevant, and contributes to helping them make an informed decision about taking the next step in the buying process.

Key difference #4: Business buying is a multi-step process.

In most consumer direct response marketing, direct marketers are geared toward producing the "package": an elaborate mailing that consists of a lengthy letter (usually four pages or longer), illustrated brochure or circular, order form, reply envelope, and additional elements such as a second letter, second brochure, second order form, or flier.

Consumer marketers rely on this one selling piece to do the bulk of their selling when it comes to getting people to subscribe to their magazine, buy their insurance policy, or purchase their mail-order product. The package is continually mailed, tested, refined, and modified. Copywriters are hired to do new test packages to mail and measure against the existing package. The package that wins the test becomes the control package and is mailed in mass quantities to as many lists as is profitable. But for many business-to-business direct marketers, the concept of *package* or *control* is simply not relevant. Why? Because, while the purchase of most consumer products is a one-step product, the purchase of most business products is a *multi-step* process.

A vice president of operations, for example, doesn't clip a coupon from a trade journal ad and order a $750,000 air pollution control system by mail. Could you imagine the response coupon for such an ad?

YES, I'M INTERESTED IN CONTROLLING POLLUTION IN MY CHEMICAL PLANT.

Please send me an XP-800 Wet Scrubbing System. Our check for $750,000 is enclosed.

I understand that if for any reason—or for no reason—the XP-800 is not for us, I may return the pollution control system, and you will refund our money in full . . . .

This example is absurd, but it illustrates the point: Most business-to-business direct marketing seeks to generate an *inquiry* or *lead,* not a direct sale. The purchase of a business product or service typically takes many steps, not a single step—unless the product or service is inexpensive ($300 or less).

Consider the chemical plant manager reading an ad for a pollution control system. First he asks for a brochure. Then a proposal. Only upon acceptance of a satisfactory proposal is the contract awarded. As a rule, the more expensive the product or service, the more steps in the buying process. Therefore, it is not a single piece of copy that wins the sale. Rather, it takes a series of letters, brochures, presentations, ads, and mailers—combined with the efforts of salespeople—to turn a prospect into a paying customer.

Unlike the consumer direct mail writer, who puts every selling argument into a one-shot "package" that has to do the entire job of getting you to subscribe to a magazine or buy porcelain dolls by mail, the business-to-business marketer has to plan a *series* of contacts with the potential customer. When writing a direct mail package for a client, for example, I have to keep in mind what we will send to prospects who respond. And, for greatest effectiveness, these two items (the lead-generating piece and the fulfillment package) should be planned and written as a series, rather than separately. We'll explore strategies for creating a maximum response lead-generating and fulfillment series later in the book.

Key difference #5: Business buying involves multiple influences.

You don't usually consult with a team of experts when you want to buy a fast-food hamburger, a soda, a bottle of shampoo, or a bag of potato chips, do you? In most consumer selling situations, the purchase decision is made by an individual. Most consumer purchases are "impulse buys." That is, the consumer sees a commercial, wants the product, and buys it. Or, the consumer sees the product in a retail outlet, remembers it favorably from the commercials, and buys it. There's not a great deal of "agonizing" over the decision; it's basically an impulse. Exceptions? Certainly. Some consumer products require a more carefully thought-out purchase decision. These include a car, home, life insurance, fine china, silverware, vacation home, health insurance plan, television, stereo, and furniture. But for most low-priced consumer products, it's basically an impulse purchase.

Most business-to-business buying involves what is called a "considered purchase," meaning the buyer carefully considers the product, the competition, and the price before making a buying decision. In most business organizations, any given executive or manager has a predefined limit of how much money he or she can spend without authorization or approval from a supervisor or someone else higher up in the organization. Therefore, most purchase decisions above small amounts are made by committee, not by individuals. People involved in the purchase decision typically perform one of three functions: recommend, specify, or buy.

Recommend means either to initiate the inquiry process or to advise others to approve the purchase. The controller at a small firm, for example, might see an ad for a new computerized accounting system, get excited about the product, send for literature, and try to convince the boss to buy it.

Specify means to make sure the product meets all requirements before purchase and to work with the vendor to ensure the product is successfully implemented after purchase. At the small firm mentioned above, the controller might recommend purchase of the software, but it's the chief computer operator or head of the information systems department who is responsible for making sure the software is compatible with the existing computer system and also for getting it installed and running on that system.

Buy means to authorize the purchase of the product or service. At a small firm, the owner, president, or general manager is the person who has the authority to purchase the new computer software. The controller and the head of IS probably don't have the authority to say to you, "OK, it's a deal," even though they may *act* as if they do.

As a result of all this, we see that selling to business successfully may require reaching *all* of the purchasing influences within a company—not just one or two. This often involves targeting *different* messages about the product or service to *different* audiences with *different* concerns.

Going back to our example: The controller is most concerned with how the software can simplify accounting procedures and wants to know in detail what accounting methods the software employs and how the numbers are treated.

The head of the computer department doesn't know or care about how the books are kept. The head of the computer department wants to know about the product from a *software* point of view. What hardware platforms does it run on? How much computer resources does it consume? What's the cost? How easy is it to install and test?

The business owner or manager is probably too busy to worry much about the technical details of either the accounting or the computing aspects (although if she is a financially oriented person, she may be interested in some of the details of the accounting system). Her primary concern might be the reputation and stability of the software vendor. She asks the controller and computer chief: "How do we know that this company will be around five years from now to support the soft-ware system we invest in today? What happens to our computing systems if they go out of business and this accounting software becomes obsolete and unsupported?" If your marketing literature hasn't provided the answers, she may put a stop to the purchasing of your software even though you thought the sale was "in the bag."

To sum up: To be successful, business-to-business marketing communications must address the needs of all parties involved with the purchase decision. In some cases, this requires separate mailings to many different people within an organization. Actually, while you almost always would benefit from separate mailings, brochures, and marketing documents aimed at each buying influence, this isn't always practical or affordable. What to do?

One solution in direct mail is to create versions of the base package aimed at different buying influences. For example, you could create a basic package—sales letter, brochure, and reply card—selling widgets to plant managers. From that, you could do different versions aimed at different buying influences: one to the purchasing agent, a second to the design engineer, a third to the chief financial officer. The brochure and reply card would be the same in each version. Only the letter would be different. This allows you to create tailored versions of your package with minimal extra cost.

The same approach could be used when doing a promotion on one product to different industries. You could have one cover letter aimed at pulp and paper plants, a second at the food processing industry, and a third at widget buyers in the electronics industry. Again, the expensive color brochure and reply card remain the same; only the letter varies.

A second solution to addressing multiple buying influences in a single promotion is a technique Steve Isaacs of the Stenrich Group calls *compartmentalization*: On one page of your brochure, you have a section listing the benefits of the product *as they apply to each of the different buying influences*. This might be a box with the headline: "BENEFITS OF THE XYZ SYSTEM." Underneath the headline is a series of subheads identifying the various buying influences or markets, e.g., "For plant managers. . . ," "For process engineers. . . ," "For purchasing agents. . . ," "For distribution managers. . . ." Under each subhead is a series of bullets (three to five is about the right number) listing the benefits of greatest interest to that particular buying influence. Some bullet points might apply to only one of the groups. Others might appear under multiple subheadings. It doesn't matter, as long as the particular reader looking under the subhead that describes his position or job function sees, at a glance, all of his most pressing concerns, needs, or wishes addressed.

The key to effective selling is to position your product or service as filling a need or want of the buyer. This is more difficult in business-to-business than consumer marketing, because we often have to reach multiple buying influences with a single piece, and therefore sometimes cannot speak as directly as we would like to the hopes, fears, concerns, and questions of each individual prospect. These two techniques—tailored versions and compartmentalization—can help overcome that problem to some degree.

Key difference #6: Business products are more complex.

Most business products—and their selection, usage, and applications—are more complex than consumer products. For example, clients I have served include a commercial bank, a manufacturer of elevator control systems, a data processing training firm, a database marketing company, a mailing list broker, and a semiconductor manufacturer.

Business-to-business marketing communications cannot be superficial. Clarity is essential. You cannot sell by "fooling" the prospect or hiding the identity of your product as is done, for example, in the get-rich-quick school of print ads found in the opportunity seeker magazines. Half the battle is explaining, quickly and simply, what your product is, what it does, and why the reader should be interested in it. "In business-to-business direct mail, the key is to educate the prospect," says Mark Toner, advertising manager for Amano, a manufacturer of computerized time-clock systems. "With a product like ours, most customers don't even know of its existence."

I am not saying here that the name and description of the product should necessarily be in the lead of the letter or the headline of the ad. In fact, it's usually better to start by addressing a need or concern of the prospect, then show how your product or service meets that need—so product talk is rarely found in the opening of your sales argument. Yet effective business-to-business marketing communications must move swiftly from the problem to how your product resolves the problem. If you take too long to get to the point, or deliberately confuse or mislead your readers, you'll lose them—fast.

I've observed that many direct response ads and direct mail packages for consumer products are successful because they make more of the product than it really is. This is necessary, I suppose, because there is so little substance to some of these products that, without embellishment and "hype" copy to create excitement, they wouldn't sell.

But for many business-to-business products, the opposite is true. The products are already exceedingly complex and difficult to understand. The marketer's job is to *simplify,* not puff up, the product description. To be sold on the product, your reader first has to understand what the product is, how it works, and what it will do for him. This is inherently difficult, given the complexity of the product. Your job is to explain it—convincingly, understandably, and quickly. You must be clear. You must be direct. You must get right to the point. You must make sure the reader understands why your product is so great, and why his or her organization simply must have it.

Key difference #7: Business buyers buy for their company— and for themselves.

This is the most overlooked aspect of business-to-business marketing communications. Most advertisers stress the benefits of what the product will do for the reader's company, assuming this is the reader's only concern. But it's not. The reader is also concerned with how the purchase decision affects him or her personally. And when corporate and personal buying motives conflict, the personal motives frequently win out. If you want to sell businesspeople something that's good for their company but bad for them, they'll probably find a way to sabotage your efforts and convince their bosses *not* to buy it. I can think of hundreds of examples of this. Let me give you a very recent one.

A close friend owns a small but well-respected ad agency here in New Jersey. Recently she had the chance to pitch a new high-tech account. The person calling her in had responded to a sales letter she had sent to about 50 such firms. His title was "Senior Writer." She visited his company. He started talking about graphics and desktop publishing and asking what software she used and what fonts she would recommend.

"Wait a minute," she said politely. "While we are happy to do graphics, we are not a design studio. We are an advertising agency. That means we do the whole advertising campaign—from planning and strategy through copywriting and design." The prospect immediately became distant and cold. "*I* do all the writing around here," he explained haughtily. "I just need someone to lay out my words. And I already know marketing, so your help is not needed there."

She thanked the prospect for his time, ended the meeting, and got out. Later, we reviewed his writing and agreed he was a terrible writer, with no understanding of selling or marketing. So why did he not retain this ad agency? The reason is that the service threatened his ego. He perceived himself as the great writer and saw the ad agency as "competition," not help. Although his company's *business* goal was to produce more effective marketing communications, this prospect's *personal* goal was to do all the writing himself—resulting in a conflict that motivated him to turn away any outside marketing service that offered advice, knowledge, or writing assistance.

The lesson here is that to motivate business buyers, you must present benefits that appeal on both the organizational and the personal level. You already know the key business benefits: to save time, to save money, to make money, to increase efficiency, to boost productivity, to make the business grow. But what are the *personal* motivations prospects respond to and should be stressed in business-to-business copy? Here are a few of the most basic appeals:

Security.

Concern for making the safe, acceptable decision is a primary motivation of business buyers. Business buyers often will buy something that involves the least risk or least chance of turning out to be a wrong decision, even if it is not the best product.

In information systems, for example, there's an old saying, "Nobody ever got fired for buying IBM." This means that if you buy a new brand of computing device that offers more power at lower cost, but the company goes out of business or there is some other problem, you'll be blamed by management for buying from a vendor nobody ever heard of. But if you have a problem with an IBM computer system, no one will criticize you because IBM is recognized as a good company: If something's wrong, it must be IBM's fault, not yours.

Recently a corporate pension fund manager, writing in *Money* magazine, noted that no money manager ever got fired for losing money invested in a blue-chip stock. A different example, but the principle is the same.

Avoiding stress or hardship.

Avoiding unnecessary headaches or work is a big concern among business buyers. Most of us have a lazy streak and do not want to get involved in things that make us work harder than we already are, even if the company would benefit in the long run.

For instance, a consultant might offer a new system for increasing productivity. But the system involves changing from the current record-keeping system to a new method. Switching from the old to the new system will save most workers time in the long run. But making the switch would involve a *lot* of extra work for Mr. Scithers, the head of record-keeping.

If Mr. Scithers has anything to say about it, and thinks no one will criticize him for it, he will work to sway his company against engaging the consultant and implementing the new system, even though current procedures are not efficient. Mr. Scithers feels he is already too busy and doesn't need this extra headache, despite the fact that it would probably help clear up some of his existing paperwork backlog.

Fear of the unknown.

Fear is an extremely powerful motivator that can either work for you or against you. A middle manager, for example, might vote against acquiring desktop publishing and putting a terminal on every manager's desk, because he himself has computer-phobia. Even though he recognizes the benefits such technology can bring to his department, he wants to avoid the pain of learning something he perceives to be difficult and frightening. Again, personal concern outweighs corporate benefit in this situation.

Fear of loss.

A traffic manager in a company that has handled its shipping and distribution in-house for the past decade may resist her president's suggestion that they retain a third-party service provider and outsource some of the company's growing distribution and logistics needs. Even if she respects the third-party logistics firm and believes they could do a good job, the traffic manager may campaign against them, fearing that bringing in a third-party service provider will diminish her own status within the company and may even result in the eventual loss of her job.

In these and many other instances, business buyers are buying for themselves first and for their companies second. To be successful, your business-to-business marketing communications must not only promise the benefits your prospects desire for their company; copy should speak to the prospect's personal agenda as well.

2

More Key Differences Between Business-to-Business and Consumer Direct Marketing

In Chapter 1 we discussed seven key differences between business-to-business and consumer marketing that apply to all forms of marketing communications—direct as well as general. These differences are fundamental and affect your entire approach to the creation of business-to-business marketing communications programs.

In this chapter, we'll explore a number of *mechanical* differences between business-to-business and consumer marketing that apply only to *direct* marketing.

As you'll see, most of these differences stem from the fact that business-to-business marketers sell to smaller, more narrow vertical markets than the typical consumer marketer, and are therefore mailing in far smaller quantities. This creates a set of unique challenges and difficulties business-to-business direct marketers must face in list selection, testing, creative fees, production, and many other areas—problems that consumer direct marketers are not burdened with.

In this chapter we'll discuss those special challenges of business-to-business direct marketing and suggestions on how to cope.

Business-to-business versus direct marketing: The volume difference

One critical difference between business-to-business and consumer marketing is the size of the audience.

In space advertising, this means that business-to-business ads are placed in specialty magazines with limited circulations, whereas consumer advertising is published in newspapers and magazines with hundreds of thousands or even millions of readers.

In direct mail, this means mailings typically of only a few thousand pieces for most business-to-business campaigns, versus tens of thousands, hundreds of thousands, or even millions for consumer direct mail. (I was once hired by a business-to-business client to write a sales letter to a market of 187 prospects.)

In the production of sales literature, this means print runs of 5,000 or fewer brochures for a business product, versus consumer catalogs printed in press runs of hundreds of thousands.

While this doesn't affect the *content* of your marketing communications as directly as the seven key differences described in Chapter 1, it does affect your budget and your approach to the *business* of marketing to business and industry. There are some big benefits to having a smaller, more spe-cialized audience. There are also some major drawbacks. Let's explore them.

Lists

If you've been in direct marketing for any length of time, you know the list industry is geared toward serving the needs of large-volume mailers. The more names you rent, the more money the list brokers, owners, and managers make. The more money they make from you, the more attention you get. Conversely, the direct marketer who mails in small volume will not get a lot of time and attention from the list professionals—even though he may be the one who needs it most.

Many experienced business-to-business marketers who get into direct mail for the first time are shocked when I explain that the reason they're not getting a lot of service from their list broker is that the rental of 5,000 names—which seems an incredible quantity to the mailer—represents an insignificant order to the broker. As one major list broker once confided to me, "My primary customer is the large consumer magazine or mail order marketer who is going to mail in the millions. I'm also interested in consumer marketers who will mail in the hundreds of thousands. Smaller accounts *are not worth cultivating.*" For this reason, the business-to-business marketer mailing only a few thousand pieces a few times a year will not get a lot of attention and help from most list brokers.

Business-to-business list rentals are difficult for the broker to make much money on, not only because the volumes mailed are smaller, but also because the lists are more specialized. Your ideal list may turn out to be the 3,200 members of some arcane professional society that doesn't even make its list available on a regular basis. It's simply not worth the broker's time to research, track down, make a deal with, and rent the list for you from the list owner. So most won't bother.

One other simple fact demonstrates that the list industry is not geared toward serving the business-to-business marketer: The minimum order quantity on most list rentals is 5,000 names, but many business-to-business direct marketers are targeting only a few thousand or a few hundred prospects. To rent 5,000 names each from five to eight lists—a very typical test quantity for consumer mailings—generates numbers beyond belief for the average business marketer.

What to do? Here are my recommendations:

1. Find a broker that specializes in business-to-business lists. There are several listed in the appendix of this book.

2. Tell the broker your needs and ask for their help in finding the right lists for you. Don't, however, be incredibly demanding. Remember that in their mind, *your request is marginally worthwhile* as opposed to the orders they are handling for large-volume mailers. So expect good service, but be a pleasant, easy-to-get-along-with client. Don't expect the list broker to jump through hoops for a mailing of 5,000 pieces. They won't.

3. If the broker reaches a dead end and seems reluctant to do more, consider hiring a direct marketing consultant to do the list research for you on a paid basis.

The difference between a broker and a consultant? Traditionally, a broker receives a commission (paid by the list owner, not the list renter) per thousand names rented. The service aspect of being a list broker, which is to research and recommend the right lists to the direct marketer, is usually provided without charge: The broker does not receive money unless names are actually rented, and there is no charge for providing list recommendations (although some brokers are experimenting with such fees).

The consultant, on the other hand, is paid a straight project or hourly rate for doing list research. Therefore, you, as the paying client, have a right to demand as much service as you want. While the broker resists spending hours researching a small list requirement because of lack of compensation, the consultant will happily do this work because he or she is paid for the time and earns money for consulting services, not list rentals.

Another reason for engaging a direct marketing consultant is that sometimes the ideal business-to-business list may be a trade show attendee list, professional society membership list, or other highly specialized list not generally available on the commercial markets and for that reason not listed in any of the standard list directories or catalogs. Often these lists are available in limited formats, such as gummed labels only or as a printed directory only, and list brokers don't want to deal with them. A consultant, however, doesn't care and will gladly get such lists for you.

A good example is a client of mine who wanted to mail to business managers at group radiology practices. The list brokers could not find any list on the market. On his own, the client discovered there was a professional group of 1,200 radiology business managers. The group didn't rent their list to brokers, only to members and associate members. My client, a vendor, joined as an associate member, got the list, and did a successful mailing. For 1,200 names, a broker wouldn't have bothered with it.

None of this is meant as a criticism of list brokers. On the contrary, my purpose is to educate you, the business-to-business direct marketer, a little bit about brokers and how they earn their money. A good business relationship has to be mutually profitable. Too often business-to-business direct marketers with small, specialized list needs complain about this broker or that broker who ignored them or gave them bad treatment. What often happens is that the marketer wants attention and service disproportionate to the meager profits the broker will make servicing the account. Be realistic about what you expect a broker to do based on your volume of business with them. And don't make false promises about "lots more business" later down the line. The broker isn't fooled. Please realize that even if you gave your broker all your business for this year and next year, it probably wouldn't add up to what they would make handling list rentals for *just one test mailing* for any major consumer magazine or catalog marketer.

Testing

"Testing" as it is meant in the traditional sense for the "classic" direct marketer (selling via mail order) is often meaningless for the business-to-business marketer. Yet some level of testing can and should be done. Classic testing in direct marketing is as follows: Say you are offering magazine subscriptions. Your list broker identifies eight lists that might work for your offer. Each list is about 200,000 names, for a total universe of 1.6 million. Yet you don't know if all the lists will work. Some will. Some won't.

So you test. You mail 5,000 names per list, for a total test of 40,000 pieces. Let's say lists "A" and "D" pay off. You then "roll out," which means you mail more names on those lists that tested successfully. But you don't mail to all 200,000 names on list A. Or on D. Instead, you roll out to no more than *ten times* the quantity of the test. That means roll out to 50,000 names maximum from a test of 5,000. If the mailing of 50,000 is successful, then you can roll out to up to 500,000 names on that list.

The reason such classic testing is not done in business-to-business is that typical quantities are so small. Let's say you have a business list that contains 6, 000 names, and a second list of 8,000 names. There's no point in testing 5,000 of each just to see which list is best. The "roll out" would be only an additional 1,000 names on the first list, and an additional 3,000 on the second. In this case I'd just mail my piece to the total universe of 14,000. I would, however, "key code" my mailings so I could identify which replies came from the first list and which from the second. For example, reply cards used in the mailing pieces going to list A are addressed to "Dept. A," so if a "Dept. A" card comes back, you know the lead is from list A. If one list pulled all the replies and the other got none, obviously we'd use only the list that worked for future mailings. So this "limited" kind of testing still has its place in business-to-business.

Let's consider another situation. You want to reach people in a specialized profession. You find that the only list available is a directory published by their trade association, and it contains 7,500 names. If there's only one list, then you can't "test" this list against others to see which is the best list. If you mail a letter to this list and it doesn't get a good response, you really don't know whether it's the list that is bad, or whether your letter missed the mark. Telephone follow-up to a few dozen people on the list who received your letter would be the best way to find out what went wrong.

On the other hand, if there were three lists to choose from, each containing 7,500 names, you could mail your letter to 2,000 or 5,000 or 7,500 names from each list, making sure to key code the reply cards so you know from which list each reply came. If the letter got good sales results on list A, but no response from list B or C, then you know that it is lists B and C—not the letter—that are at fault. Or, perhaps the three lists are not as similar as you thought, and a custom version of the letter should be tailored to lists B and C.

A frequently asked question is, "How many names must I test to get a statistically valid result?" The experts do not agree. One well-known list expert insists on 5,000 names. It's interesting that this is the same minimum quantity most list owners and brokers want to rent to you, isn't it? I think the 5,000 name figure for minimum test quantity became standard because of the list industry's 5,000-name minimum order, not because of statistical validity. Ed McLean, a leading direct mail authority, has written the definitive monograph on direct mail testing, *The Basics of Testing* (now out of print). An explanation of his method follows.

On the top line, find the deviation percentage (or *decline* percentage) you want to protect yourself against. Then go down the column until you reach the confidence level you want. The number in the box will be the number of replies you must set up your test sample to get. To find the correct sample size, divide the number of replies in the box by the percentage return you expect.

Figure 2–1   Decline Percentage

		50%	25%	12.5%	6.25%
	75%	1.8	7.3	29.2	116.8
Degree of Confidence	85%	3.5	14.0	56.0	
	90%	6.6	26.2	104.8	
	95%	11.0	42.8		
	99%	21.7	86.9		

Source: Reprinted with permission from Ed McLean, *The Basics of Testing.*

A key point is that the statistical validity of a test is determined not based on number of pieces mailed, but on *number of replies received*. Figure 2–1 shows the statistical validity of a direct mail test based on number of replies received (shown in the boxes within the table). The table lets you determine the degree of statistical validity you want from a test mailing, then tells you how many responses you must get from your test to ensure that the test results will be repeated in the roll-out.

The two factors to consider are "Decline Percentage" (horizontal line at the top of the chart) and "Degree of Confidence" (vertical line at the left of the chart). Decline Percentage tells you the maximum amount by which the roll-out results will vary from the test results. Let's say you select a 25 percent decline. That means if you get a 1 percent response from the test, the roll-out will vary from this by plus or minus 25 percent. So you can expect the roll-out to generate anywhere from 0.75 percent to 1.25 percent, based on a test result of 1 percent. Level of Confidence tells you how certain you can be of staying within the Decline Percentage you specify. If you select an 85 percent Level of Confidence and a 25 percent Decline Percentage, you are saying, "I want there to be an 85 percent chance that my roll-out will stay within plus or minus 25 percent of the response rate generated by my test."

Now go back to Figure 2–1. Read *down* the vertical column under "25 percent decline" and *across* from the horizontal row "85 percent confidence level." You see that you need 14 responses to get this level of statistical validity from your test. If you anticipate a 1 percent response, then you need to mail 1,400 pieces *per list* in your test (1 percent of 1,400 is 14). To be on the safe side, I'd make it an even 2,000. When people ask me, "How many pieces do I need to mail to get a statistically valid test result?" my recommendation is 2,000 per list, based on the above analysis.

Is this accurate? The above formula was introduced to me not by Ed McLean (who is now a good friend and valued colleague) but by a large mailing list brokerage that has been involved in thousands of mailings. "We have been using this formula for more than 30 years, and we find over and over that you can get a statistically valid test result mailing 2,000 names, not 5,000," says the president of this firm. I have since used it numerous times with clients doing smaller mailings, and have found it to be valid.

Universe

The term "universe" refers to the total size of the market, not the size of any particular list. If there are 1,200 radiology practice business managers, then the size of this market is 1,200. Most business-to-business direct marketers are dealing with markets significantly smaller than their consumer counterparts. But this is not always true. A company like Quill, for example, that sells office supplies via a mail-order catalog, has a potential universe of literally *millions* of business customers. On the other hand, a manufacturer that sells glass-lined reactor vessels for acid plants may target only a few hundred acid plants worldwide.

The size of the universe frequently dictates which marketing approach is primary. For instance, if you have a product that appeals to all chemical engineers, you might advertise in *Chemical Engineering* and other trade journals that are read by the majority of chemical engineers. On the other hand, if your product only appeals to those chemical engineers that work at *Fortune* 500 companies, you might have a com-puter extract the names of all *Chemical Engineering* subscribers that work at *Fortune* 500 firms and do a mailing just to that segment of the subscriber base. Running an ad in *Chemical Engineering* would be wasteful, be-cause it would reach thousands of engineers who are *not Fortune* 500 employees.

Now shrink the universe even smaller. One chemical company I recently consulted with made a chemical that would be of interest to only 50 to 100 companies manufacturing a certain type of automobile part. With an audience this small, it's not cost-effective to advertise in automotive magazines or to spend the money creating elaborate mailing packages. The best approach might be telemarketing or simply to have sales representatives personally visit the 50 or 100 prospects.

Single-shot versus series

As discussed earlier, consumer direct mail tends to focus on the "package": a single mailing piece that is mailed over and over to many different lists to generate direct orders for the product. The existing package—the one that currently pulls the highest response—is the *control*. The consumer direct marketer's main marketing strategy is to create a variety of different packages to test against the control. If a test package beats the control—that is, pulls a greater response—it becomes the new control and is mailed in vast quantities.

In business-to-business direct marketing aimed at limited audiences, the marketer tends to use a *series* of marketing communications rather than a single test package or control. Why? A control package for a consumer product like *Newsweek* magazine can be mailed to millions of names. But if you're mailing to radiology business managers, there are only 1,200 of them. How often can you mail the same thing over and over again before *all* the prospects who are going to respond have, and the package generates no further response? When that happens, you have to create a new mailing or find a different promotion to reach these prospects and get more of them to respond.

The size of the market, combined with the number of leads or amount of business you can handle, determines whether you can get away with having a single "package" or "control" mailing or whether you have to keep coming up with new mailings and promotional ideas to elicit sales from your universe. Let's say you create a letter that generates a 5 percent response. You have a limited number of salespeople, and therefore can only handle 20 inquiries a month. Based on a 5 percent response rate, to get 20 inquiries you would have to mail 400 sales letters per month. Say your universe for this product is 40,000 prospect names available on lists you can rent. Mailing these names at the rate of 400 per month, it would take more than *8 years* for you to exhaust the list! Therefore, if your ad agency or copywriter comes up with a letter that can generate a 5 percent inquiry rate, you need only this one letter—not a series.

Does this mean you don't test other letters? No. Why not? Because a higher response rate is always possible and translates directly into lower marketing costs. If your ad agency or copywriter can come up with a letter that pulls a 10 percent response, then you only have to mail half as many letters, which cuts your costs in half. On the other hand, suppose you have a market of 2,000 prospects, whose names are published in an annual directory you buy each year. You create a letter and mail it to the list and get a decent response. Then you mail the letter again and get a smaller response. On the third mailing, there is not enough response to justify the cost of mailing the letter. At this point, the letter has exhausted itself on this list.

The solution? Come up with a *series* of letters or mailing packages. When the first letter in the series is exhausted, you use the second letter; the fresh approach helps lift response and gets you more inquiries from this limited universe.

People frequently ask me, "What will happen if I mail the same letter or direct mail package to the same audience?" My experience is that, with a decent interval between mailings—four to eight weeks is ideal—the second mailing will pull between 40 and 60 percent of the response of the first mailing. Therefore, if the first mailing generated a 4 percent response rate, the second mailing of the same piece will pull about 2 percent. How do you determine whether to mail the same piece a second time? Well, would the mailing still be profitable if it pulls only half the response rate it originally did? If so, then it makes sense to mail the piece a second time before going to the effort and expense of creating a new mailing. This formula has been proven in repeated tests. As I write this, a client whose letter pulled a 5 percent response rate called and told me they got a 3 percent response rate (60 percent of the original) on the second mailing.

List duplication (merge/purge)

Another concern business-to-business mailers have is duplication of lists. People frequently ask me, "If we rent a subscriber list from a magazine and a trade show attendee list from a trade show in that same industry, won't there be a lot of duplication among the lists? And isn't this bad? And what do we do about it?" The answer is: Yes, there will probably be a lot of duplication. Is this bad? It's not terrible, but obviously there's some waste. And what can you do about it? Not much, if you mail small quantities.

As you're probably aware, through a service called *merge/purge,* duplicate names can be eliminated from multiple lists, preventing individuals who are on multiple lists from receiving more than one mailing piece. The problem is that this service costs money. Often the cost of a merge/purge service outweighs the cost of just mailing out the duplicate packages. How to you know when merge/purge is worthwhile? According to consultant Art Yates, it is not worth spending money on merge/purge for mailings of 30,000 pieces or less—and it's marginal for mailings of less than 50,000. The best advice is to talk with your computer shop or list broker about whether merge/purge makes sense. Another problem: Many business lists are not on computer disk, making merge/purge of these lists impossible.

Space commissions

Traditionally, ad agencies made their money based on a 15 percent commission they received when placing ads in the media for their clients. For instance, if you wanted to place an ad in Magazine X and the cost for a full-page was $10,000, the magazine would charge you $10,000 for the space. If an ad agency placed the ad for you, the magazine would give them an agency discount of 15 percent. Therefore, the ad agency would get the $10,000 ad for $8,500. The $1,500 discount represents their commission, or profit.

This made consumer advertising profitable for ad agencies and also made business-to-business advertising less profitable. For example, a full-page ad in a major national consumer magazine might cost $20,000. So the agency receives $3,000 every time they run the ad. By comparison, a full-page ad in an industry trade journal might cost $3,000, giving the agency only a $450 commission for placing the ad. Yet it theoretically takes no more time to place the $20,000 ad than it does the $3,000 ad, making the consumer account much more profitable for the ad agency. (I say "theoretically" because, in reality, consumer media buying can be more complicated and time-consuming than business-to-business media buying.)

Therefore, many business-to-business ad agencies find the 15 percent commission method of earning income either inadequate or archaic and have other ways of charging. Alexander Marketing, a Grand Rapids, Michigan, business-to-business ad agency, does not accept media commissions, choosing to return these commissions directly to the client. Instead, the agency simply bills for all of its time spent on the account at rates predetermined by contract with each client.

Business-to-business media also recognize that the 15 percent commission structure is antiquated. Many, many business publications give the 15 percent discount to you whether you're a real ad agency, an in-house ad agency for a manufacturer, or even if you're not an ad agency at all.

Creative fees

Although creative fees are not always smaller for business-to-business direct marketing than consumer marketing, often they are. This is because in a limited quantity business-to-business mailing, it's difficult to justify a high creative fee. Often, in analyzing the return on investment of a consumer mailing, the advertiser takes into account only the recurring costs of doing the mailing. These costs include printing, letter shop (putting together the pieces of the mailing and preparing it for the post office), postage, and list rentals.

What would these costs be? For an 11- by 17-inch self-mailer printed in two colors and folded to form a four-page brochure, the cost per thousand in 1991 was about $400 when mailed in quantities of 20,000 to 30,000. For a "standard" direct mail package consisting of a one- to two-page letter, folded booklet, and reply card in a #10 business envelope, the cost can easily run $500 to $700 per thousand.

Now, let's say you are doing a test mailing for a consumer product. The test quantity is 60,000 pieces. If you pay a freelance creative team (copywriter and artist) $10,000 to create the package ($5,000 for copy and $5,000 for design, type, and mechanicals), their fee represents an added cost (versus doing it yourself) of less than 17 cents per mailing. If the mailing is rolled out and eventually a million packages are mailed, your creative costs spread out over all those mailings come to a penny per mailing. Therefore, it's easy to justify spending a lot of money on the creative package; you can say, "We're reaching each prospect with a professional sales pitch for only an additional penny per prospect." That's an easy sell, isn't it?

With small-volume business-to-business mailings, it's the opposite. I recently saw a beautiful, elaborate four-color dimensional mailing that was mailed to only 200 prospects in a specialized industry. I estimated the client had spent about $10,000 to write, design, print, and mail these packages. That comes to $50 per prospect (the equivalent of a cost-per-thousand of $50,000!). If they get a 10 percent response, the mailing will have generated 20 leads at a cost per lead of $500. These figures seem steep, and I'd gulp hard before quoting them to a potential client. On the other hand, if even one sale brought in hundreds of thousands of dollars worth of business, as the client had hoped, the mailing would then pay for itself many times over.

Because the cost of creating the mailing is spread over a smaller number of prospects, business-to-business marketers are frequently more budget-conscious than their consumer counterparts when it comes to paying for creative services (copy, art, layout, photography, illustration). One way to justify the investment in such services is to design parts of the package so it can be used in more than one application. Many of my clients, for example, do mailings in #10 envelopes that consist of both a sales letter and a small folded brochure. To justify the cost, they do a larger print run of the brochure only and use the extra brochures as leave-behinds, trade show literature, and for a variety of other purposes.

What do creative services cost today? That's difficult to answer, because fees range all over. As of 1991, here are some typical fees for business-to-business direct response copywriting services:

1–2 page lead-generating sales letter	$950–$1,500
3–4 page letter to generate mail-order sales	$2,000–$3,000
Postcard for direct response postcard deck	$500–$750
Self-mailer, 8-1/2" x 11", folded twice to form six panels	$850–$1,500
Self-mailer, 11" x 17", folded to form four, 8-1/2" x 11" pages (a typical size for seminar or conference mailers)	$1,500–$2,500
Direct mail package, lead generating (consists of #10 outer envelope, 1-2 page sales letter, 8–1/2" x 11" brochure, folded to fit envelope, and simple reply card)	$1,500–$3,000+
Direct mail package, mail order (consists of a #10 or 6" x 9" outer envelope, 3-4 page sales letter, brochure, order form, business reply envelope, and possibly one or two small additional inserts, such as a buck slip)	
For a small-volume mailing for a specialized product	$2,500–$4,500
For a large-volume mailing to a mass audience	$3,000–$8,000
Direct response print ad, lead generation, full page	$850–$2,000

As a copywriter, I feel less comfortable quoting artists' fees, but in 1991, I was receiving quotes as follows. These prices include comps (layout sketches), design, mechanicals, and typography. Photography or illustration would be additional. (Often when doing a direct mail package, I like to save money by re-using illustrations or photos created for other promotions, such as the client's catalog or product brochure.)

Postcard for direct response postcard deck	$150–$300
Self-mailer, 8-1/2" x 11" folded twice to form six panels	$1,000–$1,750
Self-mailer, 11" x 17", folded to form four 8 1/2" x 11" pages (a typical size for seminar or conference mailers)	$1,500–$2,500
Direct mail package, lead generating (consists of #10 outer envelope, 1–2 page sales letter, 8-1/2" x 11" brochure, folded to fit envelope, and reply card)	$2,000–$3,000+
The above package, without the brochure (letter and reply card only)	$750–$1,500
Direct mail package, mail order (consists of a #10 or 6" x 9" outer envelope, 3-4 page sales letter, brochure, order form, business reply envelope, and possibly one or two small additional inserts, such as a buck slip)	$2,000–$6,000
Direct response print ad, lead generation, black and white, full page	$300–$2,000

If you're surprised at the wide range of fees being charged for art, there are two reasons for it:

1. Graphic artists vary widely in what they charge.

2. Those who use a desktop publishing system now quote much lower fees than those who do not.

Business reply mail

Another question that is frequently asked is, "Do I need to use a business reply permit on my reply card or reply envelope, or can I ask the recipient to affix postage?" In consumer direct mail, paying the postage by supplying a business reply envelope usually lifts response. If you are doing consumer direct mail, you should use a business reply envelope, unless your profit margin is so small that you can't afford it. (I have a small mail-order book business where such is the case with one of our product lines.)

In business-to-business direct mail, a business reply card or business reply envelope is desirable but not necessary. It's desirable because it's convenient for the prospect and conveys a professional image. If you're a small operation, for example, using a business reply card or envelope makes you look larger, more like a "real" company.

At the same time, it's not a necessity. Why not? In consumer direct mail, the logic behind using business reply envelopes is that you'll lose orders or inquiries if you don't use it and force the consumer to hunt for a stamp. But in most businesses, prospects give their outgoing mail to a secretary or assistant who runs it through the office postage meter. So the concern about not getting the replies back for lack of a stamp is not relevant. If you don't use a business reply permit, then simply place a box in the upper right corner of the address side of the reply card or envelope with copy reading "PLACE STAMP HERE."

Some people ask, "Wouldn't it be better to place stamps for the prospects on all my reply cards or envelopes?" No. It would be wasteful, and it wouldn't pay off. If you place a 29-cent stamp on 10,000 reply envelopes and, based on a 2 percent response rate, 9,800 are not returned, that represents $2,842 worth of stamps thrown in the trash. Better to use business reply mail, where you only pay the postage (plus an additional per-envelope service fee) for each envelope returned. Or just use "PLACE STAMP HERE."

I've not personally been involved in a test of "PLACE STAMP HERE" versus using a business reply card or envelope. In my direct mail seminars, several attendees have told me they tested this in business-to-business mailings in quantities of 10,000 or so with no noticeable difference in response. So you are safe with either option. But for the professional image it conveys, I recommend the slight additional expense of a business reply permit.

First class versus third class

Most large-volume consumer direct mail packages are sent third-class bulk rate. In fact, this is the preferred postage choice for most direct mail. Yet, in more and more situations, I am recommending to clients that they use first class instead—despite the higher cost. Consumer direct marketers will continue to use the cheaper third-class bulk mail rate. This is a necessity in consumer mail–order selling, where the profit margins per thousand pieces are low. In such mailings, even a small additional cost per thousand can convert the mailer from a profit–maker to a money-loser. To put it simply, the marketer selling magazine subscriptions, term life insurance, or other low–cost products via mail order simply *cannot afford* first-class mail.

On the other hand, Gary Halbert, a direct marketing expert, says that he has had success in consumer mailings using first-class mail. Others also say that if you can afford it, first class is better than third class. Why? Because third-class bulk rate is the "standard" choice for most direct mail, a third-class bulk rate mailing indicia printed on the outer envelope automatically alerts the consumer that your envelope contains "junk mail." If you are going to use third-class, use a postage meter or precanceled third-class stamp instead of an indicia, if possible.

In business-to-business direct mail, use of third-class bulk rate is an even more serious problem for three reasons. First, a certain percentage of third-class bulk rate direct mail is never delivered to the addressee. Postal employees dump it or simply never bother to deliver it. One study said the nondelivery rate for third-class bulk rate mail was 11 percent. This means one out of every ten of your packages never even gets to the address on the mailing label. Second, recent articles in *The Wall Street Journal* and other business publications report that the mail rooms of many large corporations routinely throw away mail they perceive as advertising mail rather than personal correspondence. So one reason for your low response rate is that the mail rooms are throwing your third-class mailings away. Third, even when the post office and mail room deliver the mail to your prospect's office, the secretaries screen the mail and throw away things they think are junk mail or unimportant. One study by Ogilvy and Mather showed that about half of executives and managers in business have their secretary screen their mail for them. So of the mail that does get delivered, half may be thrown away by the secretary.

In combination, these factors result in an overall low delivery rate for third-class bulk rate mail. According to an article in *The Russ von Hoelscher Direct Response Profit Report* newsletter (July 1989), "A recent study by the Direct Marketing Association showed that over 30 percent of the bulk rate ad mail mailed to business addresses never reaches the person it was intended for."

Mailing first class solves a lot of these problems. First-class mail has a much lower nondelivery rate than third class; practically all first-class mail gets delivered. First-class mail is not thrown away by the mail room. And using first class helps convince the secretary that your communication is professional, not promotional. So in much business-to-business mailing, we use first class instead of third.

Of course, a major factor that determines whether you mail first or third class for your business-to-business mailings is cost. In 1991, mailing a 1-ounce #10 envelope package first class cost 29 cents per piece, or $290 per thousand. Mailing the same package third-class bulk rate (with no carrier presort or other discounts) cost 19.8 cents per package, or $198 per thousand. Therefore, you are paying an extra $92 per thousand for the privilege of mailing first class.

If you are mailing to 500 OEMs (original equipment manufacturers) in the automobile industry, you'd probably agree the extra $46 in postage isn't a big consideration and that you should go first class for the faster delivery and greater impact. On the other hand, if you're a small business mailing 40,000 pieces per month, using third class instead of first class saves you $44,160 per year.

How long does it take for your third-class bulk rate mail to reach the prospect once your letter shop brings it to the post office? Jerry Lake, owner of Jerry Lake Mailing Services, a letter shop in Emerson, New Jersey, says two and a half weeks is average. I find it takes closer to three weeks. First-class mail is generally delivered within two to five days.

However, these figures are for delivery from your post office to the recipient's door. In a large corporation, you have to add a couple of days for the package to get from the mail room (if they deliver it at all) to your prospect's in-basket. Give the prospect a day or two to read it and respond. Wait another day for the reply card to get from the prospect's desk to his or her mail room. Then wait a week for the reply card to get back to you via business reply mail.

On a third-class bulk rate mailing, this can mean you may not get your initial replies until three to four weeks *after* you mail. So don't panic when weeks go by and you don't get any response. You have to be patient. On a first-class mailing, you will probably get some replies within a week to ten days. And you'll get the bulk of your replies within four weeks after you mail.

Screening

Another significant difference of business-to-business versus consumer direct mail is the secretarial "screening," as mentioned above.

According to the study by Ogilvy and Mather Direct, about half of all business executives have their secretaries screen their mail. Therefore, business–to–business mailers feel an extra pressure (that consumer mailers do not) to find some way to get it past a secretary to the recipient.

Is this necessary? It depends on who the prospect is and where he or she works. My experience is that the larger the prospect's company, and the higher up on the corporate ladder the prospect is, the more likely they are to have an assistant screen their mail. Therefore, when mailing to top–level executives at *Fortune* 1000 companies, you should consider who will be screening the mail and how your package will be perceived by this screener. Does it look important, or like "junk mail"?

When mailing to lower-level employees, it's less important to worry about this aspect of the mailing's appearance. With "downsizing" the trend in corporate America today, many middle–level managers and professionals either share a secretary or don't have one and open their own mail. Therefore, you don't have to design your package to get past the "gatekeeper." The same is true when mailing to small businesses. In a company with one or two or six employees, the mail is usually distributed to everyone without being screened. So you don't have to worry about getting past a gatekeeper.

Exceptions? Of course. I think nurses or other assistants in doctors' offices routinely screen mail (this opinion is based on first-hand observation). Doctors think of themselves as important, and their nurses protect and nurture this image. So it wouldn't do for "doctor" to dirty his hands with "junk mail." One day, as I was paying for a dental exam, I watched my dentist's receptionist sort through the mail. As she piled some for delivery to the dentist, and round-filed other pieces, I asked her how she made those decisions. Her simple reply: "If it looks important, I give it to him. If it doesn't, I throw it away."

So a key strategy to getting your business-to-business direct mail past the secretary or receptionist is to make it "look important." This could be accomplished in one of several ways: Through use of an elegant or expensive paper stock. Through personalization of the outer envelope (How important can it be if an address label is glued to it?). Or sometimes, simply by the nature of the subject matter.

This means if your product is important to the reader, the screener may pass on to the boss mailings that contain information about such products. If the product is not inherently vital to your prospect, your outer envelope copy should address a problem or need important to the recipient and not talk about the product itself.

Another strategy for getting direct mail past the secretary is to "disguise" your mailing so it looks like ordinary business correspondence, not promotion material. To accomplish this, do the following:

- Mail in your regular #10 business envelope.

- Mail first class.

- Use a stamp or meter (not an indicia).

- Type the recipient's name and address directly on the outer envelope using a typewriter, word processor, laser, impact, or ink jet system.

Formulas for estimating response

There are a variety of formulas for estimating total response to a direct mail package based on initial returns received after a certain number of weeks. This period is counted starting with the day you *receive your first reply*—NOT from the day you send out your mailing. Russ von Hoelscher, a mail-order consultant, says that for a direct mail package, you will get about half of your total orders or inquiries within 18 days after you receive your first reply when you mail bulk rate; 6 days when you mail first class. Therefore, to estimate total response, you take the number of replies received at the end of 18 days (or 6 days for first class) and double the figure. While this doesn't always hold true, it's a somewhat accurate indicator. However, I'm more comfortable telling clients that by four weeks after the initial response, they've probably received 40 to 60 percent of the replies they are going to get.

Another interesting phenomenon that occurs in business-to-business, especially with lead-generating direct mail, is that inquiries may continue to dribble in for many months after the bulk of them are received. This is especially true if your mailing contained a brochure, folder, or even a letter that was so interesting or valuable prospects found it worth keeping.

In my own copywriting and consulting business, I have received telephone calls and reply cards up to *one year or more* after sending out the mailing! And often these "late callers" are people who do not reply to mailings unless they have a real, immediate need. They didn't mail your reply card because they're not brochure collectors. They just kept your mailing in a reference file, and now that they need your type of product or service, they're calling. As a result, such inquiries have a high probability of converting into a sale.

The 2 percent myth

What kind of response can you expect from business-to-business direct mail? And what's the best way to measure it? It depends on whether we're talking about lead-generating mailings or mailings designed to generate a direct sale. But first, a few general guidelines that apply to both types of mailings.

Contrary to the widely held notion, there is no single figure that can be used as an "average" or "typical" direct mail response rate. At this point some of you may be thinking, "But I heard that 2 percent is the average response rate." But what does that mean? Is it leads or sales? Did 2 percent request more information, or did they actually order the product? Since it's easier to get a lead than a sale, it seems logical that response rates would differ for lead-generating versus mail-order packages.

Also, you'll hear people tell you that direct mail packages with a separate sales letter and reply card will outpull a self-mailer. So for which format is the 2 percent rate being quoted as "typical"—the self-mailer or the full package?

Another factor that varies the response rate is the *product*. Obviously, a product with broad appeal to your audience would generate a higher direct mail response rate than a product with limited appeal.

There really is no "typical" direct response rate, and it's a mistake to blindly set a 2 percent response as your target goal for every mailing. A better approach is to consider your first mailing effort on a particular product as the "baseline." Doctors frequently do this with medical tests such as EKGs and mammograms. The first test or scan in a healthy patient determines the patient's norm or baseline condition. Variations in subsequent tests indicate an improvement or deterioration in health.

It's the same with business-to-business direct mail. Let's say you get a 3 percent response with your first mailing. That becomes your baseline. If the next mailing pulls a 2 percent response, you know you haven't done as well as you can with this product. If a third mailing pulls a 3.5 percent response, you know you've got an incremental improvement in gross response rate of half a percent for your time and trouble. Ignore the "2 percent is standard" rule. The baseline tells you what's "average" or typical for your product, given your price, offer, and market.

Estimating response to business-to-business lead-generating mailings

Although, as we've just discussed, I feel it's dangerous to give "typical" response rates, I know that's what you are looking for. So let me give you some feel for what you can expect when you mail a lead-generating mailing. However, I cannot stress enough that these are rough averages only and may or may not apply to your product.

For a mailing in which the only response is a "hard" offer—that is, to respond you must take some active step, such as calling a salesperson, having a sales representative visit your office, or going to a seminar or demonstration—the response rates range from 0.5 percent to about 2 percent. For a mailing that has both a hard offer and a soft offer—the soft offer typically being "mail the enclosed reply card for a free brochure"— average response rates are from 1 to 4 percent or so. For a business-to-business lead-generating mailing that stresses the soft offer—that is, emphasizes the free booklet, report, or information kit being offered rather than the product itself—average response rates are from 1.5 to 5 percent. If the free offer is particularly enticing, or if a valuable premium (free gift as an incentive to respond) is added, response rates of 5 to 10 percent or more are possible.

Note: I define a "response" as a fax, phone call, letter, or the return of a reply card by a prospect responding to your mailing. These figures do not include prospects who do not respond to the initial mailing but are persuaded to take action after a follow-up phone call, visit, or mailing. The response rate figures also do not take into account whether the leads are of good quality (genuine prospects) or poor quality ("brochure collectors").

Here we are talking about inquiries only. But what percentage of prospects who inquire and request a brochure or sales presentation actually buy? Again, it varies. But typically, between 10 and 25 percent of the sales leads can be converted to sales within a few weeks to six months after the inquiries are received. In some cases, this is done with a simple follow-up mailing or phone call. For more expensive products or services, it may take numerous meetings, calls, letters, and follow-ups to close the deal.

Estimating response to business-to-business mail-order direct mail

The key observation that can be made about mail-order marketing over the past several years is that response rates are on the decline. One fund-raising consultant told me, "Response rates to direct mail packages seeking donations used to average 3 percent. Today we are getting a 1 percent response." In a recent issue of *The Libey Letter,* direct marketing expert Don Libey observed that while response rates used to be 2 to 4 percent years ago, today response rates of 0.25 to 0.5 percent are common.

Newsletters, magazines, and other products sold by mail have had similar declines in response rates. Combined with increases in postal rates and production costs, this has made it increasingly difficult to sell products via direct mail at a profit.

What kind of response can you expect from a "solo" direct mail package selling a single item direct via mail order? Response rates of 0.5 percent to 2 percent are typical. Offers for high-priced products, such as software, can be profitable at response rates below 1 percent. It's tough to make a profit selling directly through the mail a business product or service that sells for under $50 or even under $100.

A more meaningful measure of direct marketing success

Although percentage response is the simplest way to measure the performance of a direct mail package, it's not the truest test. What you really want to know is: Was the package profitable? Did it make money? Lose money? Break even? So you must analyze not only number of replies received, but also gross sales and net profit generated.

Measuring the sales results of business-to-business lead-generating direct mail

Example: You use a lead-generating sales letter with reply card to generate inquiries for a $2,000 business service. Your letter generates a 2 percent response. That's 20 replies per thousand pieces mailed. The cost of mailing the letter is $600 per thousand. To calculate the cost per inquiry, we divide $600 by 20 inquiries and get $30 per sales lead.

Let's say 10 percent of the 20 prospects buy the service. That's two sales at $2,000 per contact for a gross of $4,000. Your profit per thousand is the $4,000 in gross sales less the $600 per thousand mail cost, or $3,400. To put it another way, you're getting an almost 7:1 return on your investment ($4,000 sales divided by $600 mailing cost). For each $1 spent on direct mail, you make almost $7 in sales.

Measuring the sales results of business-to-business mail-order direct mail

Example: Let's say we are selling a $149 software product via mail order. The cost to manufacture and ship the product is $15 per unit. Therefore, the profit is $149 minus $15, or $134 per unit sold. Now, we have to print and mail a direct mail package to get orders. Let's say our cost for the mailing is $700 per thousand. To calculate the number of orders needed to break even:

$$\text{Break even} = \frac{\text{Cost per thousand of mailing}}{\text{Profit per order}}$$

For our example:

$$\frac{\$700 \text{ mailing expense}}{\$134 \text{ profit per unit}} = 5.2 \text{ orders per thousand pieces mailed}$$

In terms of percentage response this comes to:

$$\frac{5.2 \text{ orders}}{1,000 \text{ mailings}} \times 100 = 0.52 \text{ percent}$$

Therefore, we break even on the mailing with only 0.52 percent response rate. At a 1 percent response rate, we get $2 in income for every $1 spent on direct mail. At a 2 percent response rate, we quadruple our investment every time we mail 1,000 pieces.

Break-even objectives for business-to-business versus consumer mail order

What should your goal be? It depends. Some mailers are willing to break even or even lose money on the first order to gain a customer and build a mailing list. For them, the profits are made on the "back end"—that is, mailing additional offers to existing customers. Many consumer mail-order firms take this approach. So do large-volume businesss-to-business direct marketers that sell a broad line of products and have many thousands of customers and prospects.

Business-to-business direct marketers that have only one or two products need to make a profit from the "front end," or initial mailing, because they don't have a back end of related items to sell. Companies that have specialized, high-priced products appealing to a limited market also seek substantial profits on the front end. Also, many smaller companies simply cannot afford to lose money to acquire customers and therefore must design their direct marketing programs so that profit is made from every mailing.

Business-to-business versus consumer databases

As mentioned, back-end mailings offering related items to your "house" mailing list or database of customers are generally very profitable for two reasons:

1. They cost less. Since you own the list, the $100 per thousand or so cost of renting mailing lists is eliminated. And, because the customers already know you and your product, a less elaborate mailing piece can often be used.

2. The response is generally better—again, because the customer knows you and is already doing business with your firm.

According to Ken Morris, a mailing list expert, repeated marketing efforts to a database of customers and prospects will produce from 2 to 10 times higher response than mailings to rented lists of "cold" prospect names. Will such database marketing be important to you? Only if (a) your universe is large, (b) you can gain a big enough market share to build a sizable customer list, and (c) you have other products, services, accessories, or things to sell to these customers.

One of my clients is a management consulting firm that sells a very expensive consulting program to management at large corporations. Because the firm is small and the consulting contracts are large, they take on very few jobs in a year. Therefore, they have a small client list. So they cannot justify the cost of doing an elaborate series of database mailings to a database of only 50 to 100 clients. Instead, consultants simply keep in touch with their clients, sending personal correspondence about new services or programs from time to time. Another client, on the other hand, has an installed base of 22,000 organizations using their software. Obviously, doing direct mail programs to sell training, consulting services, maintenance and support contracts, upgrades, and new versions of the software can be extremely profitable and worthwhile for them, because the house list is big enough to justify the time and expense involved.

3

How to Make Every Marketing Communication into a Direct Marketing Communication (And Why It Pays To Do So)

Is all business-to-business marketing direct marketing?

Recall from Chapter 1 the definitions of "general advertising" and "direct marketing." General advertising is concerned with building an image or creating an awareness of a product over the long haul; direct marketing is concerned with generating an immediate, tangible response—either an inquiry or an order.

Most industrial, high-tech, and business-to-business marketers think of their marketing communications programs as "general" or "image-building" advertising. That is, we think our goal is to communicate a message, or establish a product's position in the marketplace, or make the company name well-known. And to a degree, that's desirable and should be part of your objective.

For some manufacturers, measurement is difficult. Others, frankly, don't think it's important. One large corporate client stated bluntly: "The success of our in-house advertising department is determined by whether the client (product manager) likes the ad or brochure we produce. We sell expensive capital equipment. We don't measure ad response, and I'm not sure it would be meaningful."

But in reality, 99 percent of all business-to-business marketing communications, in addition to communicating a message or building an image, also seek to elicit some response from the potential customer—a key component of any direct marketing communication. Think about it. Unlike the consumer, who can simply walk into a nearby store and buy consumer products advertised in the newspaper or on TV, the business buyer has to initiate *direct contact* with the seller of a business product or service to make a purchase. Virtually every business-to-business ad, catalog, brochure, or mailing contains *at least* a phone number or address where the reader can call or write to get more information, request a price quotation, or speak to a salesperson.

While it may not be traditional one-step direct marketing or "mail order," just about every business-to-business sale takes place as a result of the *prospect's* making a direct contact with the buyer. All marketing communications have, as one of their key objectives, the mission of persuading the prospect to make that contact.

Therefore, what I am proposing is that virtually *all* business-to-business marketing communications are *direct* marketing, whether we think of them that way or not. The difference between the business-to-business marketer who thinks in terms of direct marketing and the business-to-business marketer who doesn't is simply that the former produces communications that generate immediate response and sales results while the latter tends not to.

The premise of this chapter—and indeed, a central premise of this book—is that you can make your business-to-business marketing communications many times more effective and profitable by deliberately designing them as response-getting direct marketing promotions, not merely information-communicating general advertising pieces.

Further, you can do this not only with marketing communication vehicles that are traditionally used in direct response, such as ads and direct mail, but you can also turn *any* marketing communication into a direct response communication, even those not traditionally used to generate direct inquiries or sales. These include speeches, seminars, product brochures, press releases, magazine articles, and many others discussed later in this chapter.

What does it take to turn a regular marketing communication into a "direct response" marketing communication?

Converting a conventional marketing communication into a direct response marketing communication takes more than just slapping on a telephone number and address, although that certainly is part of it. Actually, it's a combination of techniques and mindset.

By "techniques" I am referring to the mechanical techniques direct marketers use to turn ordinary print or audiovisual communication into direct response communication. These techniques include use of business reply cards, order forms, toll-free telephone numbers, free booklets, special time-limited offers, and coupons. By "mindset" I mean that to become an effective direct marketer, you have to think differently than you may have in the past when it comes to creating advertising that sells.

A different mentality

The business-to-business marketer who enthusiastically embraces the direct response mindset to marketing communications has a different approach to creating advertising materials than the marketer who does not think in direct marketing terms. The general marketers, or "generalists," as David Ogilvy calls them, think as follows: The primary objective of an ad, brochure, or commercial is to create a favorable impression in the mind of the buyer. Marketing communications build image, create awareness, or develop preference or recognition for a particular brand or product over an extended period of time.

This calls for creating an ad, brochure, or other marketing document that is eye-catching, attention-grabbing, and extremely *memorable*. The communication has to "stand out" so that it is remembered. Also, all marketing communications should have a similar look, feel, theme, and message, so that the cumulative effect is to implant the desired ideas in the minds of the prospects.

As a result, the generalists place a great emphasis on brevity, because a shorter message is easier to remember than a longer one. They also tend to rely heavily on slogans, tag lines, themes, positioning statements, or similar devices that sum up the main selling idea in a few pithy sentences and that can be used over and over on each new ad or marketing document. Their favorite "measurement" is often a readership study that shows high reader recall of their ad or a market research study that shows high recognition of their company or product name.

The general business-to-business marketer prefers a creative approach to advertising, fearing that direct marketing techniques such as all-type designs and long-copy ads bore prospects. Many generalists will tell you that people "don't read copy" and therefore rely heavily on graphics, illustrations, pictures, and design to convey their message. Their main instruction to the copywriter: Keep it short. Their main instruction to the designer: Make it different, eye-catching.

Generalists also place heavy emphasis on "continuity"—having a consistent graphic look and style to all marketing materials. There is some validity to this approach, especially in print advertising: A uniform graphic approach builds recognition so that when readers see your ad, they immediately identify it with your company. At least one of my clients has proven this through readership studies made on a long-running series of graphically consistent print ads.

The generalist either isn't concerned with the next step in the buying process (believing prospects will take it only when they are good and ready) or else fears that asking the reader to take direct action is too crass, inappropriate, or offensive. They avoid using coupons in ads for fear of destroying the clean design of their layouts. Some even object to putting a phone number or address on a brochure, for reasons I have never fully understood.

Direct marketers think differently

The business-to-business marketers who consider themselves "direct marketers" or are fans of using direct marketing techniques approach their advertising and marketing communications programs quite differently. Like the general marketer, the direct marketer may have a variety of marketing objectives, including building image, communicating a message, and so on. But unlike the general marketer, one of the direct marketer's top objectives is to generate direct responses from every marketing communication. That is, they intend to generate inquiries that can be counted and measured, and to then convert the maximum number of inquiries to sales.

For a variety of reasons, it's often difficult to determine the source of many of the leads, and it's even harder to track which sales came as a result of a direct-marketing generated inquiry. So the business-to-business marketer doesn't always have a precise measure of how well each marketing program is performing. Realizing that, he or she still strives to track and measure results *as well as possible.* The business-to-business marketer wants to know, whenever possible, how much sales were produced for every dollar spent on advertising, public relations, direct mail, or sales promotion.

The general marketer says, "Business-to-business advertising helps build image and awareness. It doesn't produce sales. Salespeople do that." The manager with a direct marketing mindset says, "Baloney. My communications program generates direct inquiries from qualified prospects, a certain percentage of which convert to sales. Most of what I do either sells—or *helps* sell—more of our company's products and services."

While the general marketer may emphasize creativity and the quality of writing and design, the direct marketer is results-oriented. Ads and brochures are written to give the business prospects precisely the information they need to take the next step in the buying process. That next step is always spelled out, incentives are given for taking it, and mechanisms (reply cards, 800-numbers, coupons, fax forms) are provided to encourage prospects to take immediate action.

The business-to-business direct marketer says, "It's all well and good to talk about 'image' and 'positioning' and future sales, but I want an *immediate* return on every dollar spent on mailings or literature or space ads." While the general marketer thinks of herself as employed in "communications," the direct marketer would rather *sell* than just *communicate*.

Interestingly, many advertising managers working for large corporations that sell business-to-business products tend to be generalists, while entrepreneurs and managers at small to medium-size firms tend to be direct marketers. Why is this so? Several reasons. The large corporations, because of their financial resources, can afford some "waste." That is, they can spend $500,000 on a "corporate image" campaign that makes people feel good but doesn't do anything for sales, and it won't hurt them.

To the small firm, on the other hand, spending $500,000 or $50,000 or even $5,000 and not getting any return for it can hurt considerably. Entrepreneurs, in my experience, are extremely insistent on getting an immediate payback for money spent on marketing, probably because they see the money as coming directly out of their own pockets as opposed to the corporate manager, who may be spending someone else's money.

The corporate manager may also have responsibility for many different product lines, divisions, or groups, and a great deal of his or her energy goes toward coordinating multiple marketing programs and ensuring that they are consistent and of high quality. The small or medium-size business manager usually has only one product or service to sell, so sales—not consistency—is the key concern.

Another reason that small businesspeople are often advocates of measurable direct response marketing is that they actually receive and, in some cases, follow up on the leads generated. A lead is meaningful to them, because it means a sale. In large corporations, where there are many channels of distribution, marketing-generated leads may or may not be of critical importance, depending on how the company is organized. I have some clients who live and die by how many marketing-generated leads are converted to sales; I have others for whom lead generation is not of primary concern.

"Continuity," or consistency in style, tone, and design from piece to piece, is not emphasized by direct marketing types. Indeed, in some cases, response can be dampened if pieces look too much alike and increased by making each piece markedly different. For example, in magazine publishing, renewal and billing letter series perform better when each piece is a different size and has a different outer envelope. Make the pieces all the same size and format, and response goes down. Reason: Perhaps when people receive a series of mailings that all look the same, they think they are getting the initial piece over and over and just throw the subsequent pieces out.

The best of both worlds

If your marketing communications program is more geared toward general advertising and image-building now, am I telling you to scrap it? No. Effective communication, product positioning, company image, and awareness-building all have their places and shouldn't be abandoned. Don't replace your existing marketing communications program; instead, augment it. Using proven direct marketing methods, you can take an *existing* program and dramatically enhance its effectiveness by applying proven direct response techniques, while leaving its core intact. This has a number of advantages, as outlined below.

Why every marketing communication should be a direct response marketing communication

If you could leave your marketing communications program essentially unchanged and make a few simple improvements at low cost to dramatically multiply the sales and profits it generates, would you do it? Of course you would. And that's what this book shows you how to do. Converting "conventional" business-to-business marketing communications programs into direct response communications offers you these important benefits:

1. It doesn't interfere with your communications objectives.

You can convert your existing marketing communications into direct response communications without reducing their ability to communicate the messages you want to get across to your marketplace.

There's a myth general advertisers hold that says direct marketing is somehow cheap and sleazy, and using direct marketing techniques in general advertising lessens the overall impact. But it's just not true.

How does adding a coupon "destroy" an ad, as many general ad agency art directors would claim? It doesn't. Why is putting an address and phone number on a product brochure "inappropriate," as a marketing manager at a major New York bank once insisted to me? It isn't.

The thought that using direct marketing techniques (such as business reply cards, coupons, and order forms) negatively affects image, credibility, and communications effectiveness is incorrect, and there is not one shred of evidence I've seen to support it. In fact, I have found the opposite to be the case. Which brings us to our next point.

2. Using direct marketing techniques actually IMPROVES the quality of marketing communications.

Because direct marketing is measurable, the advertising manager or copywriter who produces a direct response promotion is subject to a rigorous, unforgiving scrutiny that the general advertiser is not. When you produce a general advertisement or commercial, you're measured by subjective judgment only: Your client or boss either likes it or doesn't. So you can always please them by revising according to their wishes.

In direct marketing, it's different. A sales letter that pleases the client may fail to generate a profitable response. Conversely, a copy approach the client hates may prove to be the most effective in the marketplace. Therefore, you're not held accountable only to a client's or manager's subjective standards; your success is also measured by how many leads or sales your work generates once produced.

Direct marketers are constantly under pressure to have their mailing or ad "test well" against the control or, if there is no control, to generate a high level of response. This motivates us to stop being creative and cute and concentrate instead on writing and designing promotions that *generate the highest possible response in the marketplace*. Instead of indulging creative whims or designing something that's clever or funny or that will win us an award, we concentrate on selling—and achieve it by producing materials that, while effective, are often unglamorous. Being accountable for the *marketing results* of what you design, write, or produce forces you to view what you're doing as a selling effort rather than "creating literature."

As a result, treating every marketing communication as a direct response communication forces a discipline that makes ad agencies and copywriters "sweat" over their work so that it's productive, not beautiful. Not only does this increase marketing results, but it reduces excess and waste, because the fanciest or most expensive approach, while easy to produce, is rarely the most cost-effective or profitable one for the client.

3. Direct marketing is more tangible.

When you're trying to justify a marketing budget to top management, saying that it "builds image" or helps "position the company" is a hard sell. Top management in business-to-business firms is usually not advertising oriented, and they focus on immediate results, not long-term objectives that are difficult to quantify.

By generating substantial inquiries and sales from every marketing communication, direct marketing techniques generate the kind of tangible return on investment that management can understand and appreciate.

You know that, despite what management might say about the importance of image-building or product awareness, when you spend $10,000 on an ad or a mailing, management doesn't ask "How much image did we build?" or "How's our product awareness?" They look at the ad and say, "How many inquiries did we get?" They look at the mailing piece and say, "What percentage response did we get?"

You also know that the best way to convince management of the worth of your program is not with awareness or readership studies (though those may help) but to point to a big new client or contract recently awarded to your firm and say, "That sale came from a lead generated by our ad in *XYZ Magazine*." That's the kind of real-world sales result that gets top management excited about marketing communications. That's the kind of potential result I can show you how to get from every marketing document you produce.

4. Direct marketing is self-liquidating.

Even if you're not a "pure" direct marketer—that is, you don't sell directly off the printed ad or brochure page—you should convert your marketing communications to direct marketing communications. They'll still retain their basic look, theme, and message, but you'll gain a steady flow of direct inquiries and leads from pieces that formerly were just "out there" being looked at but not responded to.

As an example, we took a press release a client had done on a specific technology issue and offered to send a lengthier summary of the key points, reprinted in the form of a simple one-page checklist, to anyone who sent us $1 plus a self-addressed stamped envelope. The release cost about $1,500 to write, print, and mail.

Generally, most clients look for press releases to generate media coverage, which this one did. But in addition, it also generated 2,500 requests for the tip sheet. Now, the purpose was not to make a big profit from selling a $1 tip sheet. But notice: We had no outgoing postage cost for fulfillment, because the prospects supplied self-addressed stamped envelopes. In addition, the $2,500 in one-dollar bills we collected more than paid for the entire promotion—making it completely self-liquidating.

5. Direct marketing is "hot."

In addition to being an independent copywriter and marketing consultant, I also give speeches, seminars, and do in-house training for corporations. Ten years ago, "Copywriting" was the most requested topic. Not any more. Today it's "Direct Mail"—by a wide margin.

Direct mail is hot. It's what today's business-to-business managers want to do more of. Sure, some people don't like it. But if you're an ad manager, self-employed marketing professional, ad agency, executive, or product manager, rest assured your client or boss will ask you someday, "Why don't we do more direct mail?"

Recent cover stories in major business magazines report that traditional advertising—magazines, newspapers, television—is in decline. On the other hand, marketing that brings a more tangible, immediate, and (some critics would say) "short-term" result—sales promotion, direct mail, telemarketing—are on the rise. So get a jump and put direct marketing into your marketing communications now. Be proactive, not reactive.

6. In business-to-business lead generation, it's relatively easy to make the program pay off.

Many consumer direct marketers—most of whom sell relatively low-priced consumer merchandise directly via mail order through direct mail, space ads, or catalogs—are having a tough time right now. With response rates down and the cost-per-thousand of catalogs and solo mailings way up, it's more difficult today than in the 1980s or 1970s to break even or make a profit. One expert even proclaimed: "The old industry standard—the #10-size third-class bulk mail direct mail package—is dead."

The truth is, making money in mail order has always been tricky. With small profit margins, a small change in percentage response can mean the difference between profit and loss. At 1 percent, you could be making money, but at 0.7 percent, you'd be out of business. Business-to-business direct marketing, because it usually involves lead generation rather than direct sales, and because the products being sold are generally more expensive than consumer merchandise, isn't as vulnerable to declining response rates or increases in production and postage costs.

For example, the typical mailing I write is a one- to two-page sales letter with a business reply card and perhaps a small booklet in a #10 envelope, all designed to generate sales leads for a business product or service costing from $2,000 to $20,000 to $200,000 or more. Let's say $20,000 is typical. At a cost per thousand of $700, if we only sell *one unit* per thousand pieces mailed (0.1 percent sales rate), we're getting a return on our marketing dollar of nearly 29:1. With a client in this situation, they don't care all that much if postage goes up and the package now costs $800 per thousand; they can still live quite nicely with one sale per thousand at that cost level.

So business-to-business lead-generating direct marketing is more immune than consumer mail order to rises in production, paper, printing, list rental, and postal costs. That's a nice advantage, and it gives you a little more room to relax than our counterparts in hard-sell mail order.

In fact, the profit potential from even a small lead-generating campaign can be enormous. One client recently hired me to write a mailing going to only 2,000 prospects to sell them a $700,000 machine. Now, it may seem like a lot of work to create a mailing to be read by only 2,000 people, especially if you're a consumer marketer used to mailing millions. On the other hand, the client will profit handsomely even if the return rate is 1/20th of 1 percent (only one prospect buys a machine for $700,000).

7. Direct marketing is more targeted.

As a rule, general or image advertising tends to be written to appeal to a broad audience, while the discipline in direct marketing calls for targeting appeals to specific audiences. This is good, because experience proves again and again that the more carefully you select your audience and tailor your message to the concerns, needs, and desires of that audience, the more your message will be read, remembered, and reacted to.

At a recent meeting, I was sitting with a young advertising manager who is enormously talented and dedicated, but not heavily experienced in direct marketing. They were doing generic mailings on their computer system; I suggested they identify specific vertical markets and target mailings to these markets. The advertising manager, who had been trained in general advertising, then asked me about the length of copy. "What is better—a one-page letter or a two-page letter?" As we talked, the president of the firm—an experienced direct marketer and student of mail order—entered the room.

"It doesn't have to be one or two pages," he said to his manager. "The letter can be eight pages long and they will read every word . . . *if it is of interest to them.*" And you can only generate this level of sustained interest when copy is targeted. Specifics captivate an audience. Generalities may roll off the tongue more trippingly, but readers soon tire of them and move on. Concretes sell; abstracts do not engage interest.

How to convert ordinary marketing communications into direct marketing communications

If you're an experienced direct marketer, this section may be a refresher or even too elementary to you. But for this book to be complete, we need to present a checklist, or formula, readers can use to convert existing marketing programs into response-getting direct marketing communications. Here then are the requirements for a successful direct marketing piece:

1. It attracts attention with a benefit-oriented or curiosity-arousing headline, teaser, or lead.

The headline of the ad, cover of the brochure, or teaser on the outer envelope of an effective direct marketing piece gains attention with a reader-centered message. Typically, the message either promises a benefit or arouses curiosity. It might also attract notice by identifying or selecting an audience.

The key point is that *the headline is designed to lure readers into the body copy*. This is in contrast to general or image advertising, where the headline is often designed to deliver a memorable message and do nothing else. The general advertiser makes the assumption that people won't read body copy and therefore the ad headline should be designed to make an impression or communicate a single easily remembered idea.

The direct marketer's approach is best summed up by mail-order guru Joseph Sugarman, who says the purpose of the headline is to get the prospect to read the first sentence of the ad; the purpose of the first sentence is to get you to read the second sentence; and so on. Marketers with mail-order backgrounds assert that genuine prospects will read long copy if it's of interest to them, and that the more you can get the prospect to read, the better your chance of making the sale.

Some examples? *The ASU Travel Guide,* a paid-subscription publication that contains information on travel discounts available only to airline employees, retirees, and their families, recently mailed a package to get former subscribers to resubscribe. The outer envelope teaser read, "WE WANT TO PUT THE WORLD AT YOUR FINGERTIPS. FOR FREE." This type of teaser arouses curiosity. What do they mean? What is being given free? The offer here was for a free mini-world atlas to those who resubscribed.

An example of a headline that promises a reward for reading the copy is this headline from a consumer magazine ad: "THE SECRET TO RICHER, MOISTER CHOCOLATE CAKE." It promises the benefit of delicious cake. And the word "secret" also works to arouse curiosity.

An example of an outer envelope teaser that gains attention by identifying the audience is a mailing recently sent to me by *Writer's Digest.* The teaser, "ATTENTION FREELANCE WRITERS," works because, if you're a freelance writer, you figure the contents are targeted to your interests. Of course this would be an utter failure if mailed to nonwriters.

The first step, then, to converting ordinary business communications to direct response communications is to take a no-nonsense, direct approach to writing headlines for article reprints, brochure covers, booklets, and whatever other materials you produce. Change all those cutesy headlines, those puns, those plays on words your agency thought were so clever! People don't get it. Be clear and direct—just say what you want to say. Business prospects will respond.

2. Appeal to the reader's self-interest.

At this point, you may be thinking, "Wait a minute, Bob. This doesn't sound right. My product or service is *boring*. If I present it in a direct, straightforward fashion, prospects won't read it. I know that *I* like clever, creative, and humorous ads and TV commercials. Aren't my prospects the same?"

I understand your concern. And I am not saying you should never be creative or clever or different. On the contrary, if you can say something of interest to your prospect in a fresh and different way, they'll respond to it. The problem is that creativity, which should be just another tool in the marketer's arsenal, has become for many advertising people the *ends* rather than the means. Too often the client starts a campaign with the commandment to the staff, agency, or freelancers, "Be different, be creative," rather than, "Be effective, be relevant, communicate this key message."

Ad agency executive John Egley, writing in *Business Marketing* magazine, said it best: "It is the unrelenting, oppressive pressure to be imaginative that is responsible for most bad advertising. It causes people to suspend judgment, to lose sight of priorities, and to forget what they're supposed to be doing."

Why does this pressure exist in business-to-business marketing? Because the people creating the advertising are not the people it is aimed at. So, for example, a liberal arts trained creative director is afraid to make the ad too "technical" for fear of boring the reader, and decides to "liven up" the subject with word-play and far-out graphics. What the creative director does not realize is that the subject of the ad, while boring to him, is not boring to the prospect. The prospect is interested in widget technology and wants to know more about it.

The headline "What you need to know about today's new widget technology" may be a formula, but formulas work. The advertising professional wants to be new and different. The business prospect just wants quick, accurate information about products and services she needs to solve problems. *So the pressure to be creative is a result of clients or advertising professionals not thinking like prospects.* Put yourself in the shoes of the doctor, chemical engineer, or grocery store manager you are writing to.

As best-selling diet-book author Samm Sinclair Baker observes, "What attracts and involves the reader primarily is his or her self-interest." *Appeal to the reader's self-interest.* If you are writing to hospital administrators who want to improve patient care while generating more revenue for the hospital, put on the outer envelope, "INSIDE: HOW TO *IMPROVE PATIENT CARE WHILE INCREASING REVENUE.*"

Another example: If you send me a catalog of running gear, I won't read it—because I don't run. But send it to my friend David Martin and he'll spend hours with it, especially if it has special gear for "hashing" or any of the other unusual running activities and races he's involved with. Same copy, different audience, different reaction. Running appeals to David's interests, not mine. Learn what interests your reader and you will be successful.

Too many marketers—the overwhelming majority—don't do this. They sit around a table and say, "What's great about our company? What's revolutionary about our product design? What makes us superior?" Or, the CEO says to stress quality . . . or safety . . . or productivity . . . or whatever this year's theme happens to be. The successful business-to-business marketer starts with the prospect, not the product. He or she asks, "What do my prospects care about? What is their biggest problem—their fears, worries, interests, concerns?" Write about that, and position your product as the solution, and you are on your way to increasing response. Dramatically.

3. Stress benefits.

A benefit is what your product or service will do for the reader. In many instances—not all, however—your prospects are primarily interested in the benefits of your product or service, not the product or service itself. For example, when I was threatened with a lawsuit recently, I wasn't buying "legal services" from my attorney (although that's what his letterhead advertises); I was buying the elimination of wasted time, headaches, money losses, and worries by having him make the lawsuit go away.

A benefit is what makes your product or service worth the price you are asking. The benefit is how the prospect comes out ahead by using your product or engaging your services. A feature is merely a factual description about a product. A feature of a plastic valve is that it is light in weight. An advantage is that it weighs less than metal valves. A benefit is that it can be used in existing piping systems without bending or stressing the supporting pipes and without the need to add reinforcing structures.

Many consumer direct marketers stress, "The consumer only cares about benefits. Talk only about benefits. Don't talk about features; no one cares." This may be true in consumer marketing, but it is not always the case in business-to-business marketing. Entrepreneurs, executives, managers, and others who are not technical specialists tend to be more concerned with benefits than features, but engineers, scientists, hackers, hobbyists, enthusiasts, and other technically knowledgeable buyers may be looking for a product that meets certain specifications, and are primarily interested in data, not "fluff."

Regardless of which group you're selling to, benefits should still be stressed. When an engineer says, "I don't read copy; I'm only looking at the specs," he or she is only telling half the truth. Technical professionals like to portray themselves as the experts, and many hold the advertising profession in contempt, so they like to tell you they "don't read all that copy." The whole truth, however, is that they *don't* fully understand the value or benefits of all of the features and can be swayed to buy a product if you explain that a certain feature delivers a desired benefit they didn't know about.

The key is that, while features and benefits have different degrees of importance depending upon the product and the audience, you should never neglect the benefits altogether, but should always stress the benefits as well as the features. Pure "spec" copy that lists only facts and features is rarely effective. It needs to be augmented with some "sell" copy that gives the reader a clearer understanding of how they can benefit from ownership of the product.

4. Don't forget the features.
One easy way to cover both features and benefits is with *cause and*

effect statements. These statements say, "Because the product has such and such a feature, it gives you such and such a benefit." For example:

Because the Fast-Flo valve has no pockets or cavities, there's no "dead space" where fluid can collect. Which means bacterial growth that can contaminate process fluids is *eliminated.*

Another technique is to create a *features/benefits table.* In the left-hand column, you list the features. In the right-hand column, you describe the benefit each feature gives the user. For a data sheet describing a high-resolution laser printer, the feature might be "1,200 dots per inch resolution." The benefit might read: "Allows you to reproduce directly from the printer output without going through a service bureau."

Again, when writing to managers, executives, entrepreneurs, and other readers who are not well-versed in your technology or don't want exhaustive details, you would stress the benefits much more than the features. When writing to engineers, scientists, enthusiasts, hobbyists, experts, and other technically sophisticated audiences, you would probably give nearly equal weight to features and benefits—depending on your audience and the objective of the piece. Original equipment manufacturers (OEMs), value-added resellers (VARs), and others who buy products for resale represent an audience that is especially interested in details, specifications, and features. Their concern is primarily whether your product fits the specifications of the larger system into which they plan to integrate it. They are also concerned with quality and reliability. Benefits, however, are often of secondary concern, since they are resellers rather than end-users.

5. Objections.

Successful direct response copy not only gives the reader a sales presentation on why they should be interested in the product; it also attempts to overcome reader resistance by dealing with objections. Objections are reasons why the prospect thinks they don't need to respond even though you say the product is good for them. Rather than avoid these objections, direct marketers tend to address them in the copy.

Not only does this help push the reader toward action, but it also makes the copy more interesting to read, because it talks about things the reader is already thinking about. Example: If you think your reader will not request information on your product because of its high cost, you might have a subhead that reads: "BUT CAN I AFFORD THE X-2000?" Copy under the subhead presents any arguments that help overcome the price objection, such as price comparisons, return on investment analysis, lease/rental options, discounts, easy payment plans, and so on. The idea is to get the reader to think, "Oh, maybe I can afford this after all. Let me mail the reply card and get their brochure."

6. The next step is clearly identified and explicitly stated.

General business communications are often vague about the next step. Many executives feel it's somehow in poor taste to clearly spell out what you want the reader to do, and when. But to increase marketing results, that's precisely what you must do: Tell the reader what the next step is and give them instructions for taking it. You should add a section of copy that provides this information to your fliers, circulars, ads, data sheets, and other printed marketing documents.

I like to introduce this "next step" section with a subhead and put it either at the end of the body copy or in a separate box on the last page of the document. The subhead might read "THE NEXT STEP," "GET THE FACTS—FREE," "TAKE THE NEXT STEP—THERE'S NO OBLIGATION," or something like that. Copy specifically tells the reader what to do next, and how. For example:

> It's easy to find out how CS/ADS can increase the productivity of your programmers and the quality of the applications they build. To request a demonstration in your office, or to receive a free brochure, mail the enclosed reply card. Or call us today at XXX-XXX-XXXX.

Avoid weak endings that are vague or uncertain. Don't end your letter with "I look forward to establishing a mutually profitable relationship with your firm." Instead, if you want them to contact you, tell them to call or write, give them a reason, and have them call or write for a specific thing: a demonstration, a free sample, a brochure, or a booklet. Always say what the next step is—and tell the reader to take it.

7. Give them a reason to respond NOW instead of later.

Why is this important? Experience shows that a decision deferred is a decision not made: If the prospect doesn't respond immediately upon receiving your mailing, chances are he or she won't respond at all. "I'll think about it" generally translates into "It's not a priority and I'll probably never get around to it."

For this reason, it pays to give the reader a reason to respond now instead of later. In fact, the best direct marketing copy not only gives the reader a reason or incentive to respond now, but also spells out the negatives that can result from failure to respond.

If there is a real reason the reader should respond now instead of later, state it in your copy. Real, pressing reasons are always the most credible. For example, if you are a small firm, and can only handle a limited number of requests for proposals, tell the prospect this. Let them know that if they are not among the first to respond, you may not be able to take them on as a client.

If there is no real reason to respond, the fallback position is to invent one. For example, if you are giving away a valuable booklet as a premium, say supplies are limited and you will fulfill requests on a first come, first serve basis. Obviously, you could always print more booklets, but saying that the supply is limited does work and gets people to respond.

Another effective technique is to put an expiration date on your offer. For example: "This offer expires December 31," or "You must respond within 10 days to receive the free bonus gift." If the client will not agree to a specific termination date for the offer, say, "This is a limited time offer, and once it expires, it may never be repeated again."

In addition to telling people why they *should* respond, you can also tell them why it is a mistake *not* to reply. Fear of pain or loss or missing out on a good opportunity is an effective motivator when telling people about the potential negatives of failing to respond. I normally throw away Publishers' Clearing House and similar sweepstakes packages without a second glance, but one headline in a recent mailing stopped me when it said: "YOU COULD BE THROWING AWAY $10 MILLION." I don't like the fuss and bother of filling out sweepstakes forms and don't think I'll ever win. But at the same time, this headline stopped me, because it indeed made me think twice about tossing a piece of paper that could be the winner to the $10 million grand prize.

8. Add an incentive for prompt response.

An *extremely* effective technique for business-to-business lead-generating direct mail and print advertising is to add an incentive for prompt response. This can be a low-cost gift item, such as merchandise, or a free booklet, special report, or other information of value to the reader.

For instance, a client asked me to write a lead-generating sales letter to motivate small businesses to request a free membership kit for the client's trade association. I suggested adding the following copy to the letter: "Respond within 10 days, and we will also send you our free special report, 'HOW TO MANAGE YOUR BUSINESS MORE PROFITABLY IN TODAY'S ECONOMY.'" In my experience, this type of free booklet almost always produces a measurable lift in response. People who are legitimate prospects but are hesitating over whether to respond to the primary offer read this copy and think, "I may as well go ahead and request the information kit," because they're curious about what's in the report, and because it's free.

It's very easy to create this type of incentive offer. Ad specialty houses have all sorts of low-cost premium and gift items, available in any price range that fits your budget, from under $2 per item to over $10. And free information can easily be written or compiled by you and published in the form of an audio cassette, video, booklet, report, or other "information premium" you offer to prospects.

What works best? If you are selling merchandise, and you are doing it in a one-step mail-order sale, a free gift of merchandise can be an enormously effective incentive offer—as can a price discount or two-for-the-price-of-one sale. On the other hand, if you are generating sales leads, especially for professional or technical services, the free booklet or other free information offer seems to work best.

Offering expensive gift merchandise, while proven to boost mail-order sales, is not as effective in lead generation. It certainly increases quantity, but at the expense of quality. So you get inquiries from people who wanted the trinket only, and salespeople become frustrated when they follow up, and find these "prospects" have no interest whatsoever in the product or service being offered.

9. Give the prospect a mechanism for responding.

At minimum, this means an address and phone number where the prospect can contact you for more information or to talk with you about making a purchase. Other response mechanisms you can add include:

- Toll-free 800 numbers

- Paid 900 numbers

- Fax numbers (more and more prospects like to fax inquiries)

- Reply cards

- Order forms

- Coupons

- Surveys or questionnaires

You will also want to emphasize and call attention to the address, phone number, and other reply information rather than obscuring them, as many general and corporate communications tend to do. This can be accomplished using any of the following graphic devices:

- Boxes (putting response information in a separate box)

- Highlighting

- Tinting or shading

- Boldface or italic copy

- Larger type

- Arrows, asterisks, dotted lines, sketches of telephones, and other graphics pointing toward the response information

And instead of just listing the address and phone number below the logo, add copy that encourages the reader to use them. For example: "For more information on any of the products described in this catalog sheet, call XXX-XXX-XXXX today. Or write to us at the address below."

10. Make each marketing document self-contained.

Every marketing document should contain not only the contact information but also your company name, a description of your product or service, and copy that tells the reader what to do next and how. Whenever possible, you should also describe any tangible offers you are making, such as a free demonstration, consultation, analysis, report, etc.

Ideally, every marketing document should contain this information— even components of larger promotions. This means in a direct mail package the contact information and offer should appear not only in the letter and reply card but also in the brochure, lift letter, and any other inserts. I have frequently extracted sales letters from direct mail packages for later reading and thrown away the rest of the package, only to discover that the sender's company address is not on the letterhead or in the body copy of the letter.

In the same way, if your literature is packaged as an information kit consisting of an outer folder with material in the pockets, all components should have your contact information—not just the brochure, but also the data sheets, article reprints, price list, even the outer folder. Marketing materials become separated, so it is important that each piece stand on its own as a direct response communication.

11. Be targeted.

Successful direct marketing delivers specific messages to specific audiences, not generic messages to mass audiences. It's better to have many letters, ads, collateral pieces, and so on, each speaking directly to the needs of a specific audience, than have one "corporate" ad, one "capabilities brochure," and one "standard letter" that attempts to be all things to all people. Chapter 4 presents the reasons why this is so as well as strategies for targeting your communications.

12. Be personal.

Because it's targeted, direct marketing tends to speak on a more personal level. It has a friendly "me-to-you" tone rather than a stiff formal tone. My personal belief after writing copy full-time since 1979 is that, while tone certainly should be suitable for the intended audience, it's better to lean toward being informal, friendly, and conversational rather than formal and corporate.

In my opinion, the widely held belief that you have to write in an ultra-dignified, upper-crust style when communicating to CEOs, doctors, Ph.D.s, the wealthy, and other upscale audiences is largely overstated. People universally have too little time and too much to read. They want the message to be simple, direct, understandable, to the point. I have never in more than 12 years of being a professional copywriter heard anyone complain that a piece of copy was too understandable or too easy to read.

Using personal pronouns in copy (we, I, you) adds warmth and personality to copy. I urge you to write in this natural, conversational style. Can you overdo it? Of course. Copy that has every other sentence beginning with *and,* has no paragraph longer than one sentence, consists mainly of sentence fragments, or in some other way sounds too slick, too much like "professional copywriting," can cause skepticism and buyer resistance by reminding the prospect that she is "reading advertising." But overall, it helps to make copy personal and to write me-to-you. Readers like and respond to it.

A quick checklist of direct response tips and techniques

Throughout this book I will give you detailed advice on how to increase response. There are complete chapters on increasing response to print ads, direct mail, postcards, brochures, catalogs, press releases, feature articles, and audio-visual communications. But to get you started right away, and for handy reference, I've abstracted these chapters and distilled them into a reference list of quick ideas you can use to boost response starting right away:

Sales letters

- Personalize the letter.

- Use a reply card or similar response device.

- Personalize the response device.

- Target different versions of a letter to the needs and concerns of specific audiences.

- Encourage both phone and mail response.

- Use subheads that communicate the key points at a glance.

- Use short paragraphs and sentences, especially in the opening.

- If you do not personalize, use a benefit-oriented headline.

- If you do not personalize, use a salutation that the reader can identify with.

- Offer something tangible for the reader to send for—a brochure, catalog, etc.

- Offer a meeting, demonstration, or appointment for those who want to buy now.

- Use a teaser on the outer envelope that arouses curiosity or promises a benefit.

- If you do not use a teaser, imprint the recipient's name and address on the outer envelope so it looks like a personal letter.

- Use a stamp or postage meter instead of an indicia.

- Omit the company logo and name on the outer envelope and print your return address in plain type.

- Make the reply card a different color than the letter (such as yellow, light blue, pink) so it stands out when the envelope is opened.

- Mail first class instead of third class.

- Use a different color or different size envelope (if everyone else is mailing 6" x 9" envelopes, use 9" x 12").

- Add an incentive, such as a bonus gift or free special report, for prompt response.

- Make the bonus gift no strings attached (they can keep it even if they don't buy the product, attend the seminar, or agree to the initial appointment).

- Write a provocative lead that engages the reader's attention.

- In your lead, talk about the prospect's needs, concerns, fears, and problems—not your product.

- In a long letter, make sure you sum up your proposition and ask for response before you get through the first half of page one.

- In a two-page or longer letter, consider summing up your offer or message in a "Johnson Box" (a rectangular box above the salutation containing brief copy).

- Print the letter in two colors, with the signature in blue.

- In a personalized letter, print each page on a separate sheet.

- In a form letter, print on both sides of the page.

- End each page in the middle of a sentence so the reader is forced to go to the next page to finish the thought.

- Write "more" or "over, please" at the bottom of each page to instruct the reader to go on to the next page.

- Prefer short paragraphs to long paragraphs.

- Use underlining, asterisks, bullets, boldfacing, ALL CAPS, and indenting to emphasize words, phrases, sentences, or paragraphs you want to call attention to.

- Do not overdo any of the above techniques or they will lose their effectiveness.

- If it's a choice between achieving a natural, conversational style and being 100 percent grammatically correct, go for the natural, conversational style.

- Do not be afraid to repeat key sales points two or three times in the same letter.

- If there is a lot of supporting data or technical detail, put it in a separate insert sheet, brochure, or additional piece.

- If your company is very well known and well respected, print the letter on your regular letterhead with your logo and name prominently displayed on page one.

- If your company is not well known, put your name, logo, and address on the last page below the signature and P.S. The first thing the reader sees should be the headline or salutation, not your logo.

Direct mail packages

- All of the techniques described above for sales letters apply equally to direct mail packages.

- In business-to-business direct mail, do not put too many elements in the direct mail package or it will be identified as "junk mail" by secretaries and not be passed on to the recipient.

- If you have a FREE offer, mention of this on the outer envelope can make an effective teaser.

- Inserts, brochures, and other materials in the direct mail package should be printed on a single sheet of paper folded to form a brochure, pamphlet, or what have you. They should not be saddle-stitched.

- The ideal business-to-business lead-generating direct mail package seems to be a one- to two-page letter in a #10 envelope with a business reply card and possibly a slim-jim brochure (8-1/2" x 11" or 8-1/2" x 14" sheet of paper folded to form six or eight panels).

- The reply card usually should be separate rather than attached to the letter or brochure.

  When personalizing the letter, you may have a reply element that is attached to the letter so you can computer-personalize the reply form as well as the letter. Include a business reply envelope for return of this detachable form.

- Use a brochure when the product is not fully understood by the prospect or is complex and you need to present more details than can be comfortably covered in a one- or two-page letter.

- Omit the brochure when the proposition or offer is simple and easily understood.

- Use the brochure when you need to establish credibility and convince the prospect that the product, offer, proposition, or the organization behind it is real, not fly-by-night.

- Use the brochure when you need to illustrate or explain things visually.

- Set the letter in typewriter style or desktop-publishing style type.

- Set the brochure in traditional type, such as Helvetica, Times Roman, etc.

- A short, simple, business reply card is usually more effective than an order form, questionnaire, or other long response device.

- Break copy in the letter and brochure into short sections, each with a selling, benefit-oriented subhead.

- Use short sentences, words, and paragraphs throughout to make your copy readable.

- In direct mail, remember, "The letter sells—the brochure tells."

- Use testimonials in both the letter and the brochure.

- Information about the company or biographical information about its founders, if it must be included, belongs in the brochure, not the letter.

Self-mailers

- Two-color self-mailers generally outpull one-color mailers.

- You can make a one-color printing job appear multi-colored by using black ink on colored stock, colored ink on colored stock, and tints.

- Making one panel or portion of the self-mailer a tear-off business reply card increases response.

- The fold attaching the reply card to the rest of the mailer should be perforated.

- Print a dashed black line along the perforation to simulate the look of a coupon.

- Use strong teaser copy on the front and back panels of the self-mailer.

- Write the inside of your self-mailer like a powerful ad or sales brochure.

- In 11" x 17" and larger self-mailers, break the copy up into sections using boxes and borders.

- In 11" x 17" and larger self-mailers, use numerous subheads and bullets to make the copy easier to read and scan at a glance.

- Use self-mailers to promote offers that cannot profitably be marketed with a full-scale direct mail package.

- Use self-mailers to reach a large universe your budget does not allow you to reach with a traditional direct mail package.

- Use self-mailers for offers that are familiar to the reader or are easy to understand and do not require a lot of explanation.

- In an 11" x 17" mailer, consider adding an extra half-flap with a tear-off business reply card.

- In a multi-page or mini-catalog type self-mailer, a letter imprinted on the inside front cover frequently increases response.

- Do not cram too much information into your mailer or set the type too small.

- Use photos or other graphics to illustrate or dramatize your message if appropriate.

Postcards

- If you want maximum inquiries, allow the reader to respond by filling in name and address and returning the card without having to do anything else (such as enclosing a check, adding a postage stamp, or using an envelope).

- When using a free offer to generate sales leads, make it really free. Don't ask for $1 or some other nominal sum to cover handling as a means of qualifying prospects; it doesn't really qualify, and it hurts response tremendously.

- Unless the cost of paying return postage is a significant factor to you, use a business reply permit on your postcard-deck postcards.

- If the offer is free, put the word free in the headline or subhead.

- Show a picture of your catalog, booklet, or other free information.

- Put a caption under the picture that says "yours FREE."

- Add a telephone number at the bottom of the card for phone response.

- Leave sufficient room for prospects to fill in their name and address.

- Make the offer simple and clear; avoid complex propositions in postcard deck marketing.

- Generally a postcard deck is good for distributing free catalogs, literature, or demo diskettes, not as effective for direct sales. Exceptions? Of course.

- Postcard decks are ideal for testing offer A versus offer B or sales message A versus sales message B.

Print ads

- Use a direct, straightforward headline rather than a cute or clever headline.

- Write the body copy like an informative article that leaves the reader hungering for more information on the same topic.

- Use a coupon.

- Put a dashed border around the coupon and place the coupon in the bottom right corner of the ad.

- Run the ad on a right-hand page.

- In a small ad, put a dashed border around the ad.

- Use a toll-free number.

- Use a bind-in reply card (a reply card bound into the magazine opposite the ad).

- Run the ad in publications known to generate high numbers of leads (such as product tabloids) or orders (mail-order publications).

- Have a free offer of a booklet, report, brochure, analysis, or something else the reader can send for.

- Stress the free offer in your copy.

- Show a picture of your free booklet, report, or kit.

- Mention the free offer in the headline or subhead.

- Use a reader service card number.

- Put your toll-free phone number in large bold type at the bottom of the ad.

- Run your ad for as long as it continues to pull well. Some ads actually generate more inquiries the longer they run.

- When the response rate declines, it is time to test a new ad.

Brochures

- Bind a tear-off business reply card into the brochure.

- Have boxes the reader can check off to request more detailed information on items mentioned in the brochure (e.g., in a general brochure, you can have a reply card offering a more complete brochure on each product mentioned).

- In your closing copy, encourage the reader to use the reply card.

- If you want the prospect to supply you with information you can use to quote a price for your product or analyze their need for your service, include a questionnaire or spec sheet the reader can fill out and return to you.

- The questionnaire or spec sheet should be printed on two sides of an 8-1/2" x 11" sheet.

- The sheet should be separate from the brochure, inserted in the brochure, and printed on a different color stock than the brochure.

- If you want to include an additional copy of the reply form as a tear-off page in the brochure, fine.

- Encourage the reader to fax the completed questionnaire to you. Display your fax number in large bold type on the reply form.

- Suggest a specific course of action and describe it in detail in the closing copy of your brochure.

- Tell the reader what you will do next for them if they contact you, and stress the benefits of this step or service.

- Write your brochure so that it answers most questions about the product or service and gets prospects to the point where they are ready to have a meeting or get a price quote.

- Make it easy to find your address and phone number.

Catalogs

- Use a title that implies value. For example, call your industrial catalog a "reference guide," "manual," or "product guide," not a "catalog."

- Design an attractive front cover.

- Put a price in the upper right corner of the front cover of your catalog to create the impression that the book has value.

- On the inside front page, put a personal letter from the owner or company president explaining the high level of service you offer or other benefits of doing business with you.

- In a large catalog that will be referred to repeatedly, put a table of contents on page 2 or 3.

- Have a page, such as the inside back cover, that gives terms, conditions, shipping instructions, and other details for ordering.

- A bound-in order form usually increases response but may not be necessary in industrial catalogs used primarily as reference guides by purchasing agents. Test it.

- Add how-to articles, technical information, or other information that gives your catalog value as a reference and therefore prompts the recipient to keep it longer.

- Encourage orders by mail, phone, and fax.

- Use a toll-free number for ordering.

- Put your order phone number on every page or every other page. The reader should instantly be able to find the phone number for ordering no matter what page they're looking at.

- Consider a "frequent buyer's discount program" that gives the customer volume discounts based on total dollar volume purchased within a year.

- Consider a "frequent buyer's credit" program where the customer receives a credit good toward future purchases based on a percentage of the total dollar amount of the current purchase.

- Design reference tables, graphs, and other graphic devices that make it easy for the customer to specify and order the correct product.

- Include cross-reference tables that make it easy for your customer to see which of your products are replacement equivalents of competing products they may now be using.

- Make it easy for the customer to establish a line of credit and buy without paying in advance.

- Include a toll-free number and encourage phone ordering for credit card orders.

- Accept MasterCard, Visa, and American Express cards.

- Allow the customer to order at any time rather than during set hours (use an answering service, answering machine, voice mail, or 800-number service bureau for accepting orders during non-business hours).

- Encourage customers to submit purchase orders by mail or fax.

- Create a form the customer can use to order if they do not want to use (or don't have) their own requisition or purchase order forms.

- Put the season or catalog number (e.g., Fall 1992) on the front cover so customers with old catalogs will call to get the new catalog.

- Distribute your catalog free rather than charging for it.

- If you charge a small fee for your catalog, rebate this with the first order.

- Consider creating versions of your catalog aimed at different markets or groups of buyers.

- If you have a large, all-purpose catalog, consider testing a mini-catalog featuring only one line of related products and aimed at people known to buy that type of product.

- The appearance of the catalog (graphics, photos, paper stock, design, printing quality) should be equivalent to other promotional materials your prospects are accustomed to receiving. Do not make it too expensive or too cheap.

- Get competitive bids for the printing of the catalog. Lowering the cost per catalog helps make more sales at less cost.

- If you operate in a metropolitan area, get at least one or two bids from out-of-town (or even out-of-state) printers.

- Consider going to a slightly thinner paper stock. It probably won't hurt response but will definitely save you money.

Inquiry fulfillment materials

- Do not mail literature without a strong, hard-sell cover letter. Including a letter is an extremely effective tool for converting leads to sales.

- On the outer envelope, stamp in large red or black letters, "HERE IS THE INFORMATION YOU REQUESTED."

- Mail brochures flat in a 9" x 12" envelope rather than folding them to fit a standard #10 business envelope.

- If you have many brochures and other materials, consider creating an attractive pocket folder for them.

- Including an audio cassette tape, product sample, or other three-dimensional enclosure makes your package more interesting than if it just contains paper literature.

- Type up favorable testimonials from 10 to 20 clients or customers, print them on one or two sides of a sheet of paper, and include this as a separate flier in your inquiry fulfillment kit.

- If you have many well-known customers, make a long list of the most famous ones and put this on a separate sheet included with the kit.

- Include a questionnaire, survey, or other response device the prospect can fill in and mail back to you to order a product, request a price quotation, or simply communicate their requirements to you.

- Print this reply form on a brightly colored stock, such as yellow, gold, or light blue.

- Encourage prospects to fax the reply form back to you and put your fax number in large bold type on it.

- Make sure the brochures you send give the prospect the information they are likely to be seeking about your product.

- If the brochures don't answer all questions, write out the questions the prospects are likely to ask. Then write an answer to each question and reprint these questions and answers on a separate sheet, and include this sheet with your inquiry fulfillment kit.

- Recent reprints of favorable or informative articles written about you or by you make excellent additions to the inquiry fulfillment kit.

- Audio cassettes of lectures by you or reprints of papers given by you also can be included with the package.

- Make sure the inquiry fulfillment kit contains everything you promised to send the prospects responding to your ad or mailer. Don't forget to include any bonus premiums or special reports you offered that are not normally included with fulfillment materials.

- Many pieces of the kit can be photocopies, desktop published, or inexpensively produced, including your client list, testimonials, and question-and-answer sheet. But there should be at least one brochure or other piece of literature that is somewhat more expensively produced. This convinces the prospect that your company is "real."

- In your inquiry fulfillment letter, spell out exactly what you are offering and what you want the prospect to do next.

- Make it as easy as possible for the prospect to respond.

- Assure the prospect that there is no risk in responding, no cost, and no obligation of any kind.

- If no salesperson will call or visit the prospect, say so.

- Make sure any response forms or devices are simple to follow, easy to complete, and not too lengthy.

- If your offer is limited, say so. Create a sense of urgency about why the prospect should respond today, not tomorrow.

- Consider designing a series of follow-up mailings to follow the original inquiry fulfillment package. Sometimes this pays off, sometimes not. You will only know by testing.

- When mailing to prospects who work at home, consider using a business card that is a refrigerator magnet.

- If your service or product will be required by your prospect in the future and at intervals rather than purchased immediately, consider enclosing a business card in the form of a Rolodex™ card.

- If your product or service is ordered only on an emergency basis, consider enclosing a telephone sticker with your name, logo, address, and a short description of the product or service.

- If you are selling professional or consulting services and have written a book on the topic, consider including a copy of your book with inquiry fulfillment packages sent to hot prospects who seem eager and ready to buy.

Press releases

- Use a headline with strong reader interest.

- Write a lead that reads like the lead of an interesting feature story.

- Put useful information in the body of your release.

- Mention that the information discussed in the release is available in more detail in a booklet or report that can be obtained from you.

- In the last paragraph, explain that readers can get a copy of the booklet or report by calling or writing you.

- Mention your free booklet or report in the lead or headline if you can.

- Write on a topic that is either controversial, deals with a "hot" issue, is timely, or gives the reader information they can use in their business.

- A two- or even three-page release with a lot of "meat" is better than a short one- or two-paragraph release that only gives a summary of the material.

- The press release must be self-contained. Do not expect the editor to write an article by interviewing you or taking copy from other materials (articles, booklets, brochures) you send along with the release.

- Including a cover letter with your press release is unnecessary and does not help convince editors to use it.

- Press releases should be typed double-spaced on white paper.

- If the release is more than one page, use a second sheet; do not type on the back of the page.

- The pages should be stapled together in the upper left corner.

- If you have a well-known company whose activities automatically constitute business news, use a special news release letterhead with your name in large type at the top (e.g., "NEWS FROM IBM").

- If your company is not famous or newsworthy in and of itself, you do not need special news release letterhead and can type your releases on plain white paper.

- Type on the release the name and phone number of someone in your company the editor can contact for more information.

- Always respond to calls from editors immediately, because they are on tight deadlines.

- If you have more than one press release, mail them separately (one per month for monthly magazines, one per week for daily or weekly publications). Do not send them all together in a single envelope.

- The most interesting word to the business editor is NEW. Always try to stress what is new in your press release (e.g., when announcing a product upgrade, your headline is "New Release of Product XYZ Now Available").

Columns/articles

- Try to get your articles or columns in the most widely read, most well respected, or largest-circulation business publications in your field.

- If you can't get into the best publications, any publication is still good. The articles and columns have enormous value as reprints that is not dependent on where they were originally published.

- Try to get the editor to run a resource box instead of a regular author's bio at the end of each article. A resource box is a box containing your name, company name, address, phone number, fax number, and a brief description of your product or service.

- If the editor will not run a resource box but only the standard "about the author" bio, make sure you get your company's *city* in the description so readers interested in knowing more about you can track down your phone number from information (e.g., "Bob Bly, an independent copywriter and consultant based in Dumont, NJ, specializes in business-to-business direct marketing.").

- If the editor will not run a resource box or pay you for the article, ask them to give you free ad space in exchange for writing the article. (The value of the ad space should be one or two times the dollar amount normally paid for an article of the type and length you are writing.)

- The ad should appear in the same issue as your article, not in a different issue, as many believe.

- The ad should appear on the same page, the page opposite, or the page immediately following your article. It should be as close to the article as possible.

- If the magazine is writing an article about you, you can often get the editor to make it the cover story by promising and then providing an attractive photo or other graphic for the front cover. Getting a cover story invariably increases readership and response.

- If you are writing an article for the magazine under your own byline, write a brief article divided into short sections by numbers, bullets, or subheads. These get higher readership than lengthy, long-winded articles.

- Use a title that promises useful ideas and quick reading (e.g., "10 tips for buying a desktop publishing system" is better than "Fundamentals of desktop publishing.").

- If the editor did not include a resource box when the article was published, add one when you make reprints.

- Offer reprints of your "10 tips" type articles to prospects who reply to your ads and mailings. Call them "special reports" or "tip sheets," not article reprints.

- Mail reprints of articles to customers and prospects.

- Write articles on subjects of strong interest to your potential customers and prospects.

- Write articles that position your company as the leader or you as the expert.

- Write articles that convince readers you are qualified to help them solve their problems.

- Plan a schedule or "matrix" of articles (topics and publications for placement) just as you would plan a print advertising campaign.

Seminars, speeches, papers, and presentations

- Make sure the content of the seminar is informative, not promotional.

- Present a solid program of information; keep the selling message brief and present it only at the end.

- If the seminar is primarily a product demonstration, first educate the audience about the problem and the correct way to handle it; then demonstrate how your product fulfills that specification.

- At a self-sponsored seminar, arrange for attendees to sit down and discuss their needs with salespeople (who are waiting patiently at the back of the room) as soon as the presentation is completed.

- At a public event, offer some hand-out free to anyone who asks. This can be an article reprint, outline of your talk, the entire text of your talk, or a booklet based on your talk. Make sure the hand-out has your name, address, and phone number on it.

- If you want to capture the names and addresses of people attending your seminar, do not bring the hand-out with you. Instead, offer to send it to anyone who gives you their business card at the conclusion of your talk.

- Ask the seminar sponsor for a list of those who attended your presentation and mail a follow-up letter immediately afterward thanking them for coming and offering more information on your product or service.

- If you tape your seminar, send copies of the tape free to attendees as a follow-up. Or, send a letter offering a free copy to any attendee who is interested in your product or service.

- Always distribute your hand-outs after you speak, not before. If you do it before you speak, people will read the hand-out and ignore your talk.

- Bring an inexpensive gift (a sample of your product, for example). After your talk, hold it up and offer it to the person who asks the first question. This ensures that questions will be asked.

- The best way to generate an enthusiastic response and potential business from a seminar, speech, or lecture is to give a great talk, packed with information and without a sales pitch.

- Let others do your sales pitch for you. Write an introduction for the person introducing you that tells who you are, the name of your company, and what you do.

- Have a small supply of brochures on hand for those who have an immediate need to know more about your product or service.

- If you have a low-priced product to sell (a book, video, etc.), have a product table at the back of the room with a supply of the items and encourage people to buy after the talk or at the break. Sales increase dramatically when the product is physically available at the talk versus giving people an order form to take home and mail in.

- Have people fill in and return to you an evaluation form they can use to rate your presentation. At the end of the form have boxes they can check if they are interested in receiving additional information on your company, product, or service.

- Promise an inexpensive surprise gift for those who complete and hand in the evaluation form.

Company newsletter or magazine

- In a large saddle-stitched multi-page magazine, bind in a reply card readers can tear out and return to request more information on products and services discussed in the articles.

- In a small four- to eight-page newsletter that is a self-mailer, turn the address panel (where the mailing label is affixed to the back page of the newsletter) into a reply form by adding boxes the reader can check to request product information. Encourage the reader to mail this page back or fax it.

- At the end of each article put a "for more information" paragraph in italic type, e.g., *For a free product brochure on the XYZ Tank Bottom Valve, call Rick Graycheck at XXX-XXX-XXXX.*

- Run small articles of two or three paragraphs that merely describe and offer materials the reader can send for: new brochures, spec sheets, videotapes, catalogs, etc. Box these articles or print them on tint blocks to make them stand out.

- On your reply form or panel, invite your readers to give their opinion of the newsletter and submit suggestions for future articles.

- Put in a quiz or puzzle related to your product and offer a prize to anyone who solves it (prize to be sent along with information on the product).

- Use the newsletter to announce and build attendance at trade show displays, seminars, demonstrations, and similar events.

- Publish the newsletter on a regular schedule, not randomly. Quarterly is ideal.

Trade shows

- Create an inexpensive one-page flier about your product or product line for distribution at the trade show.

- Put a tear-off business reply card at the bottom of this flier. Put boxes on the reply card the prospect can check off to request more detailed literature on specific products, applications, or services that the flier just touches on briefly.

- Bring a small supply of your more complete literature packages to give to prospects who have a serious interest and want immediate information.

- Put a large goldfish bowl on a table with a sign encouraging people to put their business cards into the bowl to qualify for a nice prize to be awarded based on a random drawing held at your booth at the conclusion of the show.

- Give away a nice gift (a baseball cap, a bag of fresh popcorn, a hot dog with mustard, a tee-shirt) to anyone who stops by your booth and gives you their business card.

- Send a pre-show mailing to prospects inviting them to your booth at the show. Enclose a card they can redeem at the booth to receive some sort of gift or premium item.

4

The Target Marketing Strategy

My "secret weapon" in direct marketing

Are you looking for a simple way to increase response to your marketing efforts? Something that doesn't require a lot of skill or thought, isn't terribly sophisticated, but works virtually every time? *Target marketing* is the answer.

This simple technique is one of the most *overlooked* and *underutilized* in the world of business-to-business marketing. Ninety-five percent of the marketers who could benefit from it haven't bothered to take advantage of it. The other 5 percent use it routinely to obtain superior marketing results at reduced marketing cost.

Okay. Let's say you're interested in exploring target marketing as a way to enhance your marketing program. I think I can guess your first question. . . .

What is target marketing?

Target marketing is the strategy of dividing your marketing into distinct market segments, then tailoring different marketing campaigns aimed at each of the segments.

For example, instead of just thinking of their market as "businesses," a photocopier manufacturer might target their marketing efforts at several distinct sub-markets within the business marketplace: home offices, small businesses, large corporations, engineering firms and other businesses that need to duplicate technical drawings, ad agencies and other firms that need color copying capability, and so on.

In the same way, a company manufacturing air pollution control equipment might sell to many different vertical markets: chemical plants, pulp and paper plants, food processing, iron and steel mills, and utilities.

Use of target marketing is growing

Business-to-business and direct response marketers have been doing target marketing for years. But the use of target marketing today is intensifying. Direct marketers, for example, are using such tools as demographic overlays to divide large mailing lists into categories and tailor promotions based on such market characteristics as age, marital status, and even whether a prospect has a credit card or enters sweepstakes.

Even Madison Avenue is getting into the act. Once, the giant package goods manufacturers treated all markets pretty much the same. Now they're targeting specific markets, too. For example, most of the major fast-food chains and soft drink producers have separate campaigns targeted toward blacks, and other campaigns targeted toward Hispanic consumers. Why? Because *targeting works.*

Benefits of target marketing

There are two primary benefits of target marketing:

1. It increases marketing results.
2. It decreases marketing costs.

Let's look at each advantage. But first, I have to tell you about my latest invention—the ultimate direct mail package (you'll see how this relates to the discussion of target marketing in about 3 minutes).

The ultimate direct mail package

I have recently designed the ultimate direct mail package—that is, a mailing piece guaranteed to generate almost a 100 percent response rate every time it is mailed. May I describe it?

Are you familiar with those gimmicky greeting cards that play music when they are opened? A microchip attached to the card generates the musical notes. My ultimate direct mail package also has a microchip. This microchip contains three basic components: a computer, a database stored on a miniature optical disk, and a telepathic transmitter/receiver.

The mailing presents, in print, only a brief capsule description of the product or service being sold. The rest of the information is contained on the disk database and delivered to the recipient via the telepathic transmitter.

Here's how it works: The prospect gets the mailer and reads the brief product description. Immediately he or she has a thought. This might be an objection, a question, or a reason why the prospect thinks our product isn't of interest.

The telepathic unit picks up this thought and communicates it to the computer. The computer searches the database for the appropriate response, then transmits this to the recipient via the telepathic unit. So if the prospect thinks, "I don't have time to read this right now," the computer transmits the pre-scripted message that begins, "Let me explain why it's important to consider our offer right now, even if you think you're 'too busy' or it's 'just not a priority' . . . . " If the prospect thinks, "I don't have the money right now; we can only spend a few hundred dollars," the ultimate direct mail piece responds, "You can afford to get this product at a price that will surprise you—for an initial payment of only a few hundred dollars."

Sound fantastic? Actually, this is the kind of package an experienced direct marketer will try to write every time he or she sits down to create copy. The reason that our current efforts fall short of the mark and generate only 1 or 2 percent response instead of 100 percent (as the ultimate direct mail package would) is that *we don't have the telepathic capability to read our customers' minds and tell them exactly what they need to hear to convince them to buy the product.*

Because we're not telepathic, we never know exactly what the prospect is thinking, and that's a major disadvantage we have to live with. The best copywriters spend most of their professional lives trying to think like the prospect thinks—to understand why they are interested in the product and then stress those attributes in the copy, or figure out why they aren't interested and then answer those objections in the copy.

And this is where target marketing helps. It's simple, really. If you're writing a non-targeted promotion to a mass audience, you really don't know who you're talking to. If you don't have a clear idea of your audience, how can you get inside their mind and understand what interests them (and what doesn't) about your offer? You can't. When you try to communicate with everyone in a single letter, mailing, or ad, you end up communicating with no one.

Targeting solves that problem. Narrow your focus, write to a specific audience, and you can address their specific needs, concerns, and questions. Targeting helps you get inside the mind of your prospect. If you're writing to computer programmers to sell them a subscription to a technical magazine, it's true you can't write separate letters to every programmer based on interviews with them. But by speaking to a few programmers, you can get a pretty good handle on how they think, what interests them, and how you must approach them in your letter to get them to subscribe.

Here's another example. A major software firm was interested in doing an advertising and marketing communications campaign for its mainframe software product. The ad agency they approached recommended targeted campaigns to each industry segment served: banks, hospitals, manufacturers, and so on. Each ad campaign would focus on specific software systems sold to those market segments, stressing the business benefits delivered by the software to those types of companies.

The client objected, not wanting to create so many ads and brochures, and insisted on a single ad campaign for all products and markets. But how do you talk to a banker and to a hospital administrator in the same ad or brochure and say something meaningful to both? You can't. As the ad agency president explained to the client, "If we try to reach everyone with one message, all it can be is something meaningless like, 'The leader in IBM mainframe software.'" The client did not accept this argument, and the agency did not win the account—which is fortunate, since the campaign the client insisted on would not have worked.

How targeting saves money

You have just seen how targeting increases the effectiveness of marketing communications and generates better results—namely, by allowing you to make your message more reader-oriented and prospect-focused.

But how does target marketing reduce marketing costs? Simple. By dividing the great universe of business prospects into small, easily identifiable market segments, those of us on a limited budget can do smaller "mini-campaigns" concentrated on just one or two or a few of these market segments. For most businesses, this is the only marketing that is affordable; only the *Fortune* 500 and major packaged goods manufacturers can afford mass advertising in television, magazines, and newspapers.

Targeting saves money because:

• It reduces the size of the audience you must reach.

- It increases the effectiveness and impact of each communication, eliminating the need for an expensive, mass-repetition campaign.

- It lowers your mailing costs. You have fewer names to mail to, and that means lower list rental costs, lower postage costs, and lower printing and production costs.

- It reduces advertising costs. Although you may have to create more ads, you run them in only a few specialty publications in the target industry, rather than hundreds of general-interest magazines or newspapers. There are fewer publications on your media schedule, and, because they are specialized trade publications, the cost of ad space is low.

- It reduces your telemarketing sales costs. This is because there are fewer prospects to call.

Thirteen ways to improve your marketing communications through target marketing

You can target your market in any of several ways (or a combination of these).

1. Industry.

You can target by industry, specifying industry segments by name or by SIC (Standard Industrial Code). The Standard Industrial Classification system uses a series of 8-digit codes to organize U.S. businesses into 15,000 categories and sub-categories. The definitive reference work to SIC is Dun & Bradstreet's *SIC 2+2 Standard Industrial Classification Manual,* available from the Direct Marketing Association, DMA Book Distribution Center, 1650 Bluegrass Lakes Parkway, Alpharetta, GA 30201, phone (404) 664-7284.

Here is an example of targeting by industry. A client of mine sells plastic diaphragm pumps. They asked me to write two different brochures describing the same product. Why two different brochures? Because the users in different markets were interested in different performance features. Buyers in the chemical industry were interested primarily in corrosion resistance; buyers in the pharmaceutical industry were more concerned with purity and cleanliness. Brochures to the different markets stressed these different themes. The advantage of doing this? Prospects respond better, because the brochure they receive talks about what is of interest *to them*.

2. Size of company.

Your market can be segmented according to size of company. Many commercially available mailing lists allow you to select names by size of company based on either annual sales or number of employees.

Concerning size, I see American business divided into three basic markets: small business, middle-size companies, and *Fortune* 500. How you define "small," "medium," and "large" for your marketing purposes is really up to you. But here's how I think of it:

Small companies are generally privately owned, usually family run businesses, with anywhere from one or two employees up to 30, 40, maybe 50 employees. For a manufacturer, this means sales under $10 million; for a service firm, sales under $2 million.

The small company is usually run by an owner who keeps a tight rein over all aspects of the business. A recent article in the *Record* (December 2, 1991) indicated that small business owners usually are much more aware of costs than are their corporate counterparts—probably because they view the money as coming out of their own pocket. Entrepreneurs are skeptical, pressed for time, not terribly interested in technical details, bottom-line oriented, and cost-conscious.

Home-based businesses are a distinct sub-market within the small business market. Many computer, fax, copier, telephone, furniture, and office supply companies are aggressively targeting this market segment because of the rising popularity of working at home. The disadvantage in targeting this market, however, is that home-based businesspeople are usually frugal, on a limited budget, and rarely offer opportunity for repeat business or volume sales. They tend to buy only one of everything, and that only after much deliberation. They also tend to require a lot of after-sale support and service.

The second market segment is medium-sized companies—from several dozen to several hundred or more employees, with sales usually above $10 million if a manufacturer (or above $2-3 million if a service provider) but less than $100 million. Your prospect here is probably not the owner but may very well report to the owner. Some have a lot of autonomy and authority; others have to check with the boss to spend $50 on office supplies. This market segment is difficult to put neatly into a single category, because it is so big. There's a lot of difference, for example, between a firm with $10 million in sales and one with $90 million in sales.

Large corporations make up the third segment of the market. Typically, these include the *Fortune* 500 and firms of similar size: big companies with thousands of employees and annual sales in the hundreds of millions of dollars.

Typically, managers in these firms are part of a chain of authority and must consult with others in their company to make a purchase decision of any consequence. Executives at these big firms use secretaries and mail rooms to screen mail, and so it is more difficult to reach them. Personalization of the outer envelope—making it look "personal" instead of like "direct mail"—is very effective here. Prospects at big corporations frequently are as concerned with making an "acceptable" buying decision (one that pleases the immediate supervisor or top management committee) as they are with bottom-line results. Many are risk-adverse.

3. Location.

Some business-to-business marketers target geographically; others do not. Most of my manufacturing clients, for example, sell to customers across the country, and geography does not affect their marketing efforts. Distributors, on the other hand, might market only in their immediate and surrounding states, because they can offer delivery that is both fast and economical only to prospects who are nearby.

Many companies selling professional, consulting, and technical services to businesses are often similarly restricted to serving markets within the immediate geographic area of their headquarters or branch offices.

Companies that sell to businesses from retail outlets (value-added resellers of computer systems, for example) also serve a market within "driving distance" of the shop or store, as do firms that offer on-site repair services.

Even some companies that sell products may do target marketing based on location. One of my clients, a metals firm, finds that marketing efforts do better in some states than others, and he deletes the poorer states when renting mailing lists.

In today's global marketplace, many U.S. firms are looking to expand into overseas markets. Most certainly, a separate international campaign will be developed; larger, more sophisticated marketers may have separate campaigns aimed at different regions (Europe vs. Asia) or even specific countries.

4. Job function or title of prospect within the company.

Perhaps the most common means of targeting business-to-business prospects is by job title. Direct mail, for example, can be sent only to those who are responsible for buying, recommending, or specifying your type of product or service, eliminating the waste of mailings sent to people not involved with your product or its purchase.

The most effective direct marketing often targets multiple buying influences in the same company, tailoring the message to the needs and concerns of each prospect as indicated by his or her job title or function. For instance, we would stress "quick return on investment" when talking to the chief financial officer, but "high reliability and easy maintenance" when talking to the plant manager.

If you do not know the titles of the people likely to be interested in your proposition, try addressing them by job function. In a mailing for an electronic component distributor, we used the outer envelope teaser, "ATTENTION: ELECTRONIC COMPONENT BUYER," because we could not get mailing labels with the titles of people who buy electronic components.

5. Application or use of your product.

You can target your marketing efforts based on how the prospect uses your product. A good example are the pocket planners, daily calendars, time management systems, and other pocket schedulers and diaries sold to businesses.

Some manufacturers sell them to be used personally by the buyer. Their catalogs and mailings go into elaborate detail about how the time management systems work, how they save you time, make your life more efficient, and so on.

Other manufacturers market these items as gifts to be bought by businesses and given to customers, prospects, and colleagues. When selling these same items as a gift, rather than for personal use, copy is much shorter and doesn't go into detail about how the systems work. Instead, it stresses the high value, elegant look, leather cover, personal imprint, and other aspects that make the books and diaries an appealing gift item.

6. Channels of distribution.

You can target different promotions aimed at getting response from different people in the distribution channel: end users or customers, distributors, agents, resellers, wholesalers, agents, reps, OEMs (original equipment manufacturers), VARs (value added resellers), stores, or catalog merchants.

Promotions aimed at end users or customers naturally stress the benefits of using the product, while promotions aimed at the distribution channel tend to stress how much money or profit the distributor can make by carrying the item and selling it aggressively.

Marketers sometimes use the term *push* to describe marketing to the distribution channel and *pull* to describe marketing to the end user or customer. This is because promotion to dealers is aimed at pushing the product on them and getting them to push it onto their customers, while marketing to customers creates demand that pulls the product through the distribution chain from manufacturer to distributor to end user.

Is it better to concentrate your promotional dollars toward end users or the distribution channel? It depends on the market. If customers tend to buy the product directly from the manufacturer, and distribution channels account for only a small percentage of sales, then naturally you concentrate your promotional dollars on the end user.

In other markets, distribution channels are pretty important. Take books, for example. If bookstores don't buy a particular book from a particular publisher and put it on the shelves, it has very little chance of selling. And with 50,000 new books published each year, most get little or no shelf space in bookstores. So selling the distribution channel is essential.

A similar situation exists in supermarkets. With too many products competing for limited shelf space, many packaged goods manufacturers actually *pay* the supermarket a fee to stock and display their products.

It's the same with many PC software packages. There are thousands of software packages on the market, yet most computer stores have room on the shelves for only a few dozen titles. If they don't carry yours, you either have low sales or must make sales through other channels, such as catalogs, space ads, or direct mail.

How do you overcome the challenge of getting distributors to carry your item? At first you might think heavy marketing to the distribution chain is the answer. But let's say you do this, and the bookstores carry your book. Readers might see it and snap it up. But perhaps they've never heard of it, so they walk right by it. With no demand from the end user, the title will quickly be pulled.

Often, creating a heavy customer demand is effective in getting the distribution channel to buy your product. After all, if your book gets rave reviews and dozens of people ask for it every hour, the bookstore will naturally want to order many copies from you.

For products where the distribution channel is important, then, you will probably target both the customer and the distribution chain. In most cases, the bulk of your effort will go toward end-user marketing, with a much smaller portion toward dealer and distributor promotion. Exceptions? Of course.

7. Affinity groups.

An affinity group is a group of prospects with similar interests. These might include classical music buffs, computer hackers, bodybuilders and "health nuts," and other people who vigorously and enthusiastically pursue special hobbies, interests, or activities.

When you market a product that appeals to their common interest, you get much higher results than with mass-marketing the same product to the general population, because the affinity group has a demonstrated interest in your product category or in the benefits your product provides.

A good example might be computer enthusiasts who use Prodigy, Dialog, CompuServe, electronic bulletin boards, and other on-line computer services. If you did a promotion for a bulletin board or other on-line electronic information or communications service and targeted the general population of computer users, you might be unsuccessful—not because your service or promotion are bad, but because the average computer user isn't "into" on-line communication, doesn't actively use a modem, and is intimidated by the whole idea. On the other hand, if you could target your promotion to existing users of such services, selling them an additional service—yours—might be easier, because you'd have to sell the service only, not the whole concept of on-line communication or buying a modem.

This is a good example of marketing made more efficient through targeting. We know it's always easier to "preach to the converted." That is, it makes more sense to advertise your steaks to beef lovers rather than trying to convince vegetarians that meat is good for them. Targeting to an affinity group assures that your audience is already converted before you start preaching to them.

8. Media.

You can sometimes achieve great success by targeting your copy to readers of specific business publications, members of trade or professional organizations, or specific mailing lists. For instance, I occasionally use direct mail to get new clients for my copywriting and marketing consultation services. Since I specialize in business-to-business, the list of B/PAA (Business/Professional Advertising Association) members has proven to be the best list for me.

My standard letter is a form letter with the salutation "Dear Marketing Professional." However, I find I get slightly better results with the B/PAA list by changing the salutation to "Dear Fellow B/PAA Member." The identification with their membership ("Dear *B/PAA Member*") gets their attention. The use of "*Fellow* Member" ("Dear *Fellow* B/PAA Member") shows that I am a part of their "crowd."

This approach can work easily in direct mail and print ads. In direct mail, for example, you can easily target a salutation based on membership ("Dear IEEE Member"), publications read ("Dear *Spectrum* Subscriber"), or trade show attendance ("Dear Chem Show Attendee"). You can tailor a substantial portion of your copy to the reader's profession, interests, or professional activities based on knowledge of the publication or mailing list, or you can make only minor alterations to your basic copy, as I did with the letter to B/PAA members.

You can also target to readers of a specific magazine in your space ad copy. For instance, if you're advertising only in magazines read by pharmaceutical manufacturers, put a small kicker or "eyebrow" line in bold copy above the main headline and make it read: "ATTENTION: Pharmaceutical Manufacturers." You might argue that this is totally unnecessary; if all of the people reading the magazine are pharmaceutical manufacturers, who else could the ad be for?

But the fact is, it does work, because the prospect reads the kicker and is convinced that *the ad is written specifically for him and will address the unique concerns he has as a pharmaceutical manufacturer.* You gain an enormous advantage over other advertisers, most of whom just send their generic or standard product ad to vertical-market publications, with no tailoring or slanting toward the particular audience reading the publication.

In fact, the small to medium-size business-to-business marketer can gain a significant advantage over larger competitors through use of this technique. How? Smaller firms, in my experience, are more flexible about doing "special" promotions to smaller target markets, perhaps because they don't have the budget to compete with the big corporations on a mass-marketing basis.

Large corporations, by comparison, are often committed to a year-long advertising plan that does not easily accommodate special requests for niche advertising. Also, many advertising managers at large corporations think such specialized advertising is not worthwhile, or else it is not "in the budget."

So targeting your ad or mailing to the specific publication or mailing list is one way to increase its attention-getting and selling power.

9. Adherence to certain standards, policies, or rules.

Another way to segment the market is by standards, protocols, policies, or rules—that is, to target companies that must comply with certain regulations or follow specific guidelines or procedures, usually dictated by technology, industry standards, or regulatory bodies.

Example: An industrial equipment manufacturer designed a valve that was excellent at preventing leakage to the atmosphere. This was of critical importance in chemical plants, and less so in other process applications. Therefore, an ad aimed at chemical engineers stressed how the product ensured compliance with EPA standards for controlling "fugitive emissions." This was not the primary feature stressed in ads to pharmaceutical manufacturing, biotechnology, wastewater treatment, and other industry segments.

If complying with a certain federal regulation is of extreme importance to a certain group of prospects, you can send a mailing to those prospects stressing how your product or service helps them comply with that regulation.

If concerns of interoperability among equipment require a certain segment of the market to buy equipment that adheres to certain standards of compatibility, you can do a mailing to those companies stressing how your product is designed to conform to those standards, or how its "open architecture" ensures conformance to current and future standards.

10. Users of specific devices, products, machines, systems, or technologies.

This is a simple, sensible strategy. Its premise: If you're selling fax paper, you'll do a lot better selling to people who own fax machines than to those who don't.

You might say, "You'd have to be an idiot to do otherwise," but people do this every day. For instance, a client recently asked my advice on how to select mailing lists for a promotion offering a piece of PC software that does engineering calculations. Which lists would you choose?

Your first recommendation might be lists of members of the major engineering societies, such as the American Institute of Chemical Engineers or the American Society for Civil Engineers. But wait a minute. To sell software, you want to reach people who *own and use personal computers,* and not all engineers do. (Some, for example, use workstations that can't run software written for the IBM PC or Apple Macintosh.) So when selling software, a basic rule is to target (or at least, mail to) people who own the hardware that can run your program.

In some cases, perhaps your product works exceedingly well in tandem with another product or system. You could then do a mailing to owners or prospective buyers of the system, stressing the compatibility and advantages of using your product with that system. If you could make an arrangement with the manufacturer of the primary system to have them market and sell your product as an add-on at the time of initial sale, this would be even more effective.

11. Buying habits.

Although this is not a major concern in business-to-business, there is evidence that you can increase response by tailoring your marketing efforts to fit the buying habits or patterns of the target prospects.

In consumer direct marketing, for example, results show that mailings using a sweepstakes do best when mailed to lists of people who have previously responded to sweepstakes mailings. Apparently, these people enjoy sweepstakes and will go through the trouble of entering, more so than the general population that contains a number of people who (like me) do not have patience for sweepstakes and do not respond to sweepstakes mailings.

It also makes sense to stress that you accept payment by credit card when mailing to a group of known credit card holders.

While this strategy has admittedly limited applicability in business marketing, perhaps you can make it work for you. For example, if you find that 90 percent of orders from your industrial catalog come through telephone rather than letter or order form, you might get rid of the order form and put more graphic emphasis on your phone number throughout the catalog.

On the other hand, if a significant number of people fill out and fax the order form, you should retain the order form but redesign it so that you emphasize fax rather than mail-in response.

12. Behavioral habits.

This is similar to targeting affinity groups, but it is perhaps more subtle. Targeting behavioral habits means you target prospects whose behavior would identify them as the most likely candidates to respond to your offer.

As I write this, a client called to ask me advice about marketing a series of informational audio cassettes—something I have done many, many times in the past. One of his major concerns was, "Can we sell this to anybody, or will it just appeal to those who are already sold on the idea of listening to audio cassettes?" A good question!

Although the information contained in the cassettes has wide appeal to a large business audience, he will have his best chance of success with the mailing list of SyberVision or other response lists of people who buy informational audio cassettes through direct response. Again, it's a case of "preaching to the converted." Selling a prospect on buying *your specific* audio cassette series is tough enough; to have to also sell that prospect on why he or she should be listening to audio cassettes in the first place makes it a doubly hard sell.

My recommendation in this case? Spend the bulk of your money testing lists of proven audio cassette buyers. Test a few other mail response business lists, but cautiously and in small quantities. While I won't know the results of the test for several months, I expect that the promotion will be most profitable when sent to those whose behavioral habits (i.e., audio cassette listeners) indicate a predisposition to buy the type of product being advertised.

13. Other demographic and psychographic characteristics of the prospects.

Consumer direct marketing frequently targets prospects by such demographic and psychographic characteristics as age, income, marital status, family status, zip code, sex, and so on.

While these factors don't usually come into play in targeting a business-to-business direct marketing program, there are times they may be helpful. For instance, if you created an audio cassette program that told corporate executives how to benefit from the early retirement packages now being widely offered to reduce the size of corporate payrolls, the headline of your ad or teaser of your envelope might target by age, reading "AN IMPORTANT MESSAGE FOR EXECUTIVES AGE 45 AND OVER." Managers in their 20s and 30s, of course, would not receive early retirement offers and would therefore not be prospects for buying the cassette course.

The targeting decision

Deciding how to divide your total marketing effort and expenditure among various target markets—what the markets should be, how many different target markets to address, how much time and effort to spend on each, which markets to ignore—is one of the most important and difficult decisions any marketing manager has to make.

Should you target? How broad or narrow should your focus be? Which markets are primary? secondary? Here are some questions and answers you might find useful in working through this difficult issue in your own marketing plan.

1. Does your product or service lend itself to targeting?

In my experience, most business-to-business products and services lend themselves to a targeted approach, but there are some that don't.

An example of a business-to-business service that benefits from targeting? Transportation—shipping, warehousing, freight forwarding, and so forth. One client of mine, a marketing genius, has dramatically increased the sales of his air freight forwarding business by targeting specific market segments and establishing himself as *the* transportation expert in those niches. For example, he recently formed a subsidiary that handles nothing but *medical* shipments after discovering that medical clients have specialized needs that are inadequately handled by general shipping and courier services.

An example of a product that did *not* lend itself to target marketing? A company in my area of northern New Jersey sells a software utility for improving the performance of mainframe computers. It does the same thing on every computer, it's a function every data processing manager in every company would want, and the desire for this functionality doesn't vary based on size of company, type of computer, or industry. Therefore, niche marketing does not make sense, and it is advertised in general-interest computer magazines.

Take a look at your product or service. Does it lend itself to targeting by size of prospect company, industry, SIC code, or any of the other 13 characteristics discussed in this chapter? If so, great. If not, perhaps target marketing is not for you.

2. Do clear, distinct targets emerge?

As your business progresses, certain markets may emerge as "naturals." They are attractive, lucrative, have a strong need for your product, can benefit from your service, and are a good "fit" for your company. These become the primary markets you target.

On the other hand, perhaps no distinct vertical market opportunities emerge, or no single market is clearly the right one to pursue. In this case, you must think through whether specific markets can be logically targeted, based on a combination of common sense and experience supplemented by market research.

One excellent resource for market research when targeting vertical market segments or industries is *FINDEX*. This book is a directory listing of commercially available market research reports and surveys, organized by industry. You just look up your target market, read the descrip-tions of the reports, and call the report publisher to get more details or order the material. For more information on *FINDEX,* contact Cambridge Information tion Group, 7200 Wisconsin Avenue, Bethesda, MD 20814, phone (301) 961-6750.

3. Are there distinct trade shows, mailing lists, publications, associations, and other media targeted to these markets?

If there are no specialized mailing lists, associations, directories, news-letters, or magazines covering a vertical market or industry segment, you probably will have to give up the idea of targeting it as a distinct market. After all, if there is no mailing list or directory of these prospects, no magazines they read, or no associations they belong to, how will you reach them? You can't. So for target marketing to be successful, targeted media must exist.

How can you check these resources? A good guide to mailing lists is the *Direct Mail Encyclopedia*, available free of charge from Edith Roman Associates, 253 W. 35th Street, 16th Floor, New York, NY 10001, phone 800-223-2194. This catalog contains data on thousands of commercially available mailing lists, organized by category.

For information on specialized business and professional associations, consult *The Encyclopedia of Associations*, available in your local library or from Gale Research, P.O. Box 33477, Detroit, MI 48232-9852, phone 800-877-4253.

For information on magazines and other specialized publications, organized by industry, check with the Standard Rate and Data Service, Macmillan Publishing, 3004 Glenview Road, Wilmette, IL 60091, phone (708) 256-6067. They also publish a comprehensive directory of mailing lists.

4. Does your product or service fill a need in this particular niche?

Just because a particular vertical market looks attractive to you doesn't mean you look attractive to the marketplace. If you are going to succeed with target marketing, you must offer something these prospects want—something they can't get from other vendors. Your product or service must address a need that is currently unfulfilled or else perform better than other products or services they are using now or can buy elsewhere.

Does some attribute or feature of your product or service make it especially well suited for a particular niche market? Then you have a good chance of succeeding in that market.

On the other hand, if there's no special reason why your product or service is suited to this market, you either have to change the product or service or at least create the *perception* that it was especially designed with their needs in mind. What works best is a combination of the two techniques: tailoring the product or service to the needs of the market, coupled with a promotional campaign that establishes you as a specialist in serving these unique needs.

5. Do you have credentials or credibility in these markets?

I know of several software vendors who had great products running on specific hardware platforms who thought they could expand their sales by migrating these proven winners to other platforms. But when they did so, they found it wasn't as easy as they thought it would be. Why? Because they had no *reputation* or *credibility* in these new markets. They would say, "Our software is proven in 30,000 IBM installations!" The prospects would reply, "Yes, but we're a DEC shop. Have you got any-thing running on a VAX?" Not having these reference installations made it slow going expanding into the DEC marketplace.

Do you have credentials or credibility in the marketplace you want to target? Even a small amount of prior experience, or a limited presence, can be made to seem impressive and help make prospects comfortable with you as a vendor.

But if you haven't served this market before, and they don't know you, you have to realize that extending into the market will be much tougher for you. Print advertising can help overcome this and establish a presence—if you can afford large ads and a heavy schedule. Otherwise, the best technique for gaining quick visibility in new markets is a combination of an aggressive but low-cost public relations campaign combined with networking, participation in major trade associations and professional societies, and trade show exhibits at the industry's major events.

Another good strategy for gaining credibility fast is a name change. This is usually done by establishing a division or subsidiary with a name indicating experience and specialization in a particular market. For instance, would a hospital looking for a collection agency be more likely to hire Retrieval Masters Creditors Bureau (RMCB) or American Medical Collection Agency (AMCA)? The latter, obviously. That's why RMCB's owner *formed* AMCA as a separate company when he decided to aggressively pursue the medical collections field.

6. What's your budget?

Your budget is another factor in determining whether you will do mass marketing or niche marketing. Actually, only the largest *Fortune* 500 corporations and other giants can afford mass advertising. Small and medium-size companies, having to compete with these giants on a fraction of the marketing budget, do well by avoiding mass marketing and instead concentrating on niche markets that the larger companies ignore.

A finite budget must be divided in some fashion among a finite number of target markets. If you determine that a target marketing campaign costs you $100,000 a year, and your ad budget is $500,000, then you can afford to target five niche markets, maximum. You might, however, choose to spend $200,000 on your primary target market and $100,000 each on three secondary markets. It's entirely up to you, but that's the kind of decision you'll have to make.

7. What are your resources?

Budget is one constraint on marketing activities; another is resources—usually staff and time. Do you have the time or staff to manage five ongoing campaigns? Your own resources determine how "thin" you can spread yourself. With a large staff, assistant advertising managers can each take charge of a different vertical market. If staff is limited, you may decide it's better to concentrate your energies on a smaller number of niche markets.

8. Does it work?

Target marketing usually works, but the question is, "Does it work for you?" Set objectives, measure results, and then decide. Often you find that a market segment you thought would be profitable is not, and so you switch to a different segment.

For instance, you're not making money installing turnkey computer systems for doctor's offices, but you realize the same software could work for group practices, which buy more terminals and larger systems for a higher price tag. So you switch your focus and become successful.

Target marketing almost always works, to some degree. The question is whether the incremental improvement in marketing results it generates is worth the extra time, effort, and expense of maintaining an ongoing marketing campaign aimed at that specific audience. If yes, keep going, make your money, and look to duplicate your success in similar or different markets. If not, regroup. See if the same campaign can work on a slightly different market segment, or consider switching to a different market altogether.

5

Increasing Your Response Rates with "Free Booklet" and Other Soft Offers

The importance of the offer

"YOU MAY HAVE ALREADY WON $10 million."
"The GREATEST SPORTS BLOOPERS VIDEO—yours FREE with your paid subscription to Sports Illuustrated."
"Affix the token to the reply card for your FREE sample issue."
"Buy one—get one free."
"FREE tote bag when you become a member."

Consumer direct marketers rely heavily on finding and phrasing the proper offer to wake up bored consumers, get them to take notice, and per-suade them to respond to the marketers' ads and mailings.

Business-to-business marketers have traditionally ignored offers, not considering them important. The typical "industrial ad," for example, instructs readers to circle the reply card number or telephone for "more information"; nothing more specific than that is offered. Most corporate advertising ends with smart-sounding copy that's totally vague about what you are supposed to think, feel, or do about the ad—the offer is completely absent.

This is a mistake. The offer is as critical to business-to-businesss direct marketing as it is to traditional consumer direct marketing. To get maximum response from your marketing communications, you must realize the following:

- The offer is of utmost importance to the success of any direct marketing piece or campaign.

- The strategic planning, selection, and testing of offers can make or break a campaign, regardless of how well designed or well written the piece is. As a rule, the more valuable and risk-free the offer seems to the reader, the better your response.

- The presentation of the offer—the copy used to describe it, the graphics, the emphasis it receives—is also of critical importance. As a rule, the more you emphasize and stress the offer in copy and graphics, the higher your response rate.

- The clearer and more understandable your offer, the better your response. The lack of a clear, distinct offer can significantly depress response.

This chapter explains what an offer is, lists the different types of offers you can use, and tells how to construct "free booklet" and other "soft" offers that maximize response to business-to-business direct marketing. Chapter 6 will focus on how to do the same for discount, 2-for-1, trial, free evalu-ation, and other "hard" offers.

What is an offer?

I define the "offer" as follows:

What your prospects get when they respond to your ad or mailing, combined with what they have to do to get it.

Note that the offer has two components:

1. What the prospect gets.

2. What the prospect has to do to get it.

The simplest, most popular offer in business-to-business marketing is probably the offer of a brochure describing the product or service. In direct mail, this typically reads: "For a free brochure on the Widget 2000, complete and mail the enclosed reply card today." What the prospect gets is a brochure describing your product. What they have to do to get it is fill in and mail a reply card.

This offer can and does work for many, many products and services. However, in many cases, you can come up with a much more attractive offer—one that will get many more people to be interested in your proposition and respond to your ad or mailing. Chapters 5 and 6 are written to show you how to do this.

The four basic types of offers

There are four fundamentally different types of offers: hard, soft, negative, and deferred. In this section, I'll describe them and show you how and when to use each. In the examples, I'll phrase the offers as they might be used in a typical business-to-business direct mail package; however, these can work for radio, print ads, PR, and in many other formats.

Offer #1: The soft offer

My definition of a "soft offer" is as follows:

An offer in which the prospect requests some type of printed material that is mailed or shipped to him, and makes this request using a reply card or other response mechanism that does not require face-to-face or other personal communication between the prospect and the seller.

The important thing to note about the soft offer is that it's the most painless, risk-free way for the prospect to raise his hand, get in touch with you, and say "I may be interested—tell me more" . . . without the prospect's having to subject himself to sales pressure of any kind.

The typical soft offer in a direct mail letter reads as follows: "If you're interested in learning more about what Product X can do for you, just complete and mail the enclosed reply card for a free brochure." Think about what happens: The prospect checks off a box on a reply card and mails it to you. You mail the requested literature back. The prospect has expressed interest, responded, and received information with no personal contact between you.

The soft offer appeals to those prospects who do not have an immediate need and are "just looking," or to those who have an immediate need but want to gather preliminary information without speaking to your agents or sales reps. The soft offer generates a high level of response because there is no sales pressure or risk of being "pitched" by high-pressure sales types. It promises details that can be reviewed by the prospects at their leisure.

Many business-to-business marketers mistakenly believe that all people who respond to "soft offers" are just collecting brochures and are therefore not serious, *real* prospects. For this reason, they avoid soft offers. They say, "If the prospect doesn't pick up the phone and call me, she's not really interested, and I don't want to waste time and money sending her expensive color brochures she's just going to file or throw away."

While there's some validity to this point of view, it usually turns out not to be true. "Soft" leads can be extremely profitable, and often the conversion is just as good as with hard leads. For most promotions, the best strategy is actually to give the reader a choice of *several* offers, not *only* a hard offer or *only* a soft offer. (We'll discuss the best combination of offer options to use shortly.)

Offer #2: The hard offer

The opposite of the soft offer is the "hard offer," which I define as follows:

> **An offer which requires or results in face-to-face or other personal contact between buyer and seller in a sales situation or other circumstances where the seller has the prospect "captive" for purposes of doing some selling, or an offer which actually requires payment (or promise of payment) in exchange for the product.**

In business-to-business mail order selling, the hard offer is "Send us payment and we will ship you the product." In business-to-business lead generation, the hard offer is typically something like: "Call now to schedule an appointment so we can show you how XYZ Product or Service can be of benefit to your company."

In the hard offer, the prospect typically calls or writes the advertiser to arrange a meeting, demonstration, initial consultation, or appointment. There is direct person-to-person contact between buyer and seller initially over the telephone, and usually later face-to-face. During these contacts, telemarketing representatives or salespeople attempt to persuade the prospects to buy the product or service being offered.

The hard offer is ideal for prospects who have serious interest, an immediate need, are looking to buy something fairly soon, and want to "sit down and talk" with vendors. The prospect responding to a hard offer, especially if by telephone, typically feels a fairly urgent need to gather more information for an immediate or upcoming purchase.

Use of hard offers is discussed extensively in Chapter 5. With a hard offer, the prospect is taking a definite (if tentative or uncommitted) step toward purchase of the product. A soft offer, by comparison, is more of a "let me look you over" or "we'll wait and see" response.

Negative and deferred offers

In addition to hard and soft offers, there are two other basic categories of business-to-business offers: negative and deferred.

Rather than define them, I will give you the exact wording of these offers as you would use them in a reply card in a lead-generating direct mail package.

The negative offer reads as follows:

[ ] Not interested right now because: _____.
(Please give reason—thank you.)

Typically, reference to the negative offer is made in the P.S. or elsewhere in the body of the letter, using the following language:

P.S. Even if you are not interested in [name of product or service], please complete and return the enclosed reply card. Thank you.

The negative offer provides a response option for people who are prospects (that is, they have a need or problem your product addresses), but for some reason or another, do not want to buy from you or get more information on your product. Normally, a person not interested in your offer will not respond to your mailing. By using a negative offer option, you will get response from a small portion of these people.

The negative offer should be used when you are testing a mailing on a new product, service, or offer you haven't promoted before using direct mail. The reason you use the negative offer is that without it, if you get a low or no response to your mailing, you don't know whether it's the mailing piece that's ineffective, or whether the product, service, or offer isn't right for the market.

With the negative offer option, people will *tell you* why they are not interested in your offer. Perhaps the price is too high. Or your technology is not compatible with the systems they are already using. Or they don't like your type of product, or don't use it. This information not only helps you readjust your marketing plans; it also demonstrates that the mailing was unsuccessful for reasons other than ineffective copy and design—something that's good to know if you're the person who wrote or designed it.

A second benefit of the negative option is that it can increase slightly your overall response rate. You might object and say, "But all the people who check the negative option box have told us they are not prospects."

But quite the opposite is true: If someone took the time to tell you why your offer isn't right for them, they *are* a prime prospect. They're telling you they have some sort of need, but your product *as described in the mailing* didn't seem quite right . . . and that they want you to get back to them with a product, service, or offer that *is* right for them.

Actually, your product or service may be ideal for them, but your ad or mail copy may not have communicated this effectively, or else they misunderstood or didn't read carefully enough. That's okay. By completing the negative offer option box, your prospects have set themselves up in perfect position for follow-up and closing by a skilled salesperson.

If you have ever been a salesperson, then you know the most difficult prospect to sell is the one you can't reach—the one who never responds to your letters or returns your phone calls, or the one who says they are not interested but won't say why. A prospect who fills in the blank space on your reply card where it says "please give reason why you are not interested" has framed a specific objection which can be overcome with the proper selling argument.

A deferred offer is a variation on the negative offer. Here's how it's phrased:

[ ] **Not interested right now. Try us again in** _____ .
                                          (month/year)

The deferred offer encourages response from prospects who do not have an immediate need but may have a future requirement for your product or service.

Some of these prospects won't check off the soft offer option box ("[ ] Please send me a brochure.") because they think, "If I check off this box they're going to follow-up with a phone call and pester me, and I don't have any need right now." The deferred offer option box says to this prospect, "If you have no immediate requirement but may have a future need, you can use this box to let us know that you have a future need, without getting calls and annoying follow-up from salespeople now."

When do you use the negative as opposed to the deferred offer option? Use the negative offer option when testing a new offer or when you think many prospects might not respond for specific reasons. Use the deferred offer when you think a significant number of prospects are more likely to need your services in the future rather than immediately.

Using the four basic offer options

A common mistake in business-to-business lead-generating advertising and direct mail is to have only one offer option. In most instances you should have two or three options. The best results usually come from having three offers: a hard offer, a soft offer, and either a negative or a deferred offer. At minimum, you should at least have both a hard and soft offer, with one of the two being the primary offer and the other secondary.

The primary offer is the one you hope your prospects will respond to and the one you emphasize in your copy and graphics. For example, if you want a face-to-face meeting with your prospects, you would urge them to call and arrange an appointment. A "free, no-obligation" initial appointment would be your primary offer, and the one you stress in your letter or ad.

The secondary offer is included to give those prospects who will not take you up on your primary offer a second reason to respond. If a pros-pect is not willing or ready to take you up on your offer of a free initial meeting, introduce the secondary soft offer at the end of your ad or letter copy, e.g., "P.S. For a free special report outlining six tax-saving strategies offered by our firm, just complete and mail the enclosed reply card."

Which offer should be your primary offer? Make your soft offer—the offer of free literature or information—the primary offer when:

- Requesting a brochure or catalog is the typical first step in the buying process in your particular industry or field, and circumventing that step would be counterproductive.

- You feel many prospects would be reluctant to meet or talk with you, so you need some sort of brochure or other literature to create a reason for them to respond to your mailing.

- Your product or service is complex and requires a lot of explanation that is best communicated in a standardized written format, such as a brochure or data sheet.

- You have limited staff for telephone contact with prospects and your operation lends itself more to the mailing of a standardized inquiry fulfillment brochure or package.

- Your prospects are far away and you do not have regional branch offices or sales reps who can call on them in person.

- You have a great brochure or inquiry fulfillment kit already in place that has proven its ability to (a) screen out nonqualified prospects and (b) sell effectively to qualified prospects.

Industrial equipment manufacturers are a good example of marketers who stress soft offers. Their prospects, engineers and purchasing agents, require a lot of detailed information on technical products before making a buying decision, and this information is communicated more easily in a printed brochure than over the telephone.

Also, having a brochure on your industrial product is standard practice in the industry, and most purchasers won't buy without having a brochure or other technical literature in their purchasing files. So a logical next step in industrial direct mail or ads is the offer of such a brochure or catalog at no charge.

The hard offer should be the primary offer when:

- You would prefer to get a phone inquiry rather than a written inquiry because your salespeople are more likely to close when they receive a hot lead via inbound telephone.

- Sending printed material such as a brochure or catalog is an unnecessary step that only gets in the way and slows down the selling process.

- There is not a lot of information or detail to communicate about your service or product and you can sum it up quickly and easily in a two-minute phone conversation.

- You have a special free trial offer or other special offer that enables the prospect to try your service or product on a small scale for free or for a nominal fee, and you feel you can get prospects to accept this offer if you can sell them on the phone or face to face.

- Your product or service is unique or unusual and difficult to communicate in printed material and is more easily communicated in person or over the phone or via demonstration.

- Your audience is not print-oriented.

An example of an industry that doesn't tend to use brochures is vocational training for adults—offers such as "Learn to be a computer operator in your spare time." One such marketer told me, "We have learned through experience that offering a brochure is a waste. To sell the prospect on taking our program, we have to get them to come to our facility in person for a free introductory class—otherwise it won't work."

Once you have the hard and soft offer options in place, you add either a negative offer option if you want to learn why prospects are not responding as you would have hoped, or a deferred offer option if yours is the type of product or service that is likely to be bought at a future date rather than immediately.

How will the response be split? In my mailing (reprinted in Chapter 8), the letter generated a 10 percent response. Of the total response, most people (more than 90 percent) check the soft offer ("Please send more information") box on the card. Fewer than one in ten (less than 10 percent) check the hard offer ("Give me a call") box on the reply card.

I can convert between 10 to 25 percent of inquiries to sales within 6 months of the receipt of the inquiry, if I want that much business. Interestingly, there is no difference in the *quality* of the lead (seriousness of the prospect) between those who check the hard offer box and those who check the soft offer box: percentage conversion to sales is the same in either category.

Almost all of the response to my mailing is from the reply card. I give my telephone number in my letter but do not encourage phone calls. (I prefer to speak to the prospect only after they have received a complete package of information about my service.) I do not give a fax number or encourage fax response.

People check the deferred "Not interested right now" box infrequently, and I mail so few of these letters that I can't give you a statistical result. Qualitatively, however, I can tell you that having the third box for the deferred offer has paid off. I can recall specific instances where a prospect checked off the "Try us again" option, and when I followed up, I found they did indeed have a specific project in mind to be started at a specific date. Follow-up immediately with literature and later via a phone call at the time requested resulted in a sale in at least two cases.

Enhancing the soft offer

The typical industrial marketer uses a fairly standardized soft offer that is either "more information" or "free brochure." While this is adequate in many cases and can work, there is vast room for improvement.

The key is to use the free offer as a "bait piece" and to maximize requests for this free information by making it seem highly relevant, valuable, desirable, and specific to the prospect's interests and needs. There are a number of ways to enhance the soft offer with an attractive bait piece. The most popular, and probably still the most effective, is the offer of a free booklet or special report.

"Free booklet" and other free information offers

The term *bait piece* refers to free information the advertiser offers in their mailing piece or ad to generate a high number of inquiries. The term *bait* is used because the free booklet is offered not for purposes of giving away free information or educating the reader (as the reader is led to believe) but to "hook" the reader by generating a response or inquiry which can be followed up by telephone and field sales personnel.

Here is a secret many direct marketers do not know and will find difficult to believe:

The "free booklet" (or "free report" or other free information offer) will *dramatically* increase response to your ads and mailings over what the response for essentially the same ad or letter copy would be without the free information offer.

Why are free booklet offers effective? For several reasons. First, today's business prospects, despite being overloaded with reading material, are information-seekers, always on the look-out for advice, ideas, and information to help them do their jobs better and more efficiently. Many publishers charge handsomely for such information sold as seminars, audio cassettes, books, newsletters, and manuals. So when businesspeople see that they can get similar information from you in the form of a free booklet or special report, they respond. After all, if it's free, they have nothing to lose.

Second, most businesspeople are so busy that they flip through mail and ads at a frantic rate. The free booklet offer, with perhaps a cut-out coupon in the ad and a picture of a free booklet, has attention-grabbing power. It forces the reader to slow down, stop, and peruse your copy. The reader thinks, "Oh, this is one of those ads offering something free. Let me take a look for a second and see what I can get." So they call or clip the coupon and request the booklet.

Third, businesspeople, like everyone else, like getting things for free. In the direct marketing seminars I give nationwide, there is always someone in the audience who says, "Aren't free offers much less effective in business-to-business than consumer marketing? Come on, really, how excited can an executive get about a free booklet or report?"

The fact is, whether they get *excited* is irrelevant; they do get *interested,* and the specific offer of free information dramatically increases ad and direct mail response rates.

The importance of the free booklet offer.

The free booklet offer is so effective, and so important, that for most business marketers using direct mail to generate leads, I think it's a mistake not to have such an offer as part of your mailing.

The reason is simple: Unless prospects have an immediate, urgent need to pick up the phone and call you, your mailing is largely a matter of indifference to them. It's just another "sales pitch"—one of many they will receive by mail or phone that day.

The prospect feels no need to respond, and doesn't. The free booklet offer solves that problem. It says to the prospect, "Even if you have no immediate need, don't have time to read our mailing, and don't want to think about our product right now, at least mail back the reply card. You'll receive something of value in return." Such an offer converts inaction to a response.

How to create successful free booklet offers.

What are the steps to creating and using successful free booklet offers? First, pick a topic for your free booklet or report. The topic should be something that interests the reader while at the same time helps sell the reader on your system, product, service, or idea.

For instance, to promote a line of business software, IBM published a free booklet (actually, it was a full-length paperback book) telling small businesses what to look for when evaluating software packages. The book helped readers by showing them what features to look for when "shopping" for software. At the same time, it helped IBM promote its software, because the comparison checklists highlighted many of the features found in the IBM products.

The free book "creates a specification" the reader uses to evaluate potential software. The information is believable because it is packaged in the form of a book rather than a promotional brochure. The reader then goes to IBM for a software demonstration; IBM has become a credible source in their minds because, after all, they "wrote the book." When prospects check out IBM's software, they find (surprise!) that it fulfills the specifications outlined in the book—therefore, it must be good—and a sale is made.

The topic you select can persuade the reader to favor your product or service, but the "sell" must be soft and subtle. Typically, your free report or booklet expains a certain way to do a thing or how to select a product to do it. While this discussion must appear unbiased and editorially neutral, you will slant it so the reader comes away favoring *your* approach to doing the thing, solving the problem, or selecting the product.

The booklet you write contributes to the selling process in two ways: first, by predisposing the reader to accept your methods as standard and desirable; and second, by positioning you and your firm as experts in the topic.

The topic must be interesting and relevant to the reader. A small business owner would not be interested in "How IBM Designs and Codes Its Software Systems," but would be interested in "How to Choose the

Right Software for Your Business." The booklet must appeal to the reader's self-interest while promoting your own—that's the balance you must achieve.

After selecting a topic, you need a catchy title. A title with the words "how to" in it, e.g., "How to Reduce Costs and Increase Productivity by Implementing EDI (Electronic Data Interchange)," can be effective; people want to know how to do things. Number titles, e.g., "7 ways," "6 steps," "14 winning methods," also make your booklet more attractive to the reader, because they arouse curiosity. People want to know what the 7 ways, 6 steps, or 14 methods are. Here are some typical titles from successful free booklets offered in actual business-to-business direct mail and print ads:

"15 Ways to Improve Your Collection Efforts" (RMCB)

"14 Winning Methods to Sell Any Product or Service in a Down Economy" (Bob Bly Seminars)

"Should I Personalize? A Direct Marketer's Guide to Personalized Direct Mail"   (Fala Direct Marketing)

"Choosing Business Software"   (IBM)

"Aldus Guide to Desktop Design"   (Aldus)

"Family-Owned Businesses: The 3 Most Common Pitfalls . . . and How to Avoid Them" (Consulting Dynamics)

"A Special Report: Productivity Breakthrough Projects" (JMW Consultants)

"33 Ways to Make Better Displays: What Every Marketing Executive Should Know about Point-of-Purchase Display Marketing"   (Display Masters)

"Steel Log: Glossary of Metal Terms"   (Specialty Steel)

"7 Questions to Ask *before* You Invest in DP Training . . . and One Good Answer to Each" (Chubb Institute)

The title of your "bait piece" is all-important because it determines, in large part, whether you can get prospects interested enough to send for it. So choose the title with care. If you are selling desktop publishing systems and your target market is advertising agencies, how about a booklet titled "What Every Ad Agency Executive Should Know about Choosing and Using a Desktop Publishing System to Reduce Production Costs and Increase Client Satisfaction"? If you owned an ad agency and were losing clients because you didn't offer desktop publishing capability, would you send for this free report? I should think so!

When choosing a topic and title, it's better to make it narrow and more targeted than broad and general. By narrowing the focus, you can cover one specific topic of great interest to your prospects with sufficient detail to gain their attention and whet their appetite for further contact with you. For example, Fala's booklet, "A Direct Marketer's Guide to Personalized Direct Mail" is effective because it zeros in on one specific topic of interest to direct marketers—personalizing direct mail—rather than the broader, less meaningful topic of "direct mail." It positions Fala as the expert specifically in *personalized* direct mail production.

After selecting the topic and title, think about format. Do you want to publish a booklet, report, fact sheet, or poster? Or how about a book or manual? Or do you plan on putting your information on audiotape, videotape, or computer disk?

A fact sheet or tip sheet is the most basic format. In a fact sheet, your information is typewritten or typeset and printed on one or both sides of a single sheet of 8 1/2-by-11-inch paper. Such sheets can be produced quickly and inexpensively.

For example, you can offset print or photocopy 500 single-sided tip sheets for $30 to $50. To enhance their perceived value, print on yellow, gold, or other brightly colored stock rather than white. The mechanical can be made at no cost using a typewriter or desktop publishing system. Or, you can offer reprints of articles you've written, calling them "tip sheets."

Tip sheets can be effective, but some marketers think they look cheap. One solution is to print your tip sheet as a poster, using a larger size and better stock of paper "suitable for framing." The Communication Workshop, a New York City consulting firm, has had great success promoting its business writing seminars with a series of one-page posters on grammar, sexist language, and similar writing topics.

Most marketers offering free information offer it in the form of a booklet or special report. A booklet implies a smaller size publication, either folded or saddle-stitched (staples through the spine). The information is more detailed than a tip sheet, but less detailed than a book or scholarly article.

The booklet page size can be either 4 by 9 inches to fit a standard #10 business envelope, or 5 1/2 by 8 1/2 inches to fit a 6-by-9-inch envelope. I recently produced a 16-page booklet sized to fit a #10 envelope and printed 1,000 copies saddle-stitched for $390. (To get a copy of this booklet, titled "Recession-Proof Business Strategies," send $7 to Bob Bly, 174 Holland Avenue, Dept. 109, New Milford, NJ 07646.)

A "special report" is similar to a booklet except it has full-size (8 1/2-by-11-inch) pages and is mailed in a 9-by-12-inch envelope. The report can be typewritten, desktop published, or typewritten with a desktop published cover. Often reports are simply run off on a photocopier, collated, and put in a clear plastic or other attractive cover. If you want to tailor versions of the report to different audiences, you can keep the body of it the same and simply change the introduction and front cover for each audience.

Even though you intend to give away your booklet or report for free, put a price on the front cover in the upper right-hand corner. This serves a couple of functions: First, it adds to the perceived value of the booklet or report; people are more interested in getting a $7 item for free than they are in getting a free item for free. Second, it allows you to charge for the item when you get inquiries from those who are not potential customers: students, brochure collectors, and so on. Third, it allows you to gracefully request payment from the occasional person who calls you up and wants multiple copies for a seminar, presentation, class, or to distribute in some other fashion. This does happen every once in a while and can be costly.

What should this pricing be? Say $1 or $2 for a tip sheet, $3 to $10 for a booklet, $7 to $15 for a special report, $5 to $15 for a book, $15 to $25 for a manual. These prices seem credible and fair; if you make the price too high, the prospect realizes it's a scam to make the offer seem better than it is.

If your report is long (50 pages or more), you can increase its perceived value still further by putting the pages in a three-ring binder and calling it a "manual." You can duplicate your manual in small quantities using your office copier.

If you are going to produce the manual in volume, don't imprint the manual cover directly on the binder. Instead, leave the binder cover blank and use a title page. Or print the cover on a separate glossy sheet and buy notebooks with a front cover "trap-in" (a clear plastic sleeve that allows you to easily insert and remove the cover). This way, if the report changes or becomes dated, you are not stuck with hundreds of unusable (and expensive) custom-imprinted binders.

If the free information bait piece is lengthy and a proven success, you may want to go to the next step and produce it as a self-published book. IBM did this with its *Choosing Business Software* book. CoreStates Financial Corporation similarly promotes its expertise and technology in EDI (Electronic Data Interchange) by giving away a self-published book on the subject.

A book requires more of an investment in effort, typesetting, and printing than a booklet, report, or manual. Because of printing economics, you will have to order a minimum of 500 copies of your book and will probably get the best price/volume "deal" when you order 2,000 or 3,000.

Be sure to get quotes only from printers who specialize in short-run (less than 5,000 copies) printing of books. General printers charge two to three times as much because they are not set up to print books. For a directory of book printers, contact Ad-Lib Publications, 51 1/2 West Adams Street, Fairfield, Iowa 52556, phone (515) 472-6617.

A book has an extremely high perceived value and is also perceived as being an unbiased, "legitimate" source of information. Because you want to keep the cost reasonable, you should plan to publish a small book rather than a big one. A small paperback book can contain as few as 60 to 80 pages with as little as 15,000 words of text (the equivalent of 60 double-spaced typewritten pages). Again, don't forget to put a cover price on the book—about $10 to $15 for a small paperback seems right.

Writing your bait piece

You have selected the topic, title, and format. Now it is time to determine the contents, make an outline, and write the copy for your booklet or report. The most important thing to keep in mind when writing "informational premiums" such as free booklets or reports is that the contents must deliver on the promise of the headline, convey useful information helpful to the reader, and be accurate.

It is not necessary that the contents be revolutionary or give the reader all new information. Many people read to affirm current beliefs or reinforce existing knowledge. So if your booklet mostly repeats what they already know, they'll be happy with it, and, more important, they'll think you're a wise, knowledgeable expert on the topic.

However, if you can give the reader one or two genuinely new ideas or things they may not have thought of before, so much the better. It will make your booklet or report even more valuable to them.

Do not put any selling or advertising message into the body of the booklet. The contents should be pure information. You have promised the reader knowledge; you impress the reader by conveying that knowledge. If you turn the booklet into a sales pitch, the people who sent for it expecting helpful advice will be angry, disappointed, turned off, and not inclined to do business with you. How much information should be included? It depends on the length and format. A full-length book, for example, must obviously contain more detail than a one-page tip sheet. As a rule, make your booklet or report helpful and fascinating, but don't overdo the detail. You want to tell the prospect enough to get him or her interested in hiring you to solve their problem; you don't want to tell so much in your report that it eliminates the need for the prospect to hire your firm or buy your product.

If the body is pure information, can you do any selling in the booklet? Yes, but keep it low key. On the front cover, under the title, put your firm as the author, giving the address and phone number.

Repeat this information on the back cover, adding a more complete description of your company, your product or service, how you can help the reader, and the next step they should take to learn more about your product or service. This should read like the "about the author" bios you find on nonfiction how-to books written by business experts, giving enough information to whet the reader's appetite without being too blatantly sales-oriented.

Magnetic and electronic media

One way to create additional interest and make your bait piece stand out even more is to produce your information in the form of an audio cassette, videotape, or computer-based presentation. One advantage of these formats is that they are not widely used and are therefore a bit unusual and likely to get greater notice. Also, audiotapes, videotapes, and floppy disks tend to stand out in an in-basket crowded with paper.

Other advantages? Tapes and floppy disks usually get past secretaries who screen mail and throw away lots of paper mail. Because a tape or disk has a higher perceived value and is a tangible object, it won't get thrown away.

Experience has shown that business prospects will take the time to either listen to or view the tape or disk, or at least make sure it gets passed on to the right prospect within the organization. Printed pieces are not treated with the same degree of importance. Finally, even if the prospect doesn't immediately listen to or view the tape or disk, they will probably keep it in a desk drawer, rather than throw it away. So every time they open the drawer, they see the tape or disk imprinted with your company name and phone number.

Audio cassettes

Audio cassettes are the easiest and least costly audio/visual medium to use as information bait pieces. Some marketers using audio cassettes think that briefer is better and limit the message to 10 or 20 minutes. But if the tape contains pure, useful information, it can be much longer. I have been successful promoting both my seminars and my consulting and copywriting services using cassettes on marketing and sales topics that are 90 minutes long.

Audio cassettes don't require the high level of production that video cassettes do. You can record a live presentation or speech given at work, a meet-ing, or an industry event, edit it in a studio, and offer it as an attractive bait piece on audio cassette.

What will all this cost? To hire someone with professional-quality recording equipment to record a presentation costs $100 to $200 plus travel expenses. Studio time goes for $35 to $75 per hour and should take less than half a day. To duplicate my presentations onto C-90 (90-minute) audio cassettes, including a laser-printed cassette label and soft plastic box, costs less than $1.50 per cassette in quantities of 50.

Videos

Videos are another story. You can expect to pay a professional at least $1,000 or $2,000 to record you live or in a studio. If you want a full-blown production with sets, special effects, and live location shooting, an 8-minute video can cost $5,000 to $15,000 or more, just for production.

Cost to duplicate 1,000 copies of an 8-minute video is about $2.50 per cassette with a cardboard box and typed label; plastic boxes and 4-color packaging can run much higher.

Floppy disks

A relatively new promotional medium is the floppy disk. Sales and informational presentations can be put on floppy disks that the prospect can view using a personal computer. Some direct marketers are reporting success with this medium, though I have no personal experience with it (other than conventional demo disks for software, which is a different thing).

Here are some companies that can help you create information premiums using electronic/magnetic media:

For audio cassette duplication:

Dove Enterprises
907 Portage Trail
Cuyahoga Falls, OH 44221
1 (800) 223-DOVE (3683)

For videotape duplication:

Mighty Mountain
RD #1, Box 8100
Lyndonville, VT 05851
(802) 626-8100

For presentations on floppy disk:

CompuDoc Inc.
51 Mt. Bethel Road
Warren, NJ 07059-5603
(908) 757-2888

Sources of ready-made free booklets and special reports you can offer as bait pieces

One reason that more business-to-business marketers don't use the bait-piece offer despite its proven effectiveness is as follows: "It sounds good, but we have a limited budget and staff. I don't really have the time to write and design—or commission someone to write, design, and print—a really good booklet or special report."

There are several solutions to this problem. One is to have your public relations firm or public relations department write and place a feature story on your preferred topic in an industry trade journal, then simply reprint this article as a tip sheet or booklet. This eliminates the need for you to write, typeset, and design an original piece.

Be sure the PR agency or department retains reprint rights or gets reprint permission from the magazine in which the piece is first published as an article. When you offer the reprint, call it a "tip sheet" or "special report," not an "article reprint," as the former convey higher perceived value. Somewhere in small type on the reprint, you can cite the publication and date of the article's original appearance.

A second strategy for offering free reports as bait pieces without paying to create them yourself is to reprint existing materials that deal with your topic, would be interesting to your prospects, and are in line with the service or product you sell.

If you're a member of a professional society or trade association, your group may offer informative publications that they will allow members to distribute or reprint without charge or for a reasonable sum. When reprinting, add your own front and back cover with your company name, description, and contact information.

Many medical societies and associations, as well as some pharmaceutical companies, for example, offer informative booklets on various aspects of health care that member physicians can reprint. Most doctors simply leave copies for patients on a table in the waiting room. But one orthodontist in my area reprinted such a booklet with his office address and phone number, added a personal cover letter, and mailed it, with good results, to potential patients in town.

If you're an agent, representative, distributor, or dealer, your manufacturer or wholesaler may provide you with booklets and other literature you can reprint or add your label to. These can be offered to prospects as bait pieces with no creative or other development costs on your part.

Another well-kept secret: The U.S. government is one of the biggest producers of informational booklets and special reports, and a large number of these *are not copyrighted* and may therefore be reprinted and used by you for promotional or any other purposes you choose. (The government asks but does not require you to acknowledge them as the original source of the material.) One local radon testing firm, for example, offers a report on "radon in the home," which is simply a reprint of a government publication with the firm's name and phone number imprinted on the top.

For catalogs of the various government publications available for free or at reasonable cost, contact:

Superintendent of Documents
Government Printing Office
Washington, D.C. 20402
(202) 783-3238

Consumer Resource Center
Pueblo, CO 81009
(719) 948-3334

Using existing publications as bait pieces works if you have a product or service for which a more "generic" bait piece would be an effective promotional device. For instance, if you're generating leads for an executive fitness program, you could probably increase response by offering a free package of booklets on health, diet, and exercise that are reprints of some of the copyright-free publications offered by the U.S. government.

On the other hand, if you are selling a highly specialized technical product, there is probably not an existing report you can use, and you will have to create your own. While in many cases you can "make do" using existing publications as bait pieces, I usually recommend to clients that they create their own customized information premiums, because an original publication can be made more interesting to the audience and more relevant to the client's product or service.

Four reasons why more business-to-business marketers don't use free booklet offers

Offering a free booklet, report, or other free information piece in your ads and direct mail can dramatically boost response. In fact, this is one of the few "sure-fire" rules of business-to-business direct response that works almost every time. In virtually every campaign where I have been able to persuade a business-to-business client to add a free booklet offer to the marketing program, sales lead generation has increased substantially and marketing costs were reduced. I know of few other strategies that are so basic, simple, and easy to use while consistently delivering such excellent results.

Despite this, many clients avoid using free booklet offers, based largely on the following erroneous beliefs. If you are not using the bait piece strategy because of one of these fears, this list may be helpful in overcoming your particular objection:

1. It's a cliche.

"Offering a free booklet isn't original." "It's a cliche." "Can't you think of something more creative?" The number-one reason marketers avoid free booklet offers is that they think it's old-hat and are looking for something original.

My answer is simple: So what if it's old-hat? So what if it's a "formula"? The fact is, it *works*—consistently and repeatedly, for hundreds of companies in all industries. The fact that free booklet offers are not original is true but unimportant. What's important is that it will generate more leads per ad or mailing, producing more inquiries, more sales, while lowering marketing costs.

2. It's overused.

Another common objection is, "I like the idea, but free booklet offers are so overused in our industry. Take a look at our trade magazines and you see free booklet offers in every other ad. And every other mailing I receive offers a free booklet. So how could our making such an offer compete with all this clutter?"

This argument makes sense but is refuted by experience. While there are some marketing techniques that *do* lose effectiveness in the face of clutter and overuse, free booklet offers are not one of them. In fact, the opposite is often true: Prospects in a particular industry become accustomed to seeing ads with free booklet offers and eagerly seek out such ads in their trade publications. If your ad lacks such a bait-piece offer, prospects become more likely to pass it by.

3. Our competitors already offer a free booklet.

The natural tendency is to think, "Our competitor has already published a booklet on the topic we were thinking of, so they've beaten us to it, and there's no sense going ahead with ours."

The *right* strategy, however, is to go ahead with your own booklet and either (a) choose a topic that's different but still helps promote your product or (b) choose the *same* topic and produce a report or booklet that's *better.*

How do you make your booklet better? Give tips and strategies the competition does not. Include a helpful glossary, charts, conversion tables, bibliography, checklists, names and addresses of resources, graphs, and other useful references. Use pictures and illustrations to make your point clear. Reveal inside information and details the competition keeps secret.

Even if the topic is similar, select a title that's clearly different from the competition's. Having the same or a similar-sounding title confuses prospects and isn't good for either you or your competitor.

Without a free booklet offer, your prospects are likely to respond only to your competitors' ads, which do offer booklets, while skipping over yours. Adding a free booklet offer helps ensure that you, too, will hear from prospects with a need to buy what you are selling.

4. My prospects already have too much to read.

The fourth argument against free information offers is either "My prospects already have too much to read, so the last thing they want is another booklet or report" or "My prospects are not readers."

While it is true that many business prospects already have too much to read, they will still seek out and send for yet another booklet or report *if they perceive that it contains information that is relevant, helpful, and tailored to their needs.* A prospect may have six inches of paperwork stacked in his in-basket, yet if his most pressing problem is cutting energy costs in the plant, he *will* respond to an ad or direct mail package offering a free report on "6 Proven Ways to Cut Energy Costs in Your Plant This Year."

Ideally, you want your prospect not only to send for but also to read your booklet or report. However, even if a prospect sends for but does *not* read your free information, the bait-piece offer has still done its job: generate an inquiry from a prospect who would otherwise have tossed your ad or mailing aside.

Therefore, the fact that they're too busy or not inclined to read the material you send is not a good reason not to offer such information; the key is that it overcomes inertia and gets them to respond. Once you receive the inquiry, you can start the selling process to convert the lead to a sale. But with no response, you get nowhere. And free booklet offers *increase response.*

Should you charge for your booklet or report?

In most cases, no. If you're offering a booklet or report to generate leads for a business-to-business product or service, the booklet or report should be free.

Unless your primary business is that of selling books or reports by mail, and you are offering this booklet or report to build your mailing list, you should not charge for your booklet or report. Doing so will dramatically decrease your response rate and slow down the flow of leads, which defeats the reason for offering the bait piece in the first place.

One argument for charging is the theory that people who pay for the booklet or report are better qualified as prospects. This isn't true (unless, again, your main business is the selling of books or reports by mail). For business-to-business lead generation, you can qualify the prospect by asking them their application, the type of business they're in, whether they have an immediate need, or other questions in your ad coupon or direct mail reply card. But does asking them to pay $5 for your booklet make them more qualified to buy your widget? I don't think so. In fact, it only serves to prevent a lot of qualified prospects who would have requested your widget booklet if it were free from doing so. (The reason is not the cost but the added trouble of writing a check and sending it to you.)

The basic offer options for bait pieces are as follows:

- Free booklet or report when you call or mail reply card.

- Free booklet or report available only to qualified prospects.

- Free booklet or report with self-addressed stamped envelope.

- Free booklet or report with self-addressed stamped envelope and $1 or $2 to cover handling.

- Booklet or report for a price of $5 (or whatever you want to charge).

- Booklet or report free to qualified prospects; $5 (or whatever you want to charge) to the general public and others who are not qualified prospects.

If the cost of printing and distributing booklets is a real hardship for you, you can recover that cost by requesting that the reader supply a self-addressed stamped envelope and $1 or $2 to cover shipping and handling. But I don't recommend this. For 99.99 percent of business-to-business marketers, the free booklet offer should be just that—entirely free.

6

Using Hard Offers to Generate Better Leads and More Sales

The hard offer

The term *hard offer* has a slightly different meaning in business-to-business direct marketing (especially for lead generation) than it does in traditional consumer mail-order marketing. In mail-order selling, a hard offer usually requires the prospect to pay for the product in advance. The seller ships the product only after payment is received via check, money order, or credit card. Use of a hard offer eliminates credit and collection problems, because there is no billing—everyone pays up front. By comparison, the soft offer in mail-order selling is the classic "bill-me" offer. Here, the prospect can order and receive the product with no money up front. The seller sends a bill and is paid later.

There are many intermediate ways of phrasing these offers that are neither classically hard or soft. These may be of interest to you if you are selling business books, forms, gift items, audio cassettes, office products, or other business-to-business products in a traditional mail-order or one-step promotion (i.e., your prospect orders directly from your ad, direct mail package, or catalog).

Special challenges of business-to-business mail order

Business-to-business mail order differs from consumer mail order, where you can get away with having a hard offer only. Indeed, many consumer mail-order marketers do not offer a bill-me option. They want to avoid the hassle and headache of collections, and so require payment for the product up front.

Also, with the price tag on many consumer mail-order purchases being so low, it often doesn't pay to go after deadbeats who keep your product but don't pay your bill. The deadbeat realizes it's not worth your time and effort taking him to court for a $10 past-due balance, and therefore doesn't feel an urgent need to respond to your dunning letters. A bill-me offer often will increase gross response, but how many of those who order on a bill-me basis ultimately pay up?

Many consumer mail-order firms, especially smaller operators, do quite nicely without a bill-me option. They know it's easy for the consumer to either write a check, send a money order, or charge a purchase to an American Express, Visa, or MasterCard. I run a small but profitable part-time mail-order business selling books, manuals, and audio cassettes to writers and would-be writers, and we have not had a problem with our "payment with order" policy.

In business-to-business direct marketing, on the other hand, I believe it is a mistake, in most instances, not to offer some type of soft "bill-me" offer to supplement the hard "pay-up-front" offer. Why? Because the customer is ordering for his or her company, not for personal use. And most companies are not set up to issue advance checks. Their usual procedure when making a purchase is to issue a purchase order, receive the product, verify satisfaction with it, process the invoice, and pay it when they are ready—optimally in 30 days, but more often in 60 or 90 days.

If your selling method forces business buyers to go against their company systems, they may decide that buying from you is too difficult or just not worth the extra aggravation and effort, and they may take their business to a competitor who is more flexible about payment terms and options.

For instance, if you demand payment up front, prospects may not even know how to get their accounting department to issue an advance check. Therefore, when selling to businesses, you should offer both a soft bill-me option and a hard payment-with-order option.

Variations on hard and soft offers for business-to-business mail order

Fortunately, there are a number of options for using hard offers and soft offers in business-to-business mail-order selling that may help you structure an offer that meets your customer's needs as well as your own requirements. This is done by offering a traditional hard offer (payment up front) with a second, "conditional" offer, rather than a pure, soft bill-me offer.

Let's compare the two. The traditional soft offer says, "Send us your product and bill us. If we like it, we will keep it and pay your bill. If we don't, we will return it, tear up your invoice, and not owe you any money."

Perhaps your product is expensive or easily damaged, and you are afraid of people taking advantage of you by ordering, keeping the product, and not paying for it.

One solution is to use a modified bill-me offer, in which you agree to send an invoice, but do not ship the product until the invoice is processed and payment is received. This would read as follows:

[ ] Bill me. (NOTE: Product not shipped until payment is received.)

The modified bill-me offer is similar to a soft offer in that it allows the prospect to respond without enclosing any payment and to receive an invoice from you which they can put through the system for payment. At the same time, it is similar to a hard offer in that the product is not shipped until it is paid for.

A variation of the modified bill-me offer is to agree to ship the *product* right away but to withhold shipment of any gift item or other premium until payment is received. There is a danger, if your premium is too attractive, that people will send for your product on a bill-me basis just to get the premium, then return the product and keep the free gift.

To prevent this, use a variation of the modified bill-me offer as follows:

[ ] Bill me. (NOTE: Bonus Gift is shipped when payment in full for your order is received by us.)

Even if you allow prospects to keep the premium if they return the product, this modified bill-me offer cuts down on "freebie" seekers. It requires ordering *and payment* for the product to get the gift, and few will go to that trouble just to get a free item from you, unless the premium is costly and truly fantastic.

You can even go further and state in your offer that, if they don't want to keep the product and decide to return it for refund, they must return the premium as well as the product. This provides an added degree of protection and is useful when the premium is fairly costly to you.

Another way to modify the bill-me offer to reduce the number of prospects who send for the product and don't buy it is to ask prospects to initial or sign the order card or provide a purchase order number or actual purchase order. For example:

[ ] Bill me. Our purchase order number is: _____ .
Signature (required for all bill-me orders): _____ .

For phone orders, you can't get a signature, but you can still ask for a purchase order number.

I strongly recommend that you avoid requiring prospects to send you an actual purchase order. The purchase order number itself is sufficient. If you insist on getting an actual purchase order, you will lose sales from prospects who are too busy to generate the paperwork required.

As a rule of thumb, your mailings should never force prospects to read a lot of instructions or fine print or fill out a lot of complicated paperwork. The more work you force your prospect to do to respond to your mailing, the lower your response will be.

Hard offers in business-to-business lead generation

As you will recall from the previous chapter, I define a hard offer for business-to-business lead generation as follows:

A hard offer requires or results in face-to-face or other personal contact between buyer and seller in a sales situation or other circumstances where the seller has the prospect "captive" for purposes of doing some selling.

A typical hard offer in lead generation is a check-off box on the business reply card or ad coupon that says, "Have a salesperson call me." By choosing this offer option, the prospect is saying, "I have sufficient interest in your product or service that I am willing to have your salesperson make a presentation to me or at least chat with me over the phone for a few minutes." This is a more aggressive, active response toward initiating the next step in the selling process than the soft offer of "Send me a brochure."

Enhancing the standard "Have a salesperson call" hard offer

"Have a salesperson call" is probably the most widely used hard offer in business-to-business lead generation. It paves the way for the in-person sales visit that, for many marketers, is a crucial step in getting the prospect to buy their product or service. In many cases, however, very few prospects select this offer option and ask a salesperson to call or visit. The reason for this is twofold.

First, prospects don't view salespeople as helpful or beneficial. In fact, the word "salesperson" signals to the prospect that sales pressure will be exerted—something most prospects want to avoid.

Second, most prospects don't want to hear your "sales pitch" or "presentation." Again, the word "sales" has a negative connotation, implying that the prospect will be subject to high-pressure selling tactics aimed at benefiting the seller, not the buyer.

The solution is to "repackage" the "Have a salesperson call me" offer, using skillful copywriting and a change in tactics to convert what is perceived as a "sell job" to what is perceived as a meeting that is beneficial and helpful for the prospect.

In a nutshell, this is done by replacing the words "sell" and "sales" with words that are more prospect-oriented. To start with, do not use the term *salesperson* when referring to the person who will contact or follow-up with the prospect. Replace *salesperson* with any of the following (or create your own title, as appropriate):

Account Representative
Senior Consultant
Technical Specialist
Account Manager
Account Supervisor
Industry Specialist
Program Manager
Program Planner
[name of product or service] Specialist

For example, if you are selling financial services, don't say "Have a sales representative call," say "Have a Financial Consultant call" or "Have a Financial Planner call" (if your salespeople are truly financial planners).

If you are selling a relational database, say "Have a Database Specialist call."

Next, do not use the words "sales call," "sales pitch," or "sales presentation" when referring to the initial appointment you are seeking with the prospect, because of the negative connotation of the word "sales." Instead of a sales call or sales presentation, suggest to the prospect they contact you to arrange one of the following:

Initial appointment
Free, no-obligation consultation
Free estimate
Free analysis
Needs assessment audit
Exploratory meeting
Evaluation of their requirements
Initial planning session
Free demonstration
Free executive briefing
Free seminar

Therefore, your hard offer might now read:

[ ] Please have a Technical Consultant call to arrange a free analysis of my network requirements. I understand there is no cost for this initial analysis—and no obligation.

If you phrase your offer this way or in a similar fashion, you will get more response than if you simply say "Have a salesperson call."

Why does this technique work so well? If you think about it, you'll realize that any initial contact between buyer and seller is not merely a selling opportunity for the buyer, but also has value to the seller *independent of whether the seller buys your product or service.*

For example, if a printer makes a presentation and gives you a price quotation, that price information is of value even if you do not hire the printer, since it provides a benchmark against which you can judge other quotes to see if they are in the ballpark. You might also gain some helpful pointers on the print production process, and the printer is not compensated for giving this knowledge to you unless you actually hire him to do the job.

Or, say you have an initial meeting with a financial planner during which you ask questions about investment options, your financial situation, and so on. In order to convince you that he or she is knowledgeable, the financial planner will probably answer many of those questions, and you can put that information to work even if you decide not to hire that particular person. Therefore, the initial "sales meeting" has value inherent in the meeting itself and independent of the product or service.

The strategy of offering "free consultations by experts" as opposed to the traditional "sales presentation by our salesperson" simply recognizes this inherent value and increases response by highlighting the value of the initial meeting or contact itself, rather than asking for a "sales opportunity."

Because this is a book on marketing and not on personal selling, a discussion of what takes place in such a meeting is beyond the scope of this book. It is discussed in great detail in my book *Selling Your Services,* available from my Resource Guide listed in the appendix. Basically, while you still use the initial meeting as a sales tool to get the prospect to buy, you make sure to demonstrate your expertise (and further convince the prospect that you are the right vendor for the job) by providing useful information and suggestions during your presentation.

When asking the prospect to request an initial consultation or meeting, two very important rules apply:

1. Make it clear that the meeting or consultation is free.

2. Make it clear that the meeting or consultation is given without obligation of any kind on the part of the prospect to buy from you.

Especially when your offer sounds too good and generous to be true, the prospect becomes suspicious that there is some hidden charge or implicit agreement requiring them to buy something. Always stress in your copy that "This initial consultation is absolutely free, and there is no obligation of any kind." Don't assume that your prospects understand this to be so. State it directly in your offer copy, both in your sales letter and again on the reply card.

The offer is more important than you think

A common mistake among business-to-business marketing communications professionals is to underestimate the importance of how the offer is used and phrased. The misconception is that offers are a "gimmick" used by consumer direct marketers to "trick" people into responding (such as offering a telephone or camera as an inducement to subscribe to a news, adult, or sports magazine), and that in business-to-business, such tactics are neither appropriate nor effective. The truth, however, is that the proper choice and presentation of the offer can make a *tremendous* difference in how successful your ad or mailing is in generating immediate response and sales.

For instance, a company selling business forms decided it could increase sales with the offer of "buy one, get one free." Conventional wisdom says that "FREE" is the most powerful word in direct marketing, so this offer should work well. But the marketing manager had doubts. So he tested "buy one, get one free" against a "2-for-1" offer. And guess what? The "2-for-1" offer *substantially* outpulled "buy one, get one free," contrary to what all the marketing textbooks and his own consultant had predicted.

Interestingly, the two offers are materially the same. Only the phrasing is different. But as anyone who has ever written advertising copy knows, phrasing is important. The right phrasing can lift response dramatically. And the wrong copy can destroy results for a mailing with a good product or offer.

Another firm had similar results in a mailing selling custom-imprinted executive business gifts. Here they tested "buy X quantity, get Y free" against a straightforward discount of "25% off our regular prices." Again, conventional direct marketing wisdom says the free offer is all-powerful. But test results disputed this, because the "25% off" significantly outpulled the "buy X, get Y free." A free offer in lead generation almost always increases response, but I have seen numerous instances in business-to-business mail order where "free" did not pull as well as a discount, percent-off, or 2-for-1 deal.

From these case histories we may conclude the following: Ad agencies, consultants, and other experts or authorities in direct marketing *cannot* predict with any accuracy which offer will pull best. An experienced direct marketer can recommend different offer strategies that may prove profitable and are worth testing, but no one can say for certain which offer will be the winner, nor can anyone guarantee results.

Personally, I am good at coming up with attractive offers and recommending to clients which two or three should be tested. But, while I can pretty easily spot an offer that is destined to be a loser, *I can never predict with certainty which of the better offers will be the winner*. Nor can you. Therefore, the only way to come up with the best offer for your product or service is through testing.

The need for testing

Most business-to-business marketers do not spend enough time and effort experimenting with and testing different offers. To them, the offer is more of an afterthought, with the description of the product or service as the main thrust of marketing communications.

But in reality, the offer can be the spark that overcomes the indifference barrier. Your prospects are bombarded by ads, mailings, and brochures daily, and they respond to very few of them. An enticing offer can make your communication stand out, overcome inertia, and get your prospect to take action.

Because of the small quantities being mailed, many business-to-business marketers believe they do not have sufficient quantity to justify testing their offers. But a statistically valid test of offer "A" versus offer "B" can be done even with mailings of only 4,000 or 5,000 pieces, with half offering A and half offering B. Huge volumes are not a prerequisite for testing.

Even if you do not do classic "split" or "A/B" testing (statistically valid testing of two offers with simultaneous mailing of offer "A" and offer "B"), you should still vary your offer from mailing to mailing and experiment with different variations to see which works best.

Different offers work in different media

The tendency is to assume that an offer working in one medium (e.g., direct mail) will do equally well in all other media (e.g., print advertising, radio, television, electronic bulletin board). While this is frequently true, it is not always so. As a result, if you are adapting an offer that was successful in one medium to a different medium, test cautiously before rolling out with the offer.

For instance, a client in the corporate entertainment field came up with an offer he thought would work well in a mailing, and I agreed. It involved a special promotion in which prospects could get a discount on entertainment at their next meeting or event by filling out and returning a simple form. Response to the mailing was only about one percent, less than we had both hoped. Looking back on it, I feel the form may have been too lengthy and time-consuming to fill out.

But when he made this offer in a small print ad, it generated a substantial number of inquiries—a far greater quantity than the more costly and involved mailing. (In fact, we used extras of the mailing piece as the fulfillment package for the ad.) Based on this, we did no additional mailings but continued to run the offer in small fractional ads in meetings magazines, with good results.

A one-word change increases response 15 percent

Here's another case study that demonstrates the importance of proper selection and phrasing of the offer. A company selling mainframe utility software used simple mailings to generate sales for its products, most of which sold in the range of $8,000–$12,000. The standard offer was for a free 30-day trial of the product. The prospect would call or mail the reply card to receive a magnetic tape and instructions for running the program. At the end of 30 days, they could return it and owe no money, or keep the soft-ware and be invoiced by the software firm for the license fee.

The owner of the company found that he could increase response by 15 percent (that is, go from 1 percent to 1.15 percent) by changing just one word in this offer. Can you guess what it was?

He changed "trial" to "use," so the offer was changed from "30-day free trial" to "30-day free use." What prompted the change? Explains the owner, "When we talked to data processing people, we found that the word *trial* had a negative connotation. It means coming in on evenings and weekends, interrupting normal DP operations, running tests on files, and a lot of extra work overall—and who wants to do more work?

"Based on this, we decided to try *free USE* instead of *free trial*. Our reasoning was that people buy a product to use it, so who wouldn't want to use it for free? Apparently, we were correct, because this one simple change boosted response—and, of course, cost us nothing to implement."

Interestingly, the firm achieved a second, similar lift in response by making a second change in the offer, again by changing one word. Can you guess what it was?

They changed *30*-day free use to *60*-day free use. As the owner observes, "The typical 30-day free trial in software is really not enough time for the busy DP professional to evaluate a product. A tape may very well sit for 2–3 weeks in someone's in-basket before they get around to even opening the package. At that point, they return it because the free trial period deadline is approaching and they don't want to be stuck with the product.

"We figured we could eliminate this anxiety by just extending the trial period another 30 days, and it seems to work. Our prospects feel that's a fairer amount of time to do the evaluation, and the offer increases response slightly." The company tested a 90-day period with no increase in response over the 60-day period.

Avoid confusing or difficult-to-understand offers

Although I encourage you to be creative with your offers, clarity and simplicity are essential. The offer should be straightforward, uncomplicated, easy to understand, and easy to respond to. If you make the offer difficult, confusing, a lot of hard work, or complicated, it will kill your response.

Recently, a software firm asked me to write a mailing on a fairly complicated and expensive piece of software for the DEC marketplace. At the last minute, the sales manager wanted to add to the mailing the offer of a premium: if the prospect bought the software product being advertised, they would be given another piece of software (a lower-cost program also made by my client's company) for free.

While the premium had high retail value, I discouraged testing of this offer. Why? Because the premium was not something the prospect would automatically perceive as desirable; its benefits were complex and not well known. The premium would have had to be explained at length in an additional buck slip, brochure, or other insert piece. We would, in effect, have had to sell two unrelated products in a single mailing, and I have learned from experience that you can only sell two or more products in a single mailing when the products are *related*.

Make a powerful guarantee part of your offer

If you are selling directly from your ad or mailing, be sure to back your hard offer with a powerful guarantee. This can be a guarantee of service, support, or return of money.

For a product, the best offer is a strong, long, unconditional money-back guarantee. For example: "If for any reason . . . or for no reason . . . the X-100 Widget is not for you, return it within 60 days and we will refund your money in full—no questions asked."

A longer guarantee period will generally outpull a shorter guarantee period. A 10-day or 15-day guarantee period is not long enough for the prospects to comfortably evaluate your product and decide whether it is for them. They will feel rushed and may just return your product without trying it to avoid having the deadline expire and being stuck with it.

A 30-day guarantee is sufficient for most products, and I think 60 or 90 days is even better. Many books on direct marketing say to offer a 1-year guarantee, but this can be a problem with products that are frequently updated, such as software or annual directories—the prospect could just return the old product and ask for the new one after a year.

Make your guarantee as unconditional as possible. The more conditions you put on the guarantee, the less the prospects are likely to trust you and buy from you.

For instance, one sales training firm selling a book on sales techniques offers a money-back guarantee if the sales techniques in the book do not help the reader increase income, but it adds this condition: "Just return the book along with a record of all your sales calls made using our techniques and the sample scripts you wrote following our outlines." The reader thinks, "Yeah, and you'll just say I wrote a lousy script and not refund my money."

A strong guarantee is an unconditional guarantee. The best offers contain an unconditional money-back guarantee with a long trial period. Prospects are wary of offers that seem conditional or that might obligate them in any way. The offer should be easy to take advantage of, easy to understand, risk-free, and it should not require any commitment or obligation on the part of the prospect.

Deadlines and other act-now incentives

Although it is not absolutely necessary, putting in some incentive or reason for the reader to respond now instead of later will generally increase response. Why? Because the prospect is bombarded by direct mail, sales messages, and offers daily. Your best chance of getting a response is to give her sufficient motivation to respond right now, while the piece is still in her hands.

If there is no "respond-now" incentive, the prospect may think, "I'll put this aside and get to it later." Unfortunately, a direct mail package is similar to the Sunday newspaper: If you don't read it within 48 hours of getting it, chances are you never will; too many other things surface to compete for attention. In direct-mail marketing, a decision deferred usually translates into a decision never made: no response.

How do you get the prospect to act now instead of later? The simplest mechanism is to put a time limit in your copy. This can either be a specific date ("Offer expires March 15, 1993") or a generic time limit ("You must reply within 15 days to take advantage of this special free offer").

Which is better? Both are effective. A specific date is good if you have enough control over the timing of your mailing to ensure that delays in printing and mailing don't make the deadline date obsolete. For instance, you don't want prospects to get a "reply by April 15th" mailing on April 21st. If you do not have precise control over timing, or you print your letters in large quantities and mail them regularly, a generic "respond within the next 15 days" offer may be better from a logistics perspective: No matter when the mailing drops, it's always accurate.

A client asked me today, "How long should the time limit be? Which is better—12 days or 20 days or 25 days or 30 days or 2 months or something else?" Obviously, the shorter the time frame, the more pressure there is on the prospect to respond now. On the other hand, too short a time frame may make the prospect feel rushed and uncomfortable. For business-to-business direct mail, a 20-day time limit seems reasonable: short enough to motivate action, long enough to allow some breathing space. I do not know of any tests of long versus short deadlines and would be interested in hearing from anyone who has data on this.

A variation of the specific date or time frame offer is the limited number offer: "This offer is limited to the first 200 people who respond to this letter." This tactic gets the prospect's attention because they have no idea how many pieces you mailed, and therefore want to reply right away to ensure that they are one of the first 200 to respond.

Other variations? The limited offer is most effective when you can give a legitimate, credible reason *why* the offer is limited. For instance, one computer company's offer was free prototyping of the prospect's application. Now, because prototyping takes time, and the company had a limited staff, they could handle only so many such prototypes at one time.

The sales letter pointed this out, saying, "We urge you to hurry. Based on response to previous mailings, we will get many requests for this free prototyping offer, and if you are not one of the first to respond, you may well have to wait longer than we'd both like." This works because it's specific, credible, and true.

If you don't have a real reason why the offer is limited, you can always invent one, and this can work. But when doing so, always respect the intelligence of your prospects. For instance, one mailing I received told me I had to request a certain report right away "because we have printed only 1,000 copies and supplies are limited." I suspected, though, that if requests exceeded 1,000, they would simply print more—so their act-now incentive lacked credibility for me.

Premiums for mail-order and lead-generating offers

A premium is a free gift the prospect gets for responding to your mailing. Premiums work well for mail order as well as lead-generating business-to-business direct marketing. A major question business-to-business direct marketers ask is, "Does the premium have to relate to the product or service being sold?" The answer is that it depends whether you are generating leads or sales.

Dick Benson, a successful consultant and entrepreneur, writes in his book *Secrets of Successful Direct Mail* that in mail-order selling, it is not necessary for the premium to relate to the product being sold. The most important criteria for premium selection, according to Benson, are the perceived value and desirability of the premium. If the premium relates to the product, fine, but that's of secondary importance.

In business-to-business mail order, I agree that having a desirable premium is important, probably the main selection criterion, but I put more weight on trying to select a premium related to the product. Also, you have to be careful with premiums, because many companies—especially defense contractors and subcontractors—have policies forbidding employees to accept gifts from vendors.

In fact, one of my clients, a firm selling custom-imprinted business gifts by mail, did a test mailing in which they tested a straight 25% discount on gift items against a 25% discount combined with the offer of a free clock-radio. Not only did the premium not increase response, it actually *depressed* it.

When I mentioned this at a seminar, one participant said, "It's probably because the buyers didn't want to be perceived as accepting a gift or bribe for giving the vendor his company's business." Another said, "Whenever a mail-order company attempts to bribe me with an expensive gift, I always assume they are inflating the price of their products to make up for it, and I would rather just not get the gift and instead pay less for the product."

A third participant voiced a similar observation: "In today's economy, the corporate employee increasingly looks good to his or her management by being a good purchaser. That means getting the product at the lowest price possible." His comment suggests that a larger discount would work better than a free gift intended for personal use.

This observation also suggests that if you *do* offer a premium for business-to-business mail-order offers, make it something related to the product and of value to the buyer's company, rather than an item for in-dividual use. For instance, a publisher selling technical journals and information databases on CD-ROM offers a free CD-ROM stacker and reader with the purchase of a group of its expensive CD-ROM-based information products. That's a premium that has high perceived value, is closely related to the product, and makes the prospect look like a smart buyer.

For lead generation, I think the best use of a premium is to offer something directly related to the product or service. My experience is that unrelated premiums of high value bring in large quantities of "freebie seekers" and other unqualified leads. Modest premiums that are directly related to the product or service increase the total number of responses. And, while you will always get some inquiries from those pain-in-the-neck people who seem to send for anything and everything that's free, you will also get a greater volume of qualified leads from good prospects.

As discussed in the previous chapter, I personally like the offer of a free booklet or report related to the product or service being offered. This is most often used in the soft offer ("Send for free report"), but it could conceivably be tied to a hard offer. For instance, you can offer an impressive report with the condition that it is hand-delivered by a salesperson whom prospects agree to see for an initial appointment.

Free demonstrations, seminars, and workshops

Another hard offer commonly used in business-to-business lead generation is the offer of a free demonstration, seminar, or workshop.

The advantage of a demonstration is that it clearly deals with a specific product, and therefore anyone who accepts qualifies themselves as having a significant degree of interest in that product. Another advantage of a demonstration over a seminar is that a seminar implies a scheduled event that the prospect must attend at a certain time and place, whereas a demonstration implies an event given at a time and place convenient to the prospect.

A seminar implies that the event is not a straightforward demonstration of a product but is designed to provide attendees with useful information about a certain topic. For instance, if your product is the W-100 Motionless Mixer, the seminar would not be about the W-100 but might be titled, "How to Specify Motionless Mixers in Chemical Processing Applications." Of course, the manufacturer's agenda is to get process engineers to write their specifications so that the installation requires use of a W-100 rather than a competitor's mixer.

But this agenda must be subtle, and the program must be primarily educational in nature. Otherwise, prospects will feel you have misrepresented the program by calling it a seminar instead of a sales pitch and will not be favorably inclined to do business with you.

Is the free seminar approach to business-to-business marketing right for your firm? It depends on your marketing situation. Free seminars work well when introducing new products or technologies. They are effective for products that require hands-on demonstration, such as software. If your product solves or deals with a problem or issue of interest to the prospect, a seminar is a good place to educate your prospects on the subject—and in doing so, convince them they should deal with you as an expert source of help.

Should you charge for the seminar? No. My feeling about free offers is that they should be free. If your purpose is to use the seminar to generate leads and sell your product or service, make it free. If your purpose is to make money in the seminar business, then put on a more extensive program and charge what other seminar marketers are charging.

Don't take the middle position and charge $25 or some other nominal fee to cover costs. What qualifies attendees as prospects is that they took time out to go to the program, not whether they got in free or paid some nominal registration fee. Charging instead of making it free also reduces attendance, defeating your goal of generating the greatest number of qualified sales leads.

Those who have never offered a free seminar as a marketing tool think they'll be flooded with responses because of this free offer. Sadly, that is not the case. The mere fact that the seminar is free will *not* get people to come running to your door. Executives, managers, and professionals in business are flooded with invitations to go to free seminars and don't have time to go to even a small fraction of them.

Will your seminar offer get response? If you're in an industry where free seminars are not commonly used, the uniqueness of your offer may generate a lot of interest and get a lot of response. On the other hand, if free seminars in your field are common and many of your competitors are offering them, don't expect your audience to get excited about it. The free seminar may work if the topic is attractive or your product is exciting. But don't expect adding a free seminar offer to your reply card to generate a breakthrough for you.

When writing an ad or mailing to get people to attend your free seminar, you should *not* take the approach that all you have to do is say the seminar is free and people will want to attend. Instead, you should write copy that will make the reader say, "This sounds wonderful; I would really love to go. How much does it cost?" Then, tell him or her it's free.

Free seminars need not be as comprehensive as fee-paid seminars and educational programs, nor should they be as long. Most are half-day seminars, typically 2 or 3 hours of presentation.

When making a free seminar offer to corporate types, have it on a weekday, preferably in the morning, starting with breakfast. Tuesday, Wednesday, or Thursday are the best days; avoid Monday. When making free seminar offers to self-employed and entrepreneur types, an evening or weekend is usually best. Saturday morning is better than Sunday.

Sampling, trial runs, and evaluations

Three additional hard offers you can use in your business-to-business lead-generation programs are sampling, trial runs, and evaluations.

A sampling involves offering to render your service or allow the customer to use your product on a sample basis. This may be for purposes of either demonstrating your product or service or analyzing the customer's needs to determine which of your services or products is right for them.

For example, a firm selling equipment that turns chemical powders into pellets says in its sales letter, "Send us a 5-pound bag of your compound and tell us what size pellets you want. We will run it through our pelletizer and give it back to you to show you the quality of the pellets it can produce for you."

Another company, a computer firm, sells a software program that businesses can use to quickly create customized applications that work with their databases. One potential buyer was skeptical and asked, "How long would it take to develop a so-and-so application for our database using your product?" The software firm's salesperson, instead of answering, sat at the computer, started pressing keys, and had the application prototyped and working with the database within 30 minutes. The prospect's response? "Decision made! We're buying your product!" While this took place on an individual sales call, it could be the basis of a direct mail offer.

A trial simply allows the prospect to use your product or service for a specified period at no cost and with no obligation to buy. The pelletizer manufacturer's letter went on to say that if the sample pellets were satisfactory, they would ship a pelletizer to the prospect's plant and let them use it for a month with no obligation. Then they would have the option to send it back (at the manufacturer's expense) or buy it.

A trial offer can also work with a service. If you have an on-line database, a long-distance telephone service, or another service where users are billed by the hour, a common offer is "30 minutes of use free."

In the second edition of his book *Profitable Direct Marketing* (Chicago, Ill.: NTC Business Books), Jim Kobs shows two ads from MCI. The first offers $5 off the prospect's long-distance phone bill; the second offers 30 free minutes of long-distance calls. The "30 free minutes" pulled roughly twice the response of "$5 off," because customers perceived 30 free minutes of long-distance calling as a greater value than $5 off. The 30 minutes of free service is, in essence, a free trial of the long-distance phone service.

Similar to the free trial is the evaluation. The tone of this offer is, "Let us send you the product at no cost and you can perform whatever technical evaluation is required to help you decide whether it is the right product for you. If it is not, send it back and owe us nothing. If it is, you can buy it for the list price of $X."

One problem with evaluations and free trials is that prospects send for the product to evaluate and then, because of inertia, laziness, or lack of time, don't do anything with it.

One way to overcome this problem is to combine the free trial or evaluation with an incentive to perform the evaluation or make a buying decision within a specified period of time. For instance: "If you accept our free trial offer and then decide to invest in the So-and-So System within the next 30 days, you will get 10% off the regular purchase price."

Mention of this time-limited offer in your ad or mailing will increase overall response. Periodic reminders to prospects via mail or phone during the evaluation period will help get more of them to try the product and increase the conversion rate of leads to sales.

The key points of Chapters 5 and 6 are as follows:

1. Do not underestimate the importance of offers.

2. The product or service is key, but a good offer can often mean the difference between so-so and super response.

3. Most business-to-business marketers do not spend nearly enough time on creating and testing offers.

4. You can never tell which offer will pull best; you should constantly try and test different offers.

5. When in doubt, the surest way to increase response is to make the offer free and without risk or obligation of any kind.

6. In mail-order selling to businesses, have both a hard and soft offer.

7. In lead generation to businesses, always include a free booklet or other free information offer in addition to your hard "meet-with-me-now" offer.

Part Two

Business-
to-Business
Direct
Marketing
Tasks

7

Print Advertising:
Proven Techniques for Getting More
Inquiries from Your Ads

There are hundreds of books on how to create memorable advertising, and there's no sense in my repeating what they say or trying to compete with them. So in this brief chapter, I will omit some very important topics such as positioning, graphic design, strategy, media placement, and other aspects of creating award-winning advertising.

Instead, we will focus on specific techniques, mostly mechanical, that will immediately increase the pulling power of your ads, that is, to create new ads or modify existing ones so that they generate a *lot* more leads and sales than you are now getting.

Advertising managers have often said to me, "Bob, I have a problem. Our management *say* they want advertising that reinforces the corporate image, achieves the corporate goal, and promotes brand awareness of our product. So we create the ad. They approve the ad. Then it runs. And invariably, top management complains, 'Why aren't we getting more inquiries?' Bob, is there some way we can increase the pulling power of our ads so they generate greater numbers of inquiries without altering or destroying the basic concept of the ad or campaign?"

The answer is yes, and here are some techniques you can use.

Technique #1: Put a benefit in the headline

The most successful inquiry-generating ad I ever wrote (the number-one inquiry producer in four consecutive issues of *Chemical Engineering* magazine) had the headline:

HOW TO SOLVE YOUR EMISSIONS PROBLEMS . . .
. . . at *half the energy cost* of conventional venturi scrubbers.

The headline works because it combines a powerful benefit ("half the energy cost") with the promise of useful information ("how to") addressed directly at the reader's specific problem ("solve your emissions problems"). In addition, it promises specific savings over familiar, current technology ("conventional venturi scrubbers").

A common fault of copy written by managers and technical professionals is that it discusses features only and omits benefits. Promising a benefit in the headline invites readership and increases response.

Technique #2: Ask a provocative question

My friend Bob Pallace wrote an ad that generated an immediate $1 million in increased billings for his ad agency in Silver Spring, Maryland. The headline was:

ARE YOU TIRED OF WORKING FOR YOUR AD AGENCY?

The ad ran only one time in each of three magazines (*High-Tech Marketing*, now defunct; *Business Marketing;* and *Inc.*) and immediately brought in five new clients. Apparently, advertising managers at technical companies identified with Bob's claim that conventional ad agencies don't understand high-tech, which forces the client to do many rewrites and revisions to fix the agency's inadequate copy. I would probably change "tired" to "sick and tired" in the headline, but that's a minor point.

Asking a provocative question—one that arouses curiosity, or deals with an issue on the reader's mind—almost always increases readership and response. Other examples follow:

WHEN AN EMPLOYEE GETS SICK, HOW LONG DOES IT TAKE YOUR
COMPANY TO RECOVER?
(Pilot Life Insurance)

IS YOUR PUMP COSTING YOU MORE TO OPERATE THAN IT SHOULD?
(Gorman-Rupp Pumps)

Technique #3: Be direct

An ad agency asked me to write an ad to generate sales leads for a client that repairs and rebuilds old surgical tables. When they sent me their brochure, I stole the headline from the front cover of the brochure and used it in the headline for the ad. It read as follows:

SURGICAL TABLES REBUILT
Free Loaners Available

The ad did better than many of the previous ads and demonstrates that when you are the only one advertising a particular product or service, or when the nature of your offer is hard to grasp, direct headlines can be extremely effective. Another direct headline appeared in a small ad running in *Network World:*

LINK 8 PCs TO YOUR MAINFRAME
ONLY $2,395

Donald Reddy, president of the firm, told me that the ad was extremely effective in generating a small but steady flow of highly qualified sales leads.

Technique #4: Give or promise the reader useful information

One software company has built a successful business primarily with print advertising in a niche market where the competitors are heavily into personal selling and jet-hopping to meet and "stroke" prospects in person. I asked the chief executive his secret for writing a successful ad. His answer: "Make it read like an interesting article."

One way to increase readership and response is to promise the reader useful information in your headline, then deliver it in your ad copy. For instance, an ad promoting a book on collections had this headline:

7 WAYS TO COLLECT YOUR UNPAID BILLS
New from Dow Jones–Irwin . . .
A Successful and Proven Way to Get Your Bills Paid Faster.

The information-type ad is highly effective in business-to-business advertising. Why? Because the reason your prospects read business publications in the first place is for information, and such ads fulfill that expectation.

Look at the how-to, information-packed article titles that grace the covers of *Reader's Digest* and family-oriented publications such as *McCall's* and *Family Circle.* The titles are carefully selected to get supermarket shoppers to pick up the magazine, buy it, and read the articles. Ad head-lines written in this same newsy, information-oriented style can be tremendously successful.

Technique #5: Use a news or time-related tie-in

Putting a time or date reference in the headline usually increases readership and response, perhaps because it creates a sense of timeliness and urgency. The headline "How to make $85,000 a year" is good, but "How to make $85,000 *this year*" is better.

During the recession of the early 1990s, many advertisers used, with great success, themes that directly tied into the weak economy. A major telephone company, for example, used a bill stuffer with the headline "TOUGH DECADE?" to promote a telephone system by stressing the need to keep costs down when times are tough.

Technique #6: Offer a free booklet or other bait piece in the ad

Offering something tangible—a brochure, booklet, information kit, videotape, audio cassette, book, special report, checklist, computer analysis, or other material the reader can send for—almost always increases the response to print advertisements.

The problem with most general advertising is that it starts strong but ends weak. The concept may be brilliant, the graphics clever, the copy beautifully written, but when they get to the middle or end of the ad, general copywriters don't know how to close. So they sort of wind down aimlessly; usually they close with a cute phrase or clever paragraph. But they do not have a strong call to action, because they are not trained that way.

The best way to close an ad is to stress the offer of the free booklet or bait piece. Tell the reader what it is, what's in it, why the information is important to them, and what they have to do to get it. Your response will increase dramatically.

Also, the more you stress the free booklet or bait piece offer, the higher your response will be. At the end of your ad, put in a subhead that highlights the free booklet offer (e.g., "Get the Facts—FREE"). Showing a picture of the booklet or report cover also increases response, because it makes the offer seem more tangible.

In a two-page ad, you can even run a separate sidebar stressing your free information offer. For one client, an industrial manufacturer, we used such a sidebar to offer free copies of back-issues of their newsletter, each issue dealing with one specific topic highlighted in the sidebar copy. The response was substantial.

International Paper did this with its "Power of the Printed Word" series, one of the most successful corporate ad campaigns of all time. These institutional ads featured essays by well-known figures on various communications topics, the idea being that by promoting literacy and the printed word, International Paper would ensure a future market for paper. But most of the ads also contained a box explaining the purpose of the series and offering reprints of the ads. According to one source, millions of reprint requests were generated from these sidebars highlighting the offer.

If you don't have a free booklet or report you can offer, at least add something to your product brochure or your inquiry fulfillment package that will add value and make people want to request it. For instance, if you're offering a brochure on local area networking, create and offer a glossary of networking terminology, or a table of standards, or a set of network configuration diagrams.

Also, give your bait piece a name that implies value. "Information kit" is better than "brochures and data sheets." "Resource guide" is better than "catalog." "Custom Solutions Kit" is better than "sample print-outs."

Putting the offer of your free booklet, report, or information kit in the headline of your ad will further increase response (e.g., "New FREE booklet tells how to reduce valve maintenance costs in pharmaceutical plants").

You can also increase response by increasing the perceived value of your free offer. For example, you can offer a free gift, a free product sample, a free consultation, free analysis, free recommendation, free study, free cost estimate, or free computer print-out.

If the gift is a small premium of low perceived value, say "Surprise bonus gift is yours when you mail the coupon or call us today." If the gift is a nicer premium with a higher perceived value, say what it is.

Technique #7: Put a coupon in your ad

Coupons visually identify your ad as a direct response ad, causing more people to stop and read it or at least look at the coupon to see what they can get for free. Just by adding a coupon to your ad, you can usually increase response 10 to 25 percent or more. Make the coupon large enough so that readers have plenty of room to write in their names and addresses. Give the coupon a headline that affirms positive action: "YES, I'd like to cut my energy costs in half!" Have several check-off boxes readers can use to indicate their level of interest. Include both a hard ("Have an account representative call") and a soft ("Please send me a free brochure") offer.

For a full-page ad, run the ad on a right-hand page and put the coupon in the bottom right corner. If your ad is running in a directory, rather than a monthly magazine or daily newspaper, note that people do not like to tear up directories. Therefore, for an ad running in a directory, add copy that encourages the reader to photocopy the ad and coupon before filling it in.

Your coupon should include your address and instructions telling people to mail the coupon to that address. But your address should also be printed in the body of the ad, outside the coupon. That way, someone can write to you even if the coupon has been clipped from the ad by someone else. In trade and business magazines, a bound-in business reply card, appearing opposite your ad, can increase response by a factor of 2 to 4 times or more. However, it's expensive.

Fractional ads of one-half page or less do not have enough room to allow use of a coupon. *In fractional ads, put a dashed border around the ad to simulate the look and feel of a coupon.* Your closing copy instructs the reader, "For more information, clip this ad and mail it to us with your business card."

Technique #8: Use a headline with multiple parts

Many businesspeople believe a headline must be catchy and clever, and the fewer words used, the better. But a headline doesn't have to be short to sell. In fact, it doesn't even have to be a single sentence. You can often build readership and response by using a multi-part headline. This might be a two-part headline, with a main headline and a subhead below it. Or it might be a three-part headline, with a kicker above the main headline, the main head, and a subhead.

Why do multi-part headlines work so well? A single headline communicates one key point, and if that point is not of interest to a particular prospect, you lose him or her. With a multi-part headline, you can highlight two or three different appeals without losing impact.

The kicker is an "eyebrow" or short line that goes in the upper left corner of the ad above the main headline, either straight or at a slant. Sometimes it is placed in a circle or sunburst for added emphasis. One good use of the kicker is to select a specific type of reader for the ad ("ATT: UNIX applications developers"). Another effective technique is to highlight your offer ("35% discount on all books and tapes listed in this ad").

Under the kicker, set in large type, comes your main headline. This states your central benefit, unique selling proposition, or promise. Then, in a subhead below it, you expand on the benefit or reveal the specific nature or details of the promise. An example follows:

FOR HIGH-SPEED, HIGH-PERFORMANCE DATA INTEGRATION, LOOK INTO MAGIC MIRROR.™

Now you can move data instantly from one program to another—right from your PC screen.

The headline/subhead format is especially effective in cases where your headline is written for maximum drama, perhaps at the expense of clarity. You can get away with a headline that is clever or gimmicky if you immediately follow with a subhead that makes clear the key benefit or proposal.

Benefits or offers promised in a headline should be immediately explained or presented in a subhead or within the first sentence or two of body copy. Otherwise, you risk losing the interest of the reader whose attention you worked so hard to gain. A common complaint of impartial readers and focus groups who review copy before it is printed is, "It doesn't get to the point fast enough."

Technique #9: Make the ad look like a direct response ad

Some ads look like "image" ads and don't invite response. Other ads look like "mail order" or "coupon" ads and beckon to the reader, "Please call or write." If you design your ad to look like a direct response ad instead of an image ad, you will get more responses. Following are some tricks of the trade used in designing successful direct response ads.

Long copy

A direct response ad typically has more words than a general image advertisement. In the general ad, the "concept"—the way the headline and visual work together to communicate a single message—is key. The idea is to come up with a powerful concept so readers will remember it. In direct response ads, the purpose of the headline is to get people to read the copy and order the product or request more information.

Make it look like an article

A common technique for designing long-copy direct response ads is to set them in three columns of type similar in style and format to a magazine or newspaper article. The theory is that people buy periodicals for the articles, not the ads, so you get better readership by making your ad look like an article. (NOTE: If you use this technique, most publishers will require you to print the label "ADVERTISEMENT"in small type at the top of your editorial-style ad.)

Black-and-white ads

Using a black-and-white ad instead of a four-color ad can increase response, except for certain products, such as fashion, cosmetics, or travel that must be illustrated in full color. But direct response advertisers run more black-and-white ads, while general image advertisers tend to run more four-color ads. One motivation is that the black-and-white ads look more like articles and less like ads.

Graphic techniques

Kickers, bold headlines, liberal use of subheads, bulleted or numbered copy points, coupons, sketches of telephones, toll-free numbers set in large type, pictures of response booklets, dashed borders, asterisks, copy sections in boxes, special border treatments, and marginal notes can make your ad more eye-catching, help emphasize your free offer, and increase response.

Photographs

Use clear, direct, relevant pictures to illustrate your ads. General image advertising, as created by Madison Avenue, often uses clever or breath-taking graphics that have little to do with the product. Early commercials for the Infiniti, for example, showed the ocean and never pictured the car. Direct response ads tend to have pictures either of the product or of people using and enjoying the product. Weight loss ads have before-and-after pictures of the people who lost weight. Record club ads show pictures of records and CDs.

Clear type

Use clear, easy-to-read type. The direct marketer cares whether people read the body copy, based on the theory that the more they read, the more likely they are to buy the product or respond to the offer. Therefore, type is set black on white paper, in large size, in an easy-to-read, popular type style.

This is unlike many consumer ad agencies, which set type in reverse, on colored backgrounds, against tints, in small sizes and odd, difficult-to-read typefaces, because many art directors do not believe people read, and they treat type as just one more design element.

Technique #10: A miscellany of response-boosting ideas

Here are a few more things you can do to increase your ad's pulling power:

- Ask for action. Tell the reader to phone, write, contact a sales rep, request literature, visit your trade show booth, or place an order.

- Include your address in the last paragraph of copy and beneath your logo, in type that is easy to read.

- If you have a toll-free number, put it in large type at the bottom of the ad next to a sketch of a phone, with the words "Call toll-free," followed by the phone number. Al-ways mention that it is a toll-free call.

- If you are interested in getting responses via reader service cards ("bingo" cards), be sure the magazine includes a reader service num—ber in your ad.

- To increase reader service card response, use copy and graphics that point the reader toward your reader service number. For example, an arrow pointing to the number and copy that says, "For a free bro-chure, circle the reader service number below."

- Another way to increase reader service card number inquiries is by using multiple numbers. Some advertisers use a different number for each product or piece of literature featured in the ad. Others use one num-ber for literature requests and a second number for people who want immediate contact from a sales rep.

NOTE: Portions of this chapter appeared in different form in *Direct Marketing* and *Business Marketing*.

8

How to Dramatically Boost Your Direct Mail Response Rates

In this chapter, I will present a collection of ideas and techniques for dramatically boosting the response rates of business-to-business direct mail. I'll begin with a proven five-step formula for writing powerful sales letter copy, the basis of most successful direct mail programs. And I'll illustrate with some sample letters. After that, we'll answer some common questions from business-to-business marketers who want to do successful direct mail but don't quite know what the right approach is to maximizing their response and sales.

The motivating sequence

There are a number of popular letter-writing formulas presented in books and seminars on direct marketing, and, of course, I have my own. I call it the Motivating Sequence.

The Motivating Sequence is a simple five-step formula you can use to write a persuasive lead-generating sales letter. It can also be used in writing ad copy, self-mailers, fliers, brochures, catalog copy, and other marketing documents designed to generate responses, leads, and sales. Here is the formula:

1. Gain the prospect's ATTENTION.

2. Engage the reader's interest by identifying a PROBLEM the reader has or a need that must be filled.

3. Position your product, service, or company as the SOLUTION to the reader's problem.

4. Offer PROOF to convince skeptical readers that your claim you can solve their problem is true.

5. Invite the reader to take ACTION toward implementing your solution. This might be to request more information or to order the product or service.

Model lead-generating letter following the Motivating Sequence

Let's look at two model letters that follow the motivating sequence and analyze how they follow the formula. In my seminars, I've found that going through an actual sample letter and showing how it follows the formula helps students master the sequence and use it to write persuasive sales letters.

The first example is a letter I use to generate inquiries for my own freelance copywriting services. Figure 8-1 is the complete text of the letter and the corresponding response card, with numbers indicating the five steps of the sequence. After you read the text, we'll break down the steps.

Figure 8-1 Model Lead-Generating Letter

(1) Dear Marketing Professional:

(2) "It's hard to find a copywriter who can handle industrial, high-tech, and business-to-business clients," a prospect told me over the phone today. "Especially for brochures, direct mail, and other long-copy assignments."

Do you have that same problem?

(3) If so, please complete and mail the enclosed reply card, and I'll send you a free information kit describing a service that can help.

(4) As a freelance copywriter specializing in business-to-business advertising since 1982, I've written hundreds of successful ads, sales letters, direct mail packages, self-mailers, brochures, feature articles, press releases, newsletters, and audio-visual scripts for clients all over the country.

But my information kit will give you the full story.

You'll receive a comprehensive "WELCOME" letter that tells all about my service—who I work for, what I can do for you, how we can work together.

You'll also get my client list (I've written copy for over 95 advertisers and agencies), complete with client comments . . . biographical background . . . samples of work I've done in your field . . . a fee schedule listing what I charge for ads, brochures, and other assignments . . . helpful article reprints on copywriting and advertising . . . even an order form you can use to put me to work for you.

(5) Whether you have an immediate project, a future need, or are just curious, I urge you to send for this information kit. It's free . . . there's no obligation . . . and you'll like having a proven copywriting resource on file—someone you can call on whenever you need him.

From experience, I've learned that the best time to evaluate a copywriter and take a look at his work is *before you need him,* not when a project deadline comes crashing around the corner. You want to feel comfortable about a writer and his capabilities in advance . . . so when a project does come up, you know who to call.

Why not mail back the reply card TODAY, while it is still handy? I'll rush your free information kit as soon as I hear from you.

Regards,

Bob Bly

P.S. Need an immediate price quotation on a copywriting assignment? Call me now at (201) 385-1220. The conversation is free. And there's no obligation.

YES, I WANT TO INCREASE MEETING REVENUES WHILE HELPING OUR MEMBERS COPE WITH THE RECESSION.

[ ] We have an upcoming need for a speech, seminar, or workshop on RECESSION - PROOF BUSINESS STRATEGIES. Please give me a call.

[ ] Please send complete program details including the free audio cassette.

Name_____ Title _____

Organization_____ Phone _____

Address _____

City_____ State_____ Zip _____

We are thinking of booking you: [ ] immediately [ ] next 6 months
[ ] next 6 to 12 months [ ] no immediate plans
Phone: (201) 385-1220   Fax: (201) 385-1138

Step 1: Gain the prospect's ATTENTION.

You can do this in any of a number of ways. In a form letter, you can set a headline in type above the body copy. Or put an attention-getting message in a box (called a "Johnson box") above the salutation.

In this letter, mailed to advertising and marketing managers at corporations and medium-size businesses, the salutation—"Dear Marketing Professional"—is the attention-getting device. The word *marketing* identifies the reader as someone with an interest in improving marketing results, while the word *professional* is flattering.

Could my sales letter be made stronger with a benefit-oriented headline or Johnson box stressing a sales point or free offer? Probably. But this letter generates a 10 percent or higher response when mailed as-is, so I haven't put in the effort to make it stronger. (If you feel like doing it, I'd love to see what you come up with!)

Step 2: Engage the reader's interest by identifying a PROBLEM the reader has or a need that must be filled.

This is stated in my first two paragraphs:

"It's hard to find a copywriter who can handle industrial, high-tech, and business-to-business clients," a prospect told me over the phone today. "Especially for brochures, direct mail, and other long-copy assignments."

Do you have that same problem?

It's often easiest and at the same time most direct and convincing to identify the reader's most pressing problem or key concern as a question to which you know they will invariably answer *yes*:

Are you sick and tired of paying too much for health care insurance?

But you can also phrase the problem or need as a statement:

If you're like most small business owners I know, you're sick and tired of paying too much for health care insurance for yourself and your employees.

Using a statistic or fact to dramatize the problem is another effective opening gambit:

According to a recent study by Smith & Powers Associates, 54.8% of small business owners surveyed say they will STOP PROVIDING HEALTH INSURANCE to their employees as a benefit this year because the cost is TOO HIGH. . . .

Step 3: Position your product, service, or company as the SOLUTION to the reader's problem.

The discussion of readers' problems or identification of their need should be brief—not an essay or Ph.D. thesis, but just enough to (a) get them interested and (b) show you understand their needs and problems. Then your copy should move swiftly and directly to positioning your product or service as the solution to their problem.

I usually do this with a short transition sentence such as "And that's where we can help" or "Here's a (product/service) that can solve that problem for you." In my sample letter this "we can help" theme is communicated in the third paragraph:

. . . please complete and mail the enclosed reply card, and I'll send you a free information kit describing a service that can help.

Step 4: Offer PROOF to convince skeptical readers that your claim that you can solve their problem is true.

This proof can be any of the following:

- A description of product benefits and features

- An explanation of how your service is rendered

- Testimonials from satisfied customers

- A list of prestigious clients

- Research or laboratory test results that prove the superior performance of your product

- Case histories that demonstrate the success your product or service has had solving problems similar to the prospect's problem

- The credentials, track record, and experience of your company

- Awards, licenses, degrees, certifications, affiliations, and other demonstrations of your reputation, expertise, and stability

In the example, instead of listing this information in the letter, I offer it in a free "information kit" the reader is encouraged to send for—but I do let the reader know these credentials exist and are available upon request.

Step 5: Invite the reader to take ACTION toward implementing your solution.

This is the "call to action." In this step, you discuss your offer and invite the reader to take you up on it. You also provide the reply mechanism, which may be a business reply card, order form, or telephone or fax number. Here's the "call to action" from our model letter:

> Whether you have an immediate project, a future need, or are just curious, I urge you to send for this information kit. It's free . . . there's no obligation . . . and you'll like having a proven copywriting resource on file—someone you can call on whenever you need him.
>
> From experience, I've learned that the best time to evaluate a copywriter and take a look at his work is before you need him, not when a project deadline comes crashing around the corner. You want to feel comfortable about a writer and his capabilities in advance . . . so when a project does come up, you know who to call.
>
> Why not mail back the reply card TODAY, while it is still handy? I'll rush your free information kit as soon as I hear from you.
>
> Regards,
>
> Bob Bly
>
> P.S. Need an immediate price quotation on a copywriting assignment? Call me now at (201) 385-1220. The conversation is free. And there's no obligation.

The action step is the simplest portion to write, yet it is the most frequently omitted by the inexperienced marketer. Avoid weak closes such as "We look forward to serving you" or "Let us know how we can be of service." To succeed in direct mail, you must:

- Determine *exactly* how you want readers to respond and what you want them to do.

- *Tell* readers how you want them to respond and what you want them to do.

- Make it easy and convenient for readers to respond.

- Give the reader benefits, reasons, or motivation to respond.

- Create a sense of urgency—a reason why the reader is better off responding NOW instead of later.

Model mail-order letter for the Motivating Sequence

For those of you who sell products or services direct via mail order rather than through lead generation, Figure 8-2 is a sample mail-order letter. It is longer, but it still follows the same five-step Motivating Sequence used in our shorter lead-generating letter. Although I will not go through the copy step by step as I did with the previous letter, I have annotated this letter so you can see where each step in the sequence is introduced.

Figure 8-2 Model Mail-Order Letter

[1]   HERE'S HOW I MADE $190,296 BY STAYING HOME
                    AND WRITING

Dear Writer:

The writing life is a great life. I love staying home, avoiding the rat race, and getting paid good money to sit at my beloved Kaypro computer—thinking, reading, and writing for my clients.

Now, I want to show you how to stay home writing while earning $500 a day—or $50,000 to $75,000 to $100,000 a YEAR or more.

What's the secret? I call it. . .

                    HIGH-PROFIT WRITING™

High-Profit Writing is a different type of writing. You don't usually read about it in the writer's magazines, or hear about it on TV or radio talk shows.

It doesn't have anything to do with writing books or magazine articles (although I've written 18 books and more than 100 articles in my spare time).

[2] Most writers hope to earn fame and fortune through books and articles. But it rarely works out. The pay scales are LOW (except for a handful of superstars). And the field is too crowded.

If you've ever submitted a manuscript or query letter, you know what I'm talking about.

[3] Instead, High-Profit Writing deals with the field of commercial writing: creating ads, brochures, and promotional materials for national corporations . . . local businesses . . . entrepreneurs . . . nonprofits . . . and other organizations and institutions that need written materials to sell their products, educate their audiences, raise funds, or enhance their public image.

[4]   HOW MUCH MONEY CAN YOU MAKE IN HIGH-PROFIT WRITING?

The profits are so huge in this business that to the beginner, they may seem astounding.

For example, I was recently paid $4,500 by one client to write a direct mail package. Another client paid me $5,500 to write a slightly more complex mailing consisting of a sales letter, brochure, and order form.

One bank hired me to write two brochures for two different divisions. The check they sent me was for $5,760. And, although my income is well into six figures (last year I grossed $190,296), there are others earning even more:

** Eugene Schwartz, a well-known direct mail writer, gets $24,000 (yes, $24,000) to write a sales package.

** Writer Richard Armstrong, who is also an author and actor, charges $2,500 for a 20-minute speech.

** One woman who moonlights 17 hours a week earned $30,000 in 9 months using my methods.

** I recently wrote four brochures in four weeks for one client. My fee? $18,400. That same month, another client hired me to write six simple "product data sheets" for a fee of $11,600.

And best of all, there is no querying. No outlines. No proposals to editors. No library research or "journalistic" reporting involved.

Instead, the clients come to YOU with assignments. You receive an advance retainer check and a contract. You are provided with ALL the research material and background you need. All you do is WRITE.

You are paid for your ideas and creativity—not your legwork. And if you are asked for advice, you can charge a consulting fee of <u>$50 to $400 an hour</u> (My friend Dr. Andrew Linick gets his fee up front and is booked 9 months in advance.). You don't give your ideas away for free, as magazine editors expect you to do.

NOW YOU CAN MAKE BIG MONEY THROUGH FREELANCE WRITING—STARTING TODAY!

After loving this business for 9 years, I realized that (a) there is more than enough work to go around and (b) for that reason, why not help other writers and share the wealth?

To make it easy for you, I sat down and wrote a complete PLAN, sharing with you exactly what is involved in the <u>High-Profit Writing</u> business.

You'll discover what you have to do—step by step—to break in, get started, and make a lot of money writing ads. Brochures. Booklets. Direct mail letters. Press releases. Audio-visual scripts. Speeches. Manuals. Articles. Company newsletters. And other materials for local and national clients.

Because my copyrighted plan has never been available to writers until now, I call it "SECRETS OF A FREELANCE WRITER."

My plan shows you EVERYTHING you need to succeed. Nothing is left out. For the first time, ALL the secrets of the high-paid commercial writers are revealed in full detail.

HERE'S JUST A SAMPLING OF THE SECRETS REVEALED
IN "SECRETS OF A FREELANCE WRITER":

- The best clients for freelance writers—where to find them; how to get them to hire you (p. 16).

- How to earn $1,000 to $3,000 per assignment "ghostwriting" articles and speeches for busy executives (p. 201).

- Which freelance assignments pay best? TIP: Not all pay equally well. I tell you which are lucrative—and which are losers (p. 28).

- The 7 reasons why potential clients need your services even though they already have an ad agency, staff writers, or use other freelancers (p. 21).

- How to get paid big money from local businesses for your ideas and advice (p. 261).

- How to write a sales letter that brings you 2 to 10 new potential clients (companies who want to hire you) for every 100 letters you mail (p. 40).

READERS OF "SECRETS OF A FREELANCE WRITER" SAY IT BEST!

"Your books have been a great inspiration to me. In two years, I have gone from zero customers, zero prospects, zero ad-agency experience, and zero income to working with Fortune 500 companies like Hewlett-Packard, earning $85,000+ per year—and quickly closing in on a six-figure income. Thanks."

—Steve Edwards, Carlsbad, CA

"Reading 'SECRETS OF A FREELANCE WRITER,' particularly the tips on contracts, saved me at least $10,000 in six months."

—Catherine Gonick, Jersey City, NJ

"With Bob's practical ideas and clear advice, I've been able to land jobs I would never have thought of before—and establish myself as a highly successful full-time professional freelance writer."

—Joe Vitale, Houston, TX

"I've just completed the three busiest, most financially rewarding months of my writing career—and part of the credit goes to you for sharing your 'secrets.' I've had little time for (low-paying) pieces o'cake, but no complaints. I'm having fun, and earning."

—Irwin Chusid, Montclair, NJ

[5]   TRY "SECRETS OF A FREELANCE WRITER"
                      FOR 90 DAYS RISK-FREE!

To order "SECRETS OF A FREELANCE WRITER," just fill in the coupon portion of the enclosed pink circular and mail it to me with your check or money order.

I'll rush the program to you (over 270 pages of instruction) as soon as I hear from you. And, if you are not 100% delighted with my material, simply return it within 90 days for a full, prompt refund— no questions asked.

I can't think of a fairer . . . or easier . . . way for you to sample my High-Profit Writing techniques without risking a penny.

As I said at the beginning: The writing life is a great life—especially if you are getting paid handsomely to sit home and do it. Why not enjoy the good life now instead of later?

Send for my instructions and get started today. There is no risk or obligation of any kind. And your satisfaction is guaranteed. You can't lose.

Yours for success,

Bob Bly, The High-Profit Writer™

P.S. Wondering how much to charge clients for an article, press release, brochure, booklet, ad, newsletter, or sales letter? A complete and up-to-date table of fees appears on page 26 of "SECRETS OF A FREELANCE WRITER." Consult this fee schedule before quoting your fee to a prospective client—to make sure your price is in line with what the client expects to pay.

Bob Bly / 22 E. Quackenbush Avenue / Dumont, NJ 07628 / (201) 385-1220

This letter is actually an inquiry fulfillment letter. I run small classified ads in the writer's magazines with the headline "MAKE $85,000 A YEAR" and offer "free details." People who respond get this letter, a flier that describes the book and has a tear-off order form and a reply envelope. The letter typi-cally converts 20 to 30 percent of inquiries to sales, depending on which publication the inquiries came from.

Frequently asked questions about business-to-business direct mail

If you master the five-step Motivating Sequence for persuasive writing, you won't necessarily have learned everything you need to know about direct mail. And it may not make you a creative genius. But it *will* enable you to produce competent, hard-working letters that, while they may not win awards, will generate more inquiries, leads, and sales than the letters your competitors are using.

As for the rest: In this brief chapter, I cannot give you a complete course in direct mail fundamentals. That will take many courses, seminars, and books. But I *can* hit the highlights.

The following was presented, in slightly different form, as a speech to the New Jersey Association of Advertising Agencies on February 3, 1992.

What's the most important factor affecting the response to a direct mail piece?

The mailing list. The "creative approach"—copy and graphics—might lift response 10, 20, 30, or 40 percent higher than previous mailings. In some cases, a great creative approach might even pull double previous mailings. So if you have a mailing pulling 2 percent right now, redesigning and rewriting the package might get you 2-1/2, 3, 4, possibly even 5 percent response.

But a given piece of copy, mailed to the best mailing list, might pull *4 to 10 times* the response of the same mailing piece sent to the worst mailing list. So if the response was 2 percent on the best list, using the worst list might get you a quarter-percent response or worse. Interestingly, you can get this tremendous difference in response rates even between business-to-business mailing lists that, on the surface, may seem identical and not worth testing.

For example, I wrote a mailing to sell a piece of software aimed at users of a specific kind of computer system. There are a number of trade journals serving users of this type of computer, and all are similar. They are targeted toward the same type of reader, and they run similar articles. Yet when we split our mailing among the subscriber lists of two of these magazines, we found magazine A pulled *three times the response* of magazine B. Had we not tested lists (a major mistake business-to-business direct marketers commit on a daily basis) and mailed to magazine B only, our mailing would have looked like a failure. But with the list from magazine A, the mailing was three times as profitable.

It is a mistake to think you know which list will pull best without testing, or to rent lists directly from list owners or managers, who of course want to sell you their list and won't tell you about others you might try. You should always rent your lists from a *mailing list broker,* not directly from a trade magazine, publisher, or association. Why? Because brokers act as list "consultants" to help you identify, examine, and test the right lists to maximize your response. For the most part, their services are free; brokers do not charge for their research and recommendations. They are paid only when you actually rent lists, and their fees are paid by the list owner, not you, the client.

When you put a good list broker to work for you, the broker will examine your copy, search list files, and come up with recommendations for testing a number of lists reaching your target market. Some list brokers experienced in working with business-to-business clients are listed in the appendix. For some narrow vertical markets, the list broker may not come up with any list you didn't already know about. But that's okay—at least now you have done your homework and know it's true that the one or two lists you are mailing are the only ones available. Often, however, the list broker will come up with additional lists targeted to the market when the client swore that so-and-so magazine or such-and-such association was the only list available.

Ideally, I would like the broker to recommend five to eight lists, if that many are available. The broker will send you data cards that describe the source of the list, the market it represents, and whether you can target your mailing to specific types or sizes of companies or job titles or functions. Testing as many lists as possible makes sense, because you never know until you test which list will pull best, and the differences in results among lists can be substantial—far greater than the inexperienced direct marketer may imagine is possible.

For more information on mailing lists, request a free copy of the *Direct Mail Encyclopedia,* a comprehensive catalog of mailing lists available free of charge from Edith Roman Associates, 253 W. 35th Street, 16th Floor, New York, NY 10001, phone (800) 223-2194. Also request a copy of the special report on "Computer-Aided List Selection," written by Steve Roberts, president of the firm.

What's the second most important factor affecting response to business-to-business direct mail?

It's the offer, and a major error most business-to-business direct marketers make is not spending enough time coming up with and testing enticing offers. They just say "Here's our product; call us if you want to buy it," and that seldom works.

For example, one firm selling sales training programs to associations was getting a mediocre response sending out letters saying, "If you'd like us to give a workshop or seminar at your next meeting, call us." What to do? The owner of the firm decided to try a stronger offer. In examining his selling process, he realized he was already giving away a valuable demo tape of his program to potential clients; why not highlight this in the sales letter? He added a headline that said, "YOU HAVE BEEN SELECTED TO RECEIVE A *FREE* AUDIO CASSETTE ON *SELLING IN A SOFT ECONOMY."* Letter copy was rewritten to stress the free, no-obligation offer of the audio cassette.

As a rule, you will generate maximum response in lead-generating mailings by stressing an attractive soft offer, such as a free booklet or report, and "selling" the value of the bait piece in your copy. See Chapters 5 and 6 for instructions on how to create winning direct mail offers, both soft and hard.

What is the biggest mistake clients make when doing a direct mailing?

Many clients have an unrealistic expectation that a single letter or package will solve all their problems, and that the initial theme, format, list, and offer they come up with for the first effort will be the best one. As a result they do one mailing, get mediocre results, proclaim "Direct mail doesn't work for us," abandon the whole notion of doing direct mail, and go back to their ineffective trade show exhibits and image ads—which also don't work.

The smart client realizes that (a) the first mailing is really only a test; (b) based on the test results, the mailing can be gradually modified to increase response to the point where it is profitable; and (c) it will probably take many mailings, many letters, and many contacts to penetrate the market; therefore, an integrated campaign should be planned, rather than a single mailing or promotion. As my colleague Dan Kennedy points out, if prospects are worth mailing once to, they're probably worth mailing ten times to.

It's a mistake, for most selling situations, to expect one mailing to do the whole job. Often a series of mailings is required to penetrate the market. In magazine subscription renewals, for example, almost no publisher sends just one renewal notice. Most send a series of four, five, or six letters, each of which brings more renewals and profits to the publisher.

Another mistake is to let direct mail stand alone. If you create a great free booklet offer that works well in direct mail, why not also try it as a print ad or a press release? Or present it as a paper at your industry's professional meeting or annual conference? Marketing *synergy*—the idea that the cumulative effect of various promotions is greater than the sum of their individual effectiveness—is a correct notion, in my experience.

Do you want to be successful in direct mail? Then test. Test lists. Test offers. Test sales appeals. Test product A vs. product B, or service A vs. service B. Test formats. Test copy. *Don't bet everything on one mailing.* It seldom works that way.

Which works best—a letter, a package, or a self-mailer?

This is a tough one, and the right answer is, "It depends." On what? On the market, the list, the offer, and the product. However, you need more pragmatic advice than that. You want to select the right format and get a good response.

Let's start with the question of whether to use a self-mailer or a letter in an envelope. As a rule, a letter in an envelope with a reply card (and with or without another enclosure, such as a brochure) will generally, but not always, outpull a self-mailer. In my experience, the letter in an envelope with reply card outpulls the self-mailer about 70 to 80 percent of the time.

Does this mean you never use a self-mailer? No. But when you are doing a first-time mailing for a new product or service, it's better to start with the proven, time-tested package of an outer envelope, sales letter, brochure, and reply card. This format has the best chance of success.

Once you have achieved success with the letter package, you can then test a letter and reply card *without* the enclosed brochure. Or test a self-mailer. Or a postcard. Or some other nonstandard format. But make sure you first prove that direct mail, using the standard package, will work for the product. That way, if the self-mailer doesn't pull, you know it's the format, not the product or offer. If you had started with the self-mailer and didn't get a good response, you wouldn't know whether it's the product or the offer or the format.

The reason people want to use self-mailers is primarily one of cost: Self-mailers cost less than letter packages. An economical format, self-mailers save money, and especially in today's economy, there is a growing concern for keeping promotional costs low. On the other hand, you must ask yourself if you are really saving money by using inexpensive postcards or self-mailers if they do not pull as well as letters or packages. A cheap mailing that fails to generate response is really expensive, when you think about it.

Letter packages generally outpull self-mailers, but the increased response is not always great enough to pay the additional cost of sending a full-blown direct mail package. In such cases, you make your choice depending on your goals. If you want maximum penetration of the market regardless of the cost per lead or return on dollars spent, you use the package format, because it generates the highest gross response. On the other hand, if you are concerned with the ratio of sales made to dollars spent, a self-mailer may be the best choice if a package is too costly. A good example is seminars: Most seminar and conference promoters use self-mailers because the response rate to such mailings is so low (typically one-quarter to one percent), that they can only make a profit using the lower-cost self-mailer.

One colleague who ran a major seminar operation for many years told me another reason that self-mailers are used to promote seminars is the pass-along factor. People who receive a self-mailer and are not the right prospect for the product or service tend to pass it along to others in their company who might be interested. But people who receive a letter and are not the right prospect for the product or service tend to rip up the letter and throw it away instead of passing it along. Therefore, if you are not certain you are mailing to the right person at the prospect company, and you hope to have your material passed along to the right person, you might consider a self-mailer instead of a letter.

Will the above guidelines always hold true? No. The decision of whether to use a self-mailer or a standard direct mail package largely depends on economics, and as direct mail production costs and postage continue to skyrocket, the standard direct mail package—especially the larger packages used in mail order selling, with their big brochures and multi-page sales letters—become increasingly too costly.

The skyrocketing costs of postage and production have already had a major impact on mail order entrepreneurs. For example, in the book field, where it was once possible to profitably sell a $20 book through direct mail, it no longer is. In fact, it's tough to make a profit on any item sold through direct mail that costs less than $50.

In magazine subscription promotion, the standard direct mail package (outer envelope, four-page sales letter, brochure, lift letter, order form, and business reply envelope) was always the format of choice. Now, a specific type of self-mailer, the double postcard, is beating the standard direct mail package in many tests for many publications. So, while packages are traditionally a better choice than self-mailers, they aren't always.

Should we personalize our mailings?

Again, it depends on the audience, the list, the offer, and the product or service. Still, I can provide a few suggestions that may be helpful.

As a rule, the higher up the prospect is on the corporate ladder, and the larger the company, the more it pays to personalize. Therefore, if a client were mailing to chief financial officers at *Fortune* 500 firms, I would definitely recommend personalization. If the client were mailing to process engineers at manufacturing companies, I would say that it would not be necessary to personalize.

Also, keep in mind that there are *degrees* of personalization. You can personalize every element of a package—the outer envelope, letter, reply card (I have even received mailings with my name imprinted on brochures and posters!)—or just some of the elements. If you are going to an audience that is upscale or high-level, and you do not want your mailing to *look* like "direct mail," the most important element to personalize is the outer envelope.

Some mailings seem to call for a personalized approach more than others, based on their theme or appeal. For instance, if you're doing a mailing to build membership to an organization, it's difficult to say "You have been personally selected because of your qualifications and education for membership in our society" in a letter that begins "Dear Friend."

Personalization almost always increases response, but the increase in response is not always high enough to justify the extra cost. That's why personalization is another element of the mailing that is worth testing. Another factor that determines whether you can personalize is the size and shape of the list. If you have a small list of only a few hundred prospects stored on a floppy disk, and you have in-house computer capabilities, personalization may be so cheap and easy that you personalize all letters to this group. On the other hand, if you have a large list that is available only on labels and not on computer disk, the cost, time, and effort of entering the names into a computer system or typing labels by hand may be prohibitive.

For more information on whether and how to personalize direct mail, request a free copy of the booklet "Should I Personalize?" available from Fala Direct Marketing, 70 Marcus Drive, Melville, NY 11747, phone (516) 694-1919.

Should the outer envelope be blank or have a teaser on it?

Next to the mailing list and the offer, a teaser is one of the most worthwhile items to test. Use of a teaser often will increase response, sometimes substantially. In some cases, adding a teaser won't make any difference. In many other instances, adding a teaser will actually *lower* response, and you'd be better off using a plain envelope. The most amazing thing is you can never predict this in advance. You have to test.

What is the function of an outer envelope teaser? Some experienced mailers would tell you, "That's obvious—it's to get the outer envelope opened." That sounds logical, doesn't it? But wait. Don't you open *all* envelopes that look like personal mail? Yes, most people do. So to get the outer envelope opened, you really don't need a teaser; just make your outer envelope look like personal or professional correspondence.

This means the address of the recipient is typed directly on the envelope, a first-class stamp or metered postage (not a preprinted indicia) is affixed, and there is no company logo or promotional message on the envelope—just the return address in plain type on the reverse side or upper-left corner. When going "teaserless," the idea is to make your mailing piece look as much like regular mail (not direct mail) as possible. And in fact, this approach is frequently successful and should be considered as one of your test approaches.

If you can get the recipient to open the outer envelope without using a teaser, then what purpose do teasers serve? Bob Matheo, a successful direct mail writer, says that the purpose of the teaser is not just to get the outer envelope opened but to *create a positive expectation* on the part of the reader for what is inside. A good teaser arouses curiosity, or promises a benefit, or makes an attractive offer—an offer the prospect "can't refuse." You don't want them just to open the envelope; you want them to tear into it because they're so eager they can't wait to see what's inside.

Should you use a teaser? See if you can come up with a teaser you think will make the prospect curious or eager to read further. If you can come up with such a teaser, use it. If not, if you feel your teaser isn't terribly powerful or intriguing, drop it and use a plain envelope. Don't feel you have failed if you can't come up with a great teaser, or that it's a bad idea to use a teaserless envelope. Quite the opposite is true: The plain envelope will typically outpull a teaser unless the teaser is really great.

And even with a great teaser, the teaser envelope is not the sure winner. Richard Armstrong tells of a brilliantly clever direct mail package he wrote based on the theme of an ancient Indian curse. The teaser, "ANCIENT INDIAN CURSE INSIDE," tied in beautifully with the theme of the letter. Everyone thought it would be a winner. But, just to be safe, the client mailed a small test quantity of the package with a blank envelope. Guess what? Both packages did well, but *the plain envelope outpulled the teaser,* proving that even a brilliant teaser is not always better than that old standby, the plain #10 outer envelope.

Is it better to mail first class or bulk rate?

This is discussed in detail in Chapter 1. As a rule, for business-to-business lead-generating mailings to niche markets and smaller audiences (say, fewer than 100,000 pieces), first class usually pays off, despite the extra expense, because of the higher deliverability rate. (Much third-class mail is dumped by corporate mail rooms, screened by receptionists and secretaries, or not even delivered by the postal service.) When selling a business-to-business product through mail order, where the cost per thousand of the mailing is a critical factor in determining whether the mailing will be profitable, first class is generally not affordable, especially with pieces weighing over one ounce. Most mail-order marketers mailing in large quantities (50,000 or more) use third-class bulk rate, not first class.

What's the secret to writing successful business-to-business direct mail?

It's stated best by my copywriting colleague Don Hauptman, who puts it this way: "Start with the prospect, not with the product." Another colleague, mail-order expert Sig Rosenblum, explains: "The prospect isn't interested in what *you* want, what *you* sell, how *you* run your business or make your product. The prospect is interested in what *they* want, what *they* need, what *they* fear, what's in it for them."

Most manufacturers write what is known in the trade as "manufacturer copy." Their letters typically begin as follows:

Dear Plant Engineer:

The Gillard TBV-100 is a preformed acoustic dampening material of construction fabricate to dampen acoustical overloads and minimize decibel output at maximum efficiency and with a low cost-per-square-foot expenditure enabled by retrofitting with this material vs. totally new construction.

The problem is that the reader doesn't care about the Gillard TBV-100; he or she cares about controlling noise in the plant. If we follow Don Hauptman's advice and begin with the prospect and his or her problem, and not the product, we get a letter like this:

Dear Plant Engineer:

Do you need to *control* sound in your plant to meet OSHA standards and protect your employees from noise overload . . . while at the same time *avoiding* the cost of totally tearing out and replacing the walls in your manufacturing operation?

Gillard TBV-100 "Sound-Proof Wall Add-Ons" are the answer. . . .

Always start with prospects and their concerns. This is what interests them. Business customers don't buy your product or service because they enjoy spending money or like shopping. They buy your product or service to solve specific problems.

To be successful in business-to-business selling, you cannot simply present a product; you must first show how the product relates to the needs of the prospect. This is a basic principle of selling, but one that most technically oriented managers and marketers ignore.

We are using sales letters for lead generation with mediocre response. What can we do to increase response?

First, target selectively and tailor copy to specific narrow market segments. You'll do better by offering "desktop publishing systems for ad agencies," "desktop publishing systems for printers," "desktop publishing systems for graphic artists," and for other specific markets than just offering "desktop publishing systems" and mailing broadly and generically to small businesses. Review Chapter 4 for a refresher on why this is so.

Second, if you do not now have a soft offer of a free brochure, booklet, or other information piece, add one immediately. If the only option your prospects have is to meet with you, speak with you, or see a demonstration, and there is no material they can send for, your response will continue to be low.

Third, if you do have a soft offer, beef it up. Instead of a "free brochure," create and offer a free guide or report on "How to Select the Right Voice Mail System for Your Company." Make your bait piece informative and specific, stress the offer of it in your letter copy, and response will increase substantially.

Beef up your hard offer as well. Instead of offering to "have a salesperson call," offer a free seminar on voice mail. Or a free demonstration by phone. Or a free analysis of their current message-handling procedures by a qualified Communications Consultant. Chapters 5 and 6 will refresh you on the benefits and uses of soft and hard offers.

Do pop-ups, 3-D mailings, bulky enclosures, product samples, and other such gimmicks work in direct mail?

They can, but often they're overkill. The advantage of a 3-D mailing (i.e., one which contains a gift item, product sample, videotape, or other object) is that it does get noticed. Ninety-nine percent of the direct mail your prospect receives is flat, so 3-D mailings stand out, gain attention, and get opened and looked at—more so than a lot of conventional direct mail.

The disadvantage of 3-D mailings is the expense. A regular mailing might cost anywhere from 40 cents to 70 cents apiece or so. A 3-D mailing, because of the cost of the enclosure and the additional postage, can easily run $1–3 apiece or more, and I have seen many that cost $5–10 a piece or more.

So while 3-D mailings might get more attention, be more memorable, and even generate more response, the question is whether they perform well enough to justify the added cost. Often the answer is no. For instance, one ad agency proposed to a client of mine a dimensional mailing to 6,000 prospects at a cost of $5 each (excluding production). I pointed out that for that price, we could send each prospect on the list a series of *ten* letters, and that the fancy 3-D mailing was not likely to pull anywhere near the combined response of those ten letters.

Would I ever recommend a 3-D or fancy mailing? Yes. One excellent application is when mailing to a limited number of high-level prospects. For instance, one client asked me to write a mailing sent to 2,000 large corporations. As it happened, the service being offered was one that was sound-oriented and could therefore be demonstrated quite effectively using an Evatone sound sheet or audio cassette. We created a demonstration cassette and mailed it to different executives at these 2,000 companies. In a separate package going to the CEO of each firm, we mailed the cassette *along with a Sony Walkman* on which he or she could immediately listen to it. Overall response to this campaign, which was a series of three mailings to multiple executives at each company, not a single effort, was over 50 percent.

Another good use of 3-D or gimmick mailings is mailing to prospects who are "overmailed"; that is, they receive a lot of direct mail, are jaded toward it, and don't tend to respond. A 3-D mailing can be a breakthrough in such cases, gaining attention where even the most well-written letter cannot.

9
Profits from Postcard Decks

If you're like most of my clients and seminar attendees, you don't spend a lot of time thinking about postcard decks. This cost-effective medium is ignored by 95 percent of business marketers, simply because it can't compete in excitement with running full-page ads or doing big solo mailings.

But as postage and direct mail production costs continue to skyrocket, many business marketers are taking a closer look at postcard decks. In this chapter, let's review some of the fundamentals of the medium and some ideas for getting maximum response from the cards you run.

What is a postcard deck?

A postcard deck is a group of advertising postcards mailed as a package to individuals whose names are on a mailing list. Although some decks are "dedicated" (all the cards are from one advertiser), most carry cards from many different advertisers. The advertiser pays a fee to have its card included in the deck.

The main advantage of postcard decks is the low cost. The cost-per-thousand pieces for a solo direct mail package can range from $350 to $600 or more, depending on the quantity mailed. (Some business-to-business marketers spend 75 cents to $1 or more per piece for fancier lead-generating packages.) Running a postcard in a postcard deck with a circulation of 100,000 typically costs $1,200–$1,800, so the cost is *low*—$12–18 per thousand prospects reached. That's about *thirty times cheaper* than a full-blown solo direct mail package.

Another advantage of postcard decks is that the postcards are easy to produce. They don't require copywriting genius, cleverness, or creative design. Just about anyone, even those with limited resources, can put such a card together. (Some decks, hungry for advertisers, will even do the card for you at low or no cost.)

The third advantage is that postcard decks are inherently a response medium, so if you're after pure response and don't care about things like "awareness" or "image," they make sense for you.

What kind of response can you expect? Approximately one-quarter to one-half percent is common. With a postcard deck going to 100,000 names, therefore, this would translate into 250–500 inquiries. If you paid $1,200 to run your card in the deck, that's a cost per lead of $2.40–4.80, which is *tremendously* lower than solo direct mail. (On a $500-per-thousand direct mail package pulling a 2 percent response, your cost per lead would be $25.)

The down side

Postcards are fantastically inexpensive to produce and run. They generate loads of leads. And the cost per lead is much lower than direct mail or print advertising. So why isn't everybody abandoning direct mail and print advertising in favor of postcard decks? Because there are several disadvantages that offset the advantages.

To begin with, many advertisers believe the *quality* of leads generated from postcard decks is not as good as print advertising or direct mail-generated sales leads. The reason is that the postcard tells very little about the product or service because of space constraints, so the response is from someone who hasn't really been pre-sold on the product or service. Whether postcard decks will actually produce "worse" leads than direct mail or advertising for *your* product or service can only be answered by testing them and measuring the results. Another disadvantage is that there are far fewer postcard decks than mailing lists available, so with direct mail you can reach many, many markets postcard decks don't reach.

Also, most postcard decks do mailings only two or three times a year, so you must accommodate your plans to fit their schedule. With magazine advertising, you can advertise weekly or monthly. With newspaper advertising, you can target which days your ads appear. With solo direct mail, you can mail anytime, and as often as you like. This is why these media will never be replaced by postcard decks, and why postcard decks are, for most business marketers, a *supplement* to other marketing activities rather than the main focus of the direct marketing program. There are some companies, to be sure, that do all or most of their lead generation through postcard decks, but these are the exception, not the rule. A directory of postcard decks is available from Standard Rate and Data Service, 3002 Glenview Road, Wilmette, IL 60091, phone (708) 256-6067.

Leads or sales?

Certain low-priced items such as slide duplication, business books, office supplies, and imprinted business cards and envelopes can be sold directly from the postcard. Technical products, capital equipment, and other higher-ticket items cannot, and the postcard should be used to generate an inquiry rather than solicit a direct order in such cases.

Ken Morris, a direct marketing consultant, says postcards are better for inquiry generation than for mail order. "Use card decks to build inquiry files," he advises. "While only a percentage of these may translate to direct orders, you can start to build a database of your 'affinity' groups—and down the line, repeated promotions to this database will yield 10 times the order conversion rate as opposed to rented lists."

Designing a postcard

The main advantage of the postcard deck to the recipient of the deck is convenience. You should therefore design your postcard to maximize reader convenience.

For example, the postcards measure about 5-3/8 inches long by 3-1/2 inches high. Most people hold the decks horizontally when going through them, because 99 percent of the postcards in them are designed to be read in the horizontal position (long side held horizontally). Therefore, you should design *your* postcard so that it is readable in this position. Some advertisers try to be different by designing the card vertically to force the reader to turn the card to read it. This only serves to annoy people and does not increase readership or response.

The reader flips through card decks rapidly, often with a wastebasket between his or her knees. He or she glances at each card for about 2 seconds before deciding whether to set it aside for a second read or to toss it in the basket. Therefore, your card should be clear, direct, and get the message across in 2 seconds or less. Use a short, direct headline with a picture of the product. Or, if you are generating leads for a catalog, show a picture of your catalog. Do not be clever or artsy. Be simple and direct.

Okay. The reader has set your card aside in the pile representing offers he or she might have some interest in. You want to make it as easy as possible for the reader to respond. How should you do this?

Business reply cards

First, I recommend using a business reply card permit so the reader does not have to affix postage. Many entrepreneurs in smaller offices do not have a postage meter handy and, while they may have a roll of 29-cent stamps for letters, they do not keep 19-cent stamps on hand (the first-class postage for mailing a postcard as of this writing). So when I want to send in a card that does not have a business reply indicia on it, I am forced to affix a 29-cent stamp and waste 10 cents postage. This may sound like a minor point, but I assure you if it is irritating to me, it's irritating to others in small offices. Therefore, the front should be a business reply card, not a "PLACE STAMP HERE."

Space for name and address

There should be sufficient room for the prospect to fill in name, company, and address. Although I prefer the "coupon portion" for this to be on the same side as the headline, photo, and body copy, I do see a growing trend to put a small coupon in the upper-left corner of the front (return address and business reply permit) side of the card.

Which is better? I vote for putting the name and address block on the same side as the rest of the sales copy because it logically connects the response device with the sales pitch. If the prospect has been persuaded by your sales pitch, you want them to pick up a pen and begin writing their name and address. The name and address block on the "sell side" makes this a natural progression. It also allows ample space for writing.

Putting the name and address block on the BRC side interrupts the action, forcing the prospect to search for the name and address block and turn the card over. Also, putting the name and address block in the upper-left corner of the BRC side means making it small to fit the tiny space, which makes it more difficult for prospects to write in their information.

Other details

Have one, two, or three check-off boxes so prospects can quickly indicate what they want to receive. Include your phone number and even your fax number in bold type at the bottom of the selling side so prospects too impatient to fill out the card can simply telephone. Some will.

If you are going for sales leads, make sure the postcard can stand alone as both advertisement and a response device. For example, to offset the cost of the card or the literature they are mailing, some advertisers ask prospects to pay a nominal sum ($1–3 is typical) to receive their literature or samples. But that means the prospect can no longer use the card as a stand-alone response device. He or she must now get cash, money order, or check, type an envelope, and enclose the postcard with payment. The convenience of easy response is destroyed, and response goes way down.

The offer is determined by the price of the product

We said earlier that response from a postcard deck is typically one-quarter to one-half percent of the total circulation. But this can vary tremendously, depending on the product and the offer. For those of you selling business or industrial products, here are some guidelines for structuring your offer:

- If you are selling capital equipment or other expensive technical products with long purchase cycles, use the postcard to generate a soft lead. The headline would state the main benefit offered by the product (e.g., "Reduce Energy Costs up to 40% in Your Paper Mill"). The copy would briefly explain the product and offer a free brochure. The visual would be a photo, sketch, or diagram of the product.

- If you sell a broad line of low-to-medium-priced products, and your catalog is your primary sales vehicle, use the card for catalog distribution. The headline should stress the offer and value of your catalog (e.g., "FREE Electronic Component Buyer's Guide and Reference Catalog!"). The visual should be a picture of the catalog.

- If you have a low-priced product (under $300), it may be possible to sell directly from the postcard. But test cautiously. One manufacturer of electronic equipment in the $79–400 range uses postcards frequently and has tested offering products directly versus a free catalog offer. He finds the free catalog offer gets much more response and is more profitable over the long run.

The six elements of a successful postcard

In *Secrets of Successful Response Deck Advertising,* Bill Norcutt lists the following as the essential elements for a successful postcard:

1. A powerful headline.

The headline should state a powerful benefit ("Prevent Industrial Accidents!") and also make the entire offer completely clear.

2. A clear illustration or picture.

Don't be creative. Use a picture of the product or the product in action. The headline and picture alone, according to Norcutt, should communicate instant recognition of, and understanding of, exactly what is being offered—and should get this across in one second.

3. A horizontal rather than vertical card.

This confirms what I told you earlier.

4. An overwhelmingly good deal.

Especially if you are selling a product directly from a postcard, the card must offer an overwhelmingly good deal. This is typically accomplished by offering a low price, special discount, small trial order, or free demo or sample. In a lead-generating card, copy should immediately communicate the high value of the product being promoted.

5. A wide range of response options.

For a card seeking direct orders, allow the reader to order by mailing the card or calling a toll-free 800 number. Allow the reader to pay by credit card, enclose payment, or be billed. On a lead-generating card, have response options for both a hard ("have a logistics consultant call") and soft ("send me a free catalog") offer.

6. Plenty of room.

Norcutt warns that prospects will discard postcards that force them to try to write their name in letters one-sixteenth of an inch high. Leave ample room in the coupon portion for the reader to fill in all information. Many cards try to solve this problem by encouraging the reader to "attach your business card here." But I've found business cards, especially if stapled rather than taped, can fall off, and I have gotten postcards back where a business card had been attached but came off. "Attach business card," which works well with an ad coupon that will be put in an envelope, is riskier with postcards because they are mailed with no outer envelope and can be damaged in transit.

The headline is the key element

While all elements of the postcard design are important, the one that can probably make the most difference in terms of results is the headline. In *Beyond Lead Generation: Merchandising Through Card Decks,* Robert Luedtke tells of a company promoting a seminar on management and marketing of dental practices through a postcard. They tested the following five headlines, with the rest of the postcard being otherwise identical:

A. BUILD EFFECTIVE TEAM LEADERSHIP

B. BIG MARKETING RESULTS FROM A SMALL BUDGET

C. INCREASE REFERRALS

D. CREATE A UNIQUE PRACTICE IMAGE

E. INCREASE PATIENT FLOW

One headline pulled double the response of the other four. Can you guess which? It was E, INCREASE PATIENT FLOW. (Many people I've shown this to guess B.) Again, the copy and graphics were the same for each card, proving that the right headline can significantly improve response to your copy.

10

How to Generate More Sales from Your Sales Brochures

Information dissemination versus marketing communication

Many business-to-business marketers, especially industrial manufacturers, think of brochures as purely information. But a brochure is also a marketing tool. Yes, its primary mission is to provide prospects with the information they requested; if it doesn't do that, they won't pay much attention to it. But it can also serve as a direct response vehicle to move the prospect from "merely interested" to "ready to buy."

The "next-step" theory: How a brochure moves prospects from Step A to Step B in the buying process

As discussed in Chapter 1, one factor that distinguishes business-to-business marketing from consumer marketing is the multi-step buying process. Most business products are not bought on impulse off a rack or store shelf. They are carefully considered and evaluated before purchase. This buying cycle can have many steps, and one goal of business-to-business marketing communication is to move the buyer *one step* in the buying cycle closer to a sale. Let's say our buying cycle looks like the following:

Step A ⟶ Step B ⟶ Step C ⟶ Step D

Step A: The prospect expresses some initial interest in the product.
Step B: The prospect studies and evaluates product literature.
Step C: The prospect requests a price quotation.
Step D: The prospect purchases the product.

The brochure is obviously used at Step B here. The prospect is sent literature to review. The literature serves a primary function of disseminating factual information about the product, although it is written to show the product off to best advantage, so that the prospect will want your product instead of competing products.

Looking at the diagram, it emerges that there are three ways you can improve your brochure to make it a more effective sales device:

1. You can improve the contents, organization, and clarity so that Step B, evaluation of the product based on printed literature, goes better—that is, so that the brochure gets read and helps strengthen the prospect's interest in the product.

2. You can redesign the brochure so that it increases the response to Step A, which is getting people to show interest in and request the brochure in the first place.

3. You can redesign the brochure so that you increase the percentage of brochure recipients who respond to the brochure with a request for more literature, a price quotation, an estimate, or whatever Step C is.

Let's look at each one of these tasks in more detail.

Swaying the prospect in favor of purchasing the product

The most obvious improvement to be made in a brochure is content: The brochure fails to give prospects the information they requested and need to make an intelligent buying decision. In one survey, when asked "What do you find inadequate about the brochures you request on business products and services?" prospects said their number-one complaint was that they did not contain enough information.

The reason is that such brochures are usually created by people who are not prospects for the product or service. These individuals tend to concentrate on aesthetics (graphic design and copy style), and they keep the content simple and short (because they believe that is critical to easy reading). Unfortunately, they often err on the side of being too simplistic, and they omit important technical information that the prospect is desperately seeking.

To ensure that your brochures are not superficial, here are generic outlines you can follow for the two most common types of brochures: product and service brochures. Check your copy against these outlines so that if you are leaving out one or more of the standard sections, you at least know you are doing it deliberately and not by accidental omission.

Product brochure

Here is my outline of the sections that can be included in a product brochure. They are listed in a sequence that makes sense for most products, although you may choose a different arrangement.

   I.   INTRODUCTION: A capsule description of what the product is and why prospects should be interested in it.

  II.   BENEFITS: A list of reasons why the customer should buy the product (improves business results, saves money, increases productivity, saves time, cuts pollution, conserves energy, etc.).

 III.   FEATURES: Highlights of key features, including:

- Unique features the product has that the competition does not.

- Features the product has that are superior to or different from the competition.

- Features the product has that competitors have but do not stress in their advertising.

- Features that similar products also have but are important to the prospect and should therefore be highlighted.

 IV.   HOW IT WORKS: A description of how the product works and what it can do. This section can include the results of any tests that demonstrate the product's superiority. (NOTE: Some advertising experts would tell you to omit this section, claiming readers are only interested in results and benefits. But many technical audiences, such as engineers, *are* interested in how it works.)

  V.   MARKETS: This section describes the various markets that can benefit from the product. For example, a wastewater treatment plant might be sold to municipalities, utilities, and industrial manufacturers—three distinct markets, each with its own special set of requirements. This section can also include a list of the names of well-known organizations or people that use and endorse your product.

VI. APPLICATIONS: Descriptions of the various applications in which the product can be used.

VII. PRODUCT AVAILABILITY: Lists models, sizes, materials of construction, colors, finishes, options, accessories, and all the variations in which the product can be ordered. This section may also include charts, graphs, formulas, tables, or other guidelines to aid the reader in product selection.

VIII. PRICING: Information on what the product costs, including prices for accessories, various models and sizes, quantity discounts, and shipping and handling. Often handled in a separate price sheet so as not to date expensively produced literature designed to be current for many years.

IX. TECHNICAL SPECIFICATIONS: Electrical requirements, power consumption, resistance to moisture, temperature range, operating conditions, cleaning methods, storage conditions, chemical properties, product life, and other characteristics and limitations of the product.

X. Q & A: Frequently asked questions about the product and its usage, along with the answers. This section is optional and is used to handle the presentation of miscellaneous information that does not easily fit into the other sections.

XI. COMPANY HISTORY: A brief history of the manufacturer, written to show the reader that the product is backed by a solid, reputable organization that won't go out of business.

XII. PRODUCT SUPPORT: Information on delivery, installation, training, maintenance, service, and guarantees.

XIII. THE NEXT STEP: Instructions on how to order the product, get more information, request a quotation or estimate, or take whatever action is appropriate.

Service brochure

When you are marketing a service instead of a product, you can use this outline as is or adapt it to your requirements:

I. INTRODUCTION: A summary of the services offered, types of clients handled, and reasons why readers should be interested in the services.

II. SERVICES OFFERED: Detailed descriptions of the various services offered by the firm and how they satisfy client needs.

III. BENEFITS: Describes what the prospects will gain from the services and why they should engage your firm instead of the competition.

IV. BACKGROUND INFORMATION: A discussion of the problems the service is designed to address. This section can offer some advice to the client on how to evaluate the problem or on how to select the right professional help. Such information helps the potential client evaluate you as a vendor and also adds value to the brochure, causing prospects to retain it as a reference piece. When they consult their file in the future, they find the brochure with your name and phone number and call to give you work.

V. METHODOLOGY: An outline of the service firm's method of doing business with clients.

VI. CLIENT LIST: A list of well-known companies who have used your services.

VII. TESTIMONIALS: Statements of endorsement from select clients. Testimonials are usually written in the client's own words and attributed to a specific person or organization.

VIII. FEES AND TERMS: Describes the fees for each service and the terms and method of payment. This section includes whatever guarantee the service firm offers its clients. Fees and terms are often, though not always, covered in a separate sheet or insert.

IX. BIOGRAPHICAL INFORMATION: Capsule biographies highlighting the credentials of key employees plus an overall capsule history of the firm.

X. THE NEXT STEP: Instructions on what prospects should do next if they are interested in hiring your firm or learning more about the services you offer.

Pricing Information

The *second* most common complaint of prospects requesting literature is that the inquiry fulfillment materials do not give any information about price. For off-the-shelf products with standard pricing, be sure to include a price list. For services, consider having some sort of fee schedule disclosing project or hourly rates.

For custom products, systems, and other offers that require an estimate before a price can be given, the reader should be given at least some idea of the costs involved. For example, a brochure selling power boilers had a graph showing *approximate* cost of the unit (in thousands of dollars) as a function of size (the bigger the boiler, the more expensive the system, naturally). While you could not determine exactly what your boiler would cost, in a few seconds you could get a pretty close idea. This is what the readers want and what you should give them, if at all possible.

Another way to give an approximate idea of price is to compare it to something familiar. A marketer selling computer-based imaging systems could not give a dollar price in literature because of the variations in price due to models and options and customization of software. So they chose in the price discussion simply to say the system "is about the cost of a new compact car."

Designing the brochure to increase response to direct mail packages and ads offering the brochure to prospects

Most marketers plan the creation of their sales literature and advertising/direct mail promotions separately. You get better results, however, when you design your brochures with the idea of maximizing response to ads and direct mail firmly in mind.

The primary strategy for getting more people to send for your brochure in response to ads, direct mail, and PR is to give it a title that implies value. Examples? A collection agency offered a brochure with only the name of the company on the cover. Ads said, "For a free brochure describing our services, mail the coupon today." Few did. In reprinting the brochure, the company reorganized the copy into a series of 14 numbered points, each telling how prospects could improve their collection results by using various services provided by the collection agency. The agency retitled the brochure "14 ways to improve your collections." Ads said, "For a free informative booklet, '14 ways to improve your collections,' mail the coupon today."

This offer outpulled "send for a brochure." People perceive an informational booklet as having more value than a brochure, so more will send for it. When an ad or mailing offers literature as a soft offer, you can substantially increase response by retitling and redesigning your sales literature to make it seem (a) more valuable and (b) more informative.

Another example? Two accountants produce sales brochures to be offered at local business meetings, through small newspaper ads, and in mailings to local businesses. The first brochure says "Lana Kaplan, CPA, Accounting Services." The second says, "14 questions small business owners commonly ask about reducing their tax payments... and the answers." Which would you send for?

By now you get the idea. However, one note of caution: Your brochure must, to some degree, deliver the information promised in the title, mixing in some useful ideas or tips with the sales message. If you promise the reader free, useful information, then send nothing but sales hype, they will feel cheated and will be turned off. That tactic will actually *hurt* sales.

What if your brochure doesn't take this informational approach and is a straight sales pitch? Then use a title that still implies value but doesn't mislead the reader. For example, instead of calling your catalog a catalog, call it a "product guide." I have a two-page mini-catalog offering books, tapes, and special reports of interest to business-to-business marketers. Instead of calling it a catalog, I call it the "Business-to-Business Marketing Resource Guide" (see appendix). Which sounds more valuable: "catalog" or "resource guide"?

Or let's say you have a catalog of electronic components that contains tables showing how to specify and select components for various applications. Instead of calling it a catalog, call it the "Electronic Component Selection Guide" or the "Electronic Component Buyer's Reference Guide."

As an alternative, you can always add useful information to your brochures in the next printing, then stress this value when offering them.

Many brochures I get, and this probably includes yours, have at least one or more blank panels or pages. Can you think of ways to use this space better by adding some information of use to your prospect? For example, a casino put the rules of blackjack on the back of its brochure; this makes it a "keeper" for those going to Las Vegas who, like me, do not know how to play. Similarly, a data communications equipment manufacturer added a glossary of local area networking terms to the back of its capabilities brochure, giving that piece added value.

Redesigning the brochure to increase the percentage of recipients who request more literature, a price quotation, or a cost estimate

The techniques just discussed get more people to send for your brochure when it is offered in direct response ads and mailings. But how do you get more people to respond to your sales brochures after they receive them?

The first thing is to clearly identify what action you want prospects to take after receiving and reading your brochure. Do you want them to mail you an order form with a check? Call your toll-free 800 number with their credit card information? Contact a local sales rep? Request additional literature? Send you a purchase order or a request for proposal? The specific action you want to take place after prospects receive and read your brochure must be clear in your own mind, or else you will not be able to communicate to the prospects what they should do.

Next, add these instructions to the close of your brochure. Somewhere toward the end of the brochure should be a subhead and some copy telling the prospects what to do next, how to do it, and *why* they should do it. I usually label this section with the subhead "THE NEXT STEP."

THE NEXT STEP

Installing the FunFilter 2000 in your mish-mash system can control emissions and meet EPA requirements while significantly reducing your energy costs. For more detailed technical literature . . . or to arrange to use a FunFilter 2000 FREE in your plant for 30 days . . . call our toll-free hotline 800-CLEAN-AIR. Or write us today.

Many brochures are vague about the next step and don't spell it out in this much detail. This may seem like a minor point, but you would be surprised. People are naturally lazy, and if you don't tell them to act, they won't.

Your call to action will generate more response to your brochure if you give several options, instead of just one. One software firm, for example, offers four different options:

1. A free on-line demonstration of the software via modem hook-up.

2. A free demonstration in the prospect's office.

3. 30 days free use of the product with no obligation to buy.

4. Free attendance at regional half-day educational workshops.

A brochure for an industrial product might offer more information, ask for the order, or suggest a visit from a sales rep. A brochure for a service firm might offer a free initial consultation, a free needs assessment or other free analysis of the client's situation, a free presentation in the client's office, or even free use of the service for a trial period. For example, a company in my county that rents mailboxes offers three months use free to new customers.

Finally, to get even more people to respond to your brochure, give them not only a clear action step and specific instructions, but also provide the mechanism or vehicle they can use to respond, for example, a reply card, questionnaire, specification sheet, check-off survey, or other form of response device the recipient can complete and return to you. This can be inserted in the brochure or actually printed as a part of the brochure.

In its capabilities brochures selling process equipment, one major manufacturer incorporates a tear-out business reply card into the back cover. The card offers additional information on specific products described in the more general overview brochures.

Another engineering firm, selling a motionless mixer, requires certain technical information about the prospect's process—fluid viscosities, flow rates, pipe diameters, temperature, and so forth—before they can design the right mixer and quote a price to the prospect. Note pads containing fill-in-the-blank specification sheets are on every salesperson's desk, so when a prospect calls, the salesperson can ask the right questions, fill in the sheet, and hand it to engineering for an immediate quote.

When a graphic design firm was hired to redo the company's product brochure, the designer suggested incorporating the spec sheet as a tear-off page in the back of the brochure, reasoning that it would encourage prospects to take the initiative in requesting a cost estimate and providing the necessary technical data. And indeed, many engineers took the time to fill in the lengthy spec sheet and mail it back for a quotation.

Nowadays, prospects can return such a form either by mail or fax. Make it as easy and painless as possible for them to respond. One company, selling an expensive product to a limited and highly targeted group of prospects, enclosed a prepaid Federal Express label for the prospect to use to return the application form for the service being offered.

Another solution is to incorporate into your brochure a tear-off business reply card, similar to the subscription cards you find in magazines. If your brochure is saddle-stitched (stapled through the spine), this can be inserted as a separate piece. In a smaller brochure folded to fit a #10 business envelope, you can make one of the panels a separate business reply card.

11

How to Get More Orders from Business-to-Business and Industrial Catalogs

Catalogs versus brochures

A catalog is a comprehensive directory describing all the products a company sells. The main difference between a brochure and a catalog is that brochures typically describe a single product in detail, and catalogs cover more products in less detail. The brochure promotes an individual item; the catalog is a single source of information on your company's entire product line. A brochure is narrowly focused; a catalog is comprehensive.

Catalogs have several uses. By inserting a catalog in the shipping envelope or box when you pack and ship products ordered by customers, you educate those customers about other products you offer that may be of interest to them. Catalogs can also be mailed separately to your customer list one or more times a year to remind those customers of your existence and get them to buy more from you.To expand your catalog sales, you can mail the catalog unsolicited to potential buyers whose names you rent from mailing list brokers. You can offer your catalog, either at no cost or for a nominal fee, in print ads.

Types of business-to-business catalogs: Mail order and industrial

Business-to-business mail-order catalogs typically offer low-priced or medium-priced items that a business would buy via mail order sight unseen. Envelopes, business cards, shipping supplies, gloves, uniforms, safety equipment, signs, posters, business gifts, software, computer supplies, office supplies, labels, and office furniture are some items sold via business-to-business mail-order catalogs.

The catalog will contain complete pricing information so the customer can place a direct order by returning an order form or calling a toll-free 800 number. Most catalog operations allow buyers to establish an account and be billed, although some require payment in advance for the initial order.

The business-to-business mail-order catalog is sent primarily to end users, that is, to people who use the product or order it for their boss or supervisor. So a catalog of business software would be mailed to PC users. A catalog of office supplies would go to the office manager.

An industrial or commercial catalog is used to sell technical products such as ball bearings, machine components, nuts and bolts, and a wide range of products used in factories, machine shops, and other manufacturing operations. Often they are targeted at the "professional buyer"—a purchasing agent whose job it is to purchase these products.

The purchasing agent has a direct telephone relationship with the vendor and will typically make a purchase by phone call or by issuing a purchase order. These catalogs often do not have pricing, and buyers will call to get a quote before placing an order.

The first impression: The front cover

The concept of improving readership and response to sales literature by giving the literature a title that implies value, as discussed in the previous chapter on sales brochures, also applies to catalogs. A business-to-business mail-order catalog can look more promotional, like a consumer catalog. But an industrial catalog should have a title and cover design that implies value.

The title should sound official and important, e.g., "The Metal Buyer's Guide to Specialty Steel and Forgings." The cover should either have a striking design or be made to look more like a directory than a catalog. If the cover has the look of an expensive directory, buyers will tend to view it as a reference piece rather than sales literature. Some who issue big reference catalogs put a cover price on their catalogs. Although the catalog is still sent free upon request, the cover price enhances the perceived value of the material.

Speaking of cover price, you may be thinking, "My catalog is very expensive to print and distribute, so should I charge a dollar or two to cover the cost and prevent people from requesting it who aren't really prospects but just like to collect catalogs?"

My opinion is that you should not charge; the catalog should be free. Although charging would eliminate the freebie seekers, it would also prevent many legitimate prospects from sending for it. So you lose much more than you gain. If you get an inquiry from someone who is obviously not a prospect, having a cover price allows you to tell that person he or she will have to pay for the material. That usually puts the freebie seeker off.

Making it easy for prospects to order

Industrial catalogs must make the buyer's job easier by providing the technical data and specifications needed to order the correct product. Graphs, guides, tables, and other devices that simplify the selection process are critical. Often people ordering different grades or types of a specific product are not sure which type to order for their application. Or they may think they know what to order, but they are actually not ordering the proper item and so will be dissatisfied when they try to use what you send them. The solution is to put selection guides in your catalog explaining the various grades, models, or types, what they are used for, which applications you recommend them for, and how to select them.

You should also include charts listing the sizes and weights of different models in a series. By showing your full product line in a single illustrated table, you enable readers to see at a glance all the sizes available, so they can select the size that fits their requirements.

In many product categories—semiconductors, for example—there are standard sizes or specifications to which all manufacturers conform, and the customer can specify any manufacturer's product in a given size or model. When one brand can be automatically substituted for another brand, it is called "drop-in" technology, because you can simply remove one brand and drop in another. The confusion for the customer is knowing which model number of your product to order as a replacement for a specific model number of a competitor's product now being used. A cross-reference table makes it easy for the customer to see which model numbers of various manufacturers are interchangeable with one another.

Whenever you can convert long paragraphs of complicated instructions into easy-to-use tables or charts, do it. Visual tools provide easy reference guides and make your catalog more useful to the buyer. The key is to make the catalog as easy to read, use, and order from as possible. If a purchasing agent deals with three vendors, and one has a superior catalog that is clear and easy to follow, and the other two vendors have complicated, hard-to-follow catalogs, the purchasing agent will naturally tend to use the easy catalog more.

Organizing the catalog for quick reference

Industrial catalogs should be organized in a fashion that is logical and makes reading and ordering easy and natural for the buyer. At the same time, you want to organize your merchandise and present it in the order likely to generate maximum sales. Here are some ways you can organize your catalog:

- Group products by type or category of product.

- Feature your most popular items.

- Feature scarce, hard-to-get items.

- Organize products in sections according to the functions they perform.

- Group products according to price.

- Group products by application.

- Group products depending on where they fit into the customer's process, system, or flow loop.

- Group products by dimensions, weight, power, or some other unit of measure related to size or performance.

- List products by model or part number.

- Organize your products according to alphabetical order.

Determining the type of response you want

You must determine whether your catalog is a traditional mail-order catalog that buyers can order from without assistance, or whether you need an industrial catalog that can assist the purchasing agent but may require personal contact between buyer and seller to facilitate the purchase of complex components, products, or systems. Rule of thumb: If the ordering process is too complicated to explain in the catalog, don't try to create a mail-order catalog. Instead, encourage the buyer to call you for explanations, pricing, quotes, or technical assistance.

Suggestions for order forms

A little-known but effective technique is to use not one but two identical order forms. One is bound into the catalog or printed on one of the regular catalog pages, and the second is loose and inserted between the front cover and first page. The loose order form falls out when the prospect opens the book, so it gains more attention and encourages immediate ordering. However, if the prospect is not ready to buy immediately, the loose order form may become lost, or it may get thrown away. When the prospect turns to the catalog later to place an order, the bound-in order form is ready and waiting.

Add a line to the bottom of your order form that says, "In a hurry? Simply complete this form and FAX to [fax number] for immediate action." Since most businesses today have fax machines, this provides the prospect with a convenient method of ordering.

Humanizing

Many business catalogs include a one-page letter printed on the inside front page. The letter provides an ideal opportunity to sell your catalog as a whole or your company as a quality supplier, rather than merely promoting individual items. A letter also adds a personal touch to what may otherwise be a rather impersonal, cold book of facts and figures.

Also, many prospects are bombarded by technical literature and may not remember why they requested your catalog in the first place. A letter quickly orients prospects, helping them understand what the catalog contains and how to benefit from these products.

Another technique to generate reader interest is testimonials, either within the cover letter or on other pages of the catalog. Testimonials are one of the most powerful advertising techniques, yet few catalogs contain them. Testimonials are quotations from satisfied customers saying how good your company, product, or service is.

The best testimonials are not general, but rather they address specific advantages of your products or concerns other buyers may have. Some marketers sprinkle testimonials throughout the catalog, using only one or two per page. Others group them all on one or two pages. I think the latter technique has more power and impact.

Increasing orders with a strong guarantee

In industrial marketing today, a strong guarantee of performance, service, quality, or delivery is critical. People do not want to order unless they know they will get their money back or receive some other compensation if you don't deliver as promised.

Many marketers object to guarantees, saying, "Doesn't adding a guarantee put into the reader's mind the notion that something can go wrong, alerting him to possible negatives he wasn't thinking of?" No, because today's buyers are not naive. They realize full well the possibility of problems and are comforted by the fact that you are prepared to stand behind your catalog and do something to correct mistakes. A guarantee is critical. Use graphic techniques such as a special border treatment or tint to make the guarantee stand out.

Encouraging prospects to keep your catalog

An obvious factor affecting response is whether prospects receiving your catalog keep it or throw it away. If you want your catalog to be kept and referred to often, add valuable how-to information and reference data that will make prospects want to hold on to it.

What to include? Your buyers want to know: How to install insulation. How to check valves for signs of corrosion. How to select the right size mixer. How to monitor air quality. How to set up a company-wide safety program. How to design an office automation system. And so on.

Give them how-to information that is genuinely useful and answers the most pressing technical questions they have, and your catalog will double or triple in perceived value.

Designing the catalog

Today's prospects, especially younger people, are more graphics-oriented than the previous generation. So your catalog should be designed not only to facilitate ordering but also to look good and convey a positive professional image.

Avoid fancy typefaces. Keep type simple and legible. Use readable type for your body copy, in at least a 9-point type size. Use subheads to break up copy and to aid readers who merely scan your copy.

Use a number of small tables rather than fewer, all-inclusive ones. Large tables of numbers intimidate the reader. Avoid technical-looking, highly complicated graphics unless you are sure your readers need and understand them. Use well-prepared photographs and illustrations. They communicate better and give a quality image.

Design your layout in two-page spreads rather than page by page. This is how your reader sees them. Use color functionally to describe how products work, to highlight features, provide organization, or illustrate products that need to be shown in full color for maximum sales effectiveness.

12

Press Releases as a Direct Response Tool

Why conventional press releases don't generate response

More than 99 percent of the press releases issued by PR firms and corporate PR departments fail to generate significant response. There are several reasons for this.

First, most corporate PR departments, and the PR firms serving them, go about creating press releases in the wrong way. Namely, they decide that they should be doing press releases, then look around the company to see what's news and what they can use. Finding nothing, but still having a quota of press releases to issue, they write the allotted number of press releases on the most mundane, non-newsworthy, useless topics imaginable. They mail the press releases to the publications they think management would like to see the company name mentioned in, then complain when editors don't use their material.

What you should do is the *reverse* of what these PR departments and firms are doing. That is, you should look for newsworthy items of interest *first,* and only when you find one should a press release be written and distributed. If there are no newsworthy events or items to be found within the company, you create your own. I'll tell you how shortly. When you do this, you ensure that every press release has strong appeal to both the editors and their readers. This is the only way to get editors to use your material.

The second reason most press releases fail to generate significant response is that they are not designed to. Most PR professionals view their objective as "getting ink." Generally this means getting the company and its products mentioned in as many publications as often as possible. Their belief, which has some truth to it, is that over time this builds an image of credibility and makes the company more visible in the marketplace. But why settle for mere "ink" when you can get leads and sales? This chapter demonstrates the Direct Response Press Release—a unique type of press release designed to generate direct responses as well as plenty of media coverage.

Choosing a topic that excites editors as well as readers

To get publicity in the trade press, you must write press releases that appeal not only to your ultimate prospect—the reader of the business magazine or trade journal—but also to the *editor* of the publication. No matter how much appeal your message has to prospects, they won't respond if they don't see it. They won't see it if the editor doesn't print your story. And editors won't print your story if it doesn't grab their attention.

At this point you might object and say, "Wait a minute. The editor's responsibility is to the *readers*—my prospects—and my product is very important to them. If editors don't run my press release, they're doing readers a disservice." But you are not taking into account the fact that editors receive *many* more press releases than they can use. Therefore, putting together a story that is relevant to your market is only half the battle of getting ink. Getting the editor to publish it is the other half.

Seven themes for press releases

There are seven story themes that have the greatest appeal to editors and business journalists:

1. News

2. Interesting information

3. Useful advice

4. Controversy

5. Celebrity

6. Human interest

7. Timeliness

A press release built around any of these seven themes has a far greater chance of catching an editor's eye and seeing print than a release that does not contain any of these elements. How might you build a news story around some of these themes?

News.

The most interesting word to a trade journal editor is *new*, and you are coming up with new products and services all the time. Every time you produce a new model, new release, new version, or upgrade, send out a release announcing it as a new product.

Interesting information.

Editors and readers are fascinated by facts. For instance, if your firm performs surveys of certain markets or industries, release some of the more interesting findings in one or more press releases. Drake Beam Morin, a consulting firm, does surveys to determine the average number of months it takes for professionals who are terminated to find new jobs; editors come to rely on Drake Beam Morin as *the* source for this important piece of data. As a result, the firm gets a lot of publicity from it.

Useful advice.

How-to information appeals to editors because they know their readers love checklists, resources, free booklets, guidelines, and other how-to-do-it information. If you can tell the readers how to do something to enhance their business operations, editors of the magazines going to these readers will print it and cite you as the source.

Controversy.

Look at the positions gurus, editors, and columnists take on issues important to your industry. If your views are opposite, you can get a lot of press by going public with those views and creating controversy.

Celebrity.

Famous personalities are a bit more difficult to use in business-to-business, but it is not impossible. As Lee Iacocca and Frank Perdue have proven, making a celebrity out of the CEO is possible and can make a company more visible. Perhaps you can use publicity to make your company president a mini-celebrity in your particular industry or market.

Human interest.

Although not used much in business-to-business public relations, human interest stories abound in any company. Can you find something to use here—perhaps an employee with an unusual background or hobby or colorful past?

Timeliness.

Editors like material that fits in with special theme issues, is related to major industry events, or is in some way tied to current news.

As you can see, any of the seven themes can make for an interesting (and therefore effective) press release. I have used most of them for myself and my clients, though I tend to focus on interesting information and useful advice. These are the easiest to do, editors love them, and they generate the greatest reader interest. We'll look at examples later in the chapter.

Creating

More often than not, when you decide it's time to do some public relations, there isn't much going on that would be of real interest to an editor. So when there is no news peg or "hook," you must go out and create the event, the story, the news, or the information.

Here's an example of how this was done for one technology firm using controversy as the news hook. The company made a technology product designed to conform to a certain industry-accepted standard. Their competitors made similar products and also claimed that these products satisfactorily met the standard. In closely examining the competing products as well as the detailed multi-page industry specification, the company marketing director discovered that while his product did indeed meet all the specifications, the competing products did not.

What to do? An editor will not print a press release from one vendor in which he identifies his competitors' products and criticizes them. Instead, the marketing director took the broader view. Using the company president, a well-respected figure in the industry, as spokesman, he issued a press release with a headline something like this:

MOST XYZ SYSTEMS PHONY, CLAIMS JOE BIG, PRESIDENT OF JOE BIG TECHNOLOGY

Says almost all systems fail to conform to ABC Committee Standards for XYZ products.

If you wrote a press release that just said your product was better than your competitors' products, I doubt any editor would run it. This headline positions the story not as a product comparison but as an "industry alert"—a warning to buyers to check their XYZ systems for conformance to approved standards. In this way, the company positions itself as the leader. (Its product, of course, does conform to the standard, and this is mentioned in the body of the release.)

Writing a "free booklet" press release

The easiest and most effective type of Direct Response Press Release is the free booklet release. This release is based on the offer of a free booklet, report, or other information. The booklet or report can be the same bait piece you're offering in ads and mailings. Or if you don't currently have such a piece, you can create it specifically for PR purposes.

The free booklet release has strong appeal not only to your prospects, who want valuable information, but also to editors, for the following two reasons. First, the contents of the booklet can be edited and published as an article in their magazine. Second, editors like to run short blurbs offering their readers free things like booklets, audiotapes, checklists, samples, and so on. They view it as a service to the reader and are glad to have your free item to offer as a giveaway. Here are the elements necessary for a successful free booklet press release:

1. A headline that grabs attention by targeting an important issue or area of concern. The headline should also communicate that you have a new booklet and are offering it free.

2. A lead that can stand on its own as a short article. Some editors will print your lead only, without excerpts from the actual contents of the booklet, then give the address where readers can send for your material. The lead should be written like a short feature article on the topic addressed by the booklet.

3. A body that gives a sampling of the useful information contained in the free booklet. This can be taken as is or edited from the booklet. Bullets can be used to separate the points. Do not use numbers as you might in a booklet, because editors might want to change the

order or omit some items. This section should be long enough so the editor can reprint all or part of it as a short article on the topic.

4. A close that tells readers how they can get your booklet. Invite the reader to request the booklet by calling or writing. You might want to put a "key" in your address (e.g., "Dept. P-1"), so when an inquiry addressed to that key comes in, you know it is from press release 1.

Figure 12–1 is a sample three-page press release I used to promote a booklet called "Recession-Proof Business Strategies." It fits the above criteria in almost every respect except that I charged $7 for my booklet.

This press release was sent to several hundred publications, including business magazines, syndicated business columnists, and business editors at large daily newspapers during the height of the recession of the early 1990s.

I chose to send each editor a copy of the booklet along with the press release because I felt it was impressive and would catch the editor's attention. However, it is not necessary to include your booklet to get the editor to use such a release, and, because it's expensive to mail booklets with press releases, I normally don't do it.

This press release was picked up in dozens of publications. Some ran very short blurbs, others ran it almost word for word. The release generated sales of more than 3,000 booklets at $7 each.

Figure 12–1   Sample Press Release

FROM: Bob Bly, 174 Holland Avenue, New Milford, NJ 07646
CONTACT: Bob Bly (201) 385-1220

For immediate release

NEW BOOKLET REVEALS 14 PROVEN STRATEGIES
FOR KEEPING BUSINESSES BOOMING IN A BUST ECONOMY

New Milford, NJ—While some companies struggle to survive in today's sluggish business environment, many are doing better than ever—largely because they have mastered the proven but little-known strategies of "recession marketing."

That's the opinion of Bob Bly, an independent marketing consultant and author of the just-published booklet, "Recession-Proof Business Strategies: 14 Winning Methods to Sell Any Product or Service in a Down Economy."

"Many businesspeople fear a recession or soft economy, because when the economy is weak, their clients and customers cut back on spending," says Bly. "To survive in such a marketplace, you need to develop recession-marketing strategies that help you retain your current accounts and keep those customers buying. You also need to master marketing techniques that will win you *new* clients or customers to replace any business you may have lost because of the increased competition that is typical of a recession."

Among the recession-fighting business strategies Bly outlines in his new booklet:

- Reactivate dormant accounts. An easy way to get more business is to simply call past clients or customers—people you served at one time but are not actively working for now—to remind them of your existence. According to Bly, a properly scripted telephone call to a list of past buyers will generate approximately one order for every ten calls.

- Quote reasonable, affordable fees and prices in competitive bid situations. While you need not reduce your rates or prices, in competitive bid situations you will win by bidding toward the low end or middle of your price range rather than at the high end. Bly says that during a recession, your bids should be 15 to 20 percent lower than you would normally charge in a healthy economy.

- Give your existing clients and customers a superior level of service. In a recession, Bly advises businesses to do everything they can to hold onto their existing clients or customers—their "bread-and-butter" accounts. "The best way to hold onto your clients or customers is to please them," says Bly, "and the best way to please them is through better customer service. Now is an ideal time to provide that little bit of extra service or courtesy that can mean the difference between dazzling the client or customer and merely satisfying them."

- <u>Reactivate old leads.</u> Most businesses give up on sales leads too early, says Bly. He cites a study from Thomas Publishing which found that although 80 percent of sales to businesses are made on the fifth call, only one out of ten salespeople calls beyond three times. Concludes Bly: "You have probably not followed up on leads diligently enough, and the new business you need may already be right in your prospect files." He says repeated follow-up should convert 10 percent of prospects to buyers.

To receive a copy of Bly's booklet, "Recession-Proof Business Strategies," send $8 ($7 plus $1 shipping and handling) to: Bob Bly, Dept. 109, 174 Holland Avenue, New Milford, NJ 07646. Cash, money orders, and checks (payable to "Bob Bly") accepted. (Add $1 for Canadian orders.)

Bob Bly, an independent copywriter and consultant based in New Milford, NJ, specializes in business-to-business, hi-tech, and direct response marketing. He is the author of 18 books, including <u>How To Promote Your Own Business</u> (New American Library) and <u>The Copywriter's Handbook</u> (Henry Holt). A frequent speaker and seminar leader, Mr. Bly speaks nationwide on the topic of how to market successfully in a recession or soft economy.

The release in Figure 12–2 was done to generate inquiries for my consulting and copywriting services and to promote my name as an expert in the specific field of software marketing. It was sent to about a hundred publications, some general advertising and marketing journals, some magazines specifically about marketing computers and software. The release was picked up by half-a-dozen publications and generated more than 150 requests for the tip sheet. The tip sheet was nothing more than a reprint of a two-page article I had written on how to market software.

Figure 12–2 Sample Tip Sheet Press Release

FROM: Bob Bly, 174 Holland Avenue, New Milford, NJ 07646
CONTACT: Bob Bly (201) 385-1220

For immediate release

NEW TIP SHEET SHOWS ESTABLISHED AND START-UP
SOFTWARE PRODUCERS
HOW TO MARKET AND PROMOTE THEIR
PRODUCTS EFFECTIVELY

New Milford, NJ—With the glut of software products flooding the marketplace, it's essential to produce mailings, brochures, ads, and other printed materials that quickly, clearly, and dramatically communicate the key functions and benefits of your software to potential buyers.

That's the opinion of Robert W. Bly, a New Milford, NJ–based consultant specializing in software marketing and promotion. He is also the author of a new tip sheet, "How to Sell Software," which presents advice on how both established and start-up software producers can effectively advertise, promote, and market software for PCs, mainframes, and minicomputers.

One of the most difficult marketing decisions facing software sellers, says Bly, is whether to use a one-step or two-step marketing approach—that is, whether to sell the product via mail order directly from the ad or direct mail piece, or instead to generate a sales lead to be followed up by mailing a brochure or sending a salesperson for a face-to-face meeting.

"PC software products in the $59 to $299 price range are good candidates for one-step mail-order selling," advises Bly. "In the $399 to $899 price range, you may want to test a one-step against a two-step approach and see which works best." And at $1,000 and up, says Bly, the two-step lead-generating method is best. "Few people will send payment for a $1,999 software package without some extra convincing by a salesperson, free trial, or demo diskette," he notes.

Some additional software marketing tips from the fact sheet:

- Early in your ad copy, tell the prospective purchaser what type or category of software you are selling. "People are usually in the market for a product to handle one of the known, identifiable, major applications—project management, word processing, accounts payable," says Bly.

- Talk in terms the reader can visualize. Instead of writing "2,400 bps modem," say "The SuperSpeedy modem transmits data at a rate of 2,400 bits per second—about seven seconds for a full page of text."

- The headline or teaser copy should select the right audience for the ad or mailer. For example, if you are selling C compilers, the teaser copy might read, "Attention C programmers."

One of Bly's all-time favorite headlines is from a small black-and-white display ad for Winterhalter Incorporated, a manufacturer of coax boards and controllers that enable micro-to-mainframe communication. The headline reads, "LINK 8 PCs TO YOUR MAINFRAME— ONLY $2,395." Says Bly, "Computer magazines are filled with 'clever' ad headlines that give the reader no idea whatsoever what the product is or who it is for. This headline tells you *exactly* what the product will do for you and what it will cost."

For a copy of Bly's software marketing tip sheet, "How to Sell Software," send $1 and a self-addressed stamped #10 envelope to: Bob Bly, Dept. 105, 174 Holland Avenue, New Milford, NJ 07646.

You will note that this press release calls for the reader to send a self-addressed stamped envelope. If your goal is to get the maximum number of people to request your booklet, make it free; do not charge a dollar to cover costs or require a self-addressed stamped envelope. Just ask them to call, fax, or write; you send the booklet free and provide the envelope and postage. The reason I asked for a return envelope is that I have only one assistant. Having the reader provide an envelope for us saved time in fulfilling the requests.

Another advantage of using these press releases is that you can add hundreds of names to your prospect database at low cost. Not everyone who requests the booklet is a possible customer or client, but many are. As consultant Ken Morris pointed out in Chapter 9, repeat promotions to an inquiry database will yield better results than promoting to rented mailing lists. Press releases, along with postcard decks, are the lowest cost means of generating such leads and building such an inquiry database.

Preparing your press release for distribution

The press release should be cleanly typed, with no typos or white-outs. Type it double-spaced, on plain white paper. Some PR agencies send out releases single-spaced, but I think this is a mistake. Single-spaced material is more difficult to edit, which may discourage an editor from using the release as the basis of a story.

You should type it so the last paragraph on the page ends on that page; do not break and "jump" paragraphs to the next page. Many editors will rewrite your press release and like to be able to cut it apart with scissors, rearrange the paragraphs, and tape it together to change the order of your material. You should print on one side of the page only, never on both sides, for the same reason.

There is no need to use a special PR letterhead or to type the release on your company letterhead, although if you want to do so, it does no harm. I type my releases on plain white paper, with information on where the editor can contact me or my client at the top of page one (see the sample press releases in this chapter for style). Under this contact information comes the headline, typed in all caps and taking one, two, or three lines.

Some argue that it is not necessary to have a headline on a press release, because editors will not use it and will make up their own headline to fit the page layout. While it is true that editors almost never use the headline you put on your press release, you should still write one, because that headline is what grabs the editor's attention. A strong headline can make the difference between an editor's reading your material or throwing it away. So always come up with a powerful headline that contains an item of interest or strong news hook.

For example, one company did a press release to promote an IBM PC software program that did resumes, cover letters, and other tasks related to finding a job. The headline of the press release, LET YOUR PC FIND A

JOB FOR YOU, attracted editors, although it probably wasn't used when the stories appeared. The headline arouses curiosity—how can a computer find a job for you?—and gets you to read on. After the headline, leave some space, then begin your story. Again, see the samples in this chapter for format. The pages should be stapled in the upper right corner.

Mail the press release in a plain #10 business envelope, first class. Some PR counselors advise including a cover letter with the press release, but this is unnecessary and will not increase coverage. Also, if you feel the need to explain your press release in a cover letter, you probably haven't written your release clearly enough. The press release *is* the story and should stand on its own without explanation.

Finding business magazines for press releases

There are many lists, directories, and services for distribution of press releases. Some companies publish directories of newspaper and magazine editors, and you can type your envelopes using the information in the directory. Some companies provide the names on mailing labels. This doesn't give you telephone numbers for follow-up. However, if you send out the free booklet release as shown in this chapter, you won't need to follow up; your press release will receive wide coverage. One advantage of labels over directories is that labels are more current (editors move around a lot). Some companies handle the distribution of the press release for you. You send them one clean typed copy of the release. They print, staple, fold, stuff, and mail the releases to the publications you specify.

Some companies offer two or three of these services. One of the biggest and best known of these companies is Bacon's. They sell PR directories of newspapers, magazines, and TV and radio shows, and they will also provide labels or do the distribution for you. I use them frequently and am satisfied with their service. For more information, contact Bacon's PR Service, 332 S. Michigan Avenue, Chicago, IL 60604, (800) 621-0561.

13

Feature Articles and Resource Boxes

Free advertising from feature articles

The problem with advertising and direct mail is that they are expensive. The cost of direct mail especially has skyrocketed in recent years. And print advertising has always been expensive, often prohibitively so for the small-to medium-sized marketer. The alternatives are to use such low-cost advertising vehicles as postcard decks and inquiry-generating press releases. Another alternative is the *planted feature story*.

The planted feature story is an article written by your company or about your company, the publication of which was initiated and pursued by you as a means of gaining visibility, promoting your product, and attracting new customers. This is a common practice in the business world, and many companies are already using such planted feature stories as marketing vehicles. This chapter will explain not only how to write and place such stories, but also how to maximize their use in your direct response program as a bait piece and an inquiry-generating device.

Selecting a topic

The first step in marketing your product or service directly through planted feature stories is to determine what topic or topics should be the focus of the articles. To be successful, the article must be written on a topic that: (1) is of interest to your potential customers, (2) fills a gap in the reader's knowledge (tells them something they want or need to know), and (3) is related to your product or service in such a way that publication of the article helps promote your product or service.

Feature articles can have titles and contents similar to the free booklets, special reports, and other bait pieces we talked about in Chapter 5. Examples include:

"Specifying motionless mixers in process applications"
"How to improve your collection efforts"
"3 steps to creating a winning business plan"
"How to run a successful employee awards program"
"7 questions to ask before you invest in a DP training program"
"Choosing business software for accounts payable and accounts receivable"

When you pick a topic of interest to your potential customers, organize it as a series of points, steps, or ideas, and then give it an attractive title similar to the examples above, you convert your article from "just an article" to a powerful direct-response bait piece that can be offered in ads, direct mail, press releases, postcards, and other promotions to attract prospects like a magnet.

When offering an article reprint as a bait piece, refer to it as a "tip sheet," not an "article reprint." "Tip sheet" sounds more important and has higher perceived value. Or you can reset the text of the article and print it as a booklet. You can then offer it as a "free booklet" rather than an "article reprint." Again, "free booklet" is a stronger offer than "free article reprint." Another variation is to take one or more articles, create a title page, and put them in a binder or report cover. This allows you to offer your article reprints as a "special report."

By offering your article as a free tip sheet, booklet, or special report, you can use it to increase response to direct mail, ads, and press releases featuring the article as a bait piece.

Here's a real-life example. Years ago I wrote a half-page article presenting 31 quick tips on how to increase ad response. It was published in *Business Marketing* as a sidebar to another, longer article on print advertising. Bob Donath, then editor of *Business Marketing*, gave it the catchy title "31-derfully simple ways to get more inquiries from your ads." I reprinted the article as a four-panel booklet designed to fit a #10 envelope. The inside two panels contained the article, reprinted directly from the original magazine—I didn't even reset the type. The Bob Donath title and my byline were on the front cover. The back cover had my photo and an "About the Author" bio promoting my copywriting and marketing consultation services. My address and phone number were on both the front and back covers.

I sent out a press release to 50 advertising trade publications and another 50 or so general business magazines. This was a free booklet release similar to the ones shown in Chapter 12. The result was 18 published articles and more than 2,500 requests for the booklet. One article in *Nation's Business* alone generated more than 400 responses.

To use reprints of your article as a bait piece to increase responses to lead-generating promotions, give your article an attractive title promising useful information and advice. However, one difference between the article and the self-published booklet or report is that the article cannot be promotional in any sense. It should not mention your company more than once or twice, and the information should be useful to the readers even if they do not buy your product. For example, an article on how to maintain process equipment should give maintenance tips that apply to many different valves and pumps, not just yours.

How, then, does such an article promote your product or service? *Subtly.* Each company selling a product or service is promoting a particular way to do something: control fluid flow in a pipeline, train technicians to safely operate nuclear power plants, access the corporate database, mold plastic, or whatever. When you write the article, you highlight *your* methodology or technology. If you're selling an application development tool, you might write an article on how to design database applications. Of course, the steps in the article just happen to conform to how your application development tool works. The person who reads your article and likes your advice is now pre-sold on the way your product or service works and is eager to get more help from you in the form of advice, service, products, systems, or some combination of these.

Advertising expert Bruce Bloom says this is "creating a specification." Your prospect reads your article and follows your advice on how to select, implement, or use a particular type of product or service. He or she naturally comes to you predisposed to buy from you, because you are the expert. And when the prospect evaluates your product, lo and behold—it perfectly meets the criteria set forth in your article. Competitive products do not meet all the criteria, so yours is selected.

To promote a line of business software, IBM published an entire book (really a big article) called *Choosing Business Software*. The book set forth guidelines for shopping for and selecting accounting and other business software applications. Naturally, the features and functions the book said were essential in business software were features and functions you could find in the IBM programs. The book created a specification for the reader which only IBM's product could fulfill. Feature articles work much the same way. *Choosing Business Software* could easily have been an article or series of articles.

Writing the article

When writing a feature article for placement, I intend from the start to use the article as a reprint, so I am concerned with length. What length is best? The standard business magazine or trade journal page (7 by 10 inches), set in two or three columns of type, carries about 800 to 900 words per page. That's on a page with mostly text, not a lot of graphics. So a one-page article would be 750 to 800 words, or about three double-spaced typewritten pages. A two-page article would be 1,500 words, or about six double-spaced typewritten pages.

Keep these lengths in mind as you write if you want an article that is easy and inexpensive to reprint. Most articles that appear as one or two pages in a magazine are published without carrying over to other pages, so the entire article can be reproduced without cutting and pasting, and it fits neatly on one or two sides of a sheet of 8-1/2-by-11-inch paper. You can make reprints on a good quality photocopier or take the article to a print shop for small quantities of inexpensive offset reprints.

So one reason to keep articles short is ease of reprinting. An article that runs three, four, or five pages in the magazine will have to be printed on an 11-by-17-inch or 11-by-25-inch sheet of paper and folded, and that gets more expensive. An article that runs seven or eight pages must be printed as a saddle-stitched eight-page booklet or brochure, and that costs even more. Another reason to keep articles short is that readers prefer short articles. If you can communicate the salient points in one or two tightly written pages instead of five, so much the better. Does this mean you should never write a long article? No. Some topics might require more explanation. Or perhaps you need photos and illustrations to explain your story, and this adds to the length.

When writing, try to break your material into short sections with many subheads, and use bullets and numbers to separate your key points. There are two reasons why numbering points is especially useful. First, it makes for easy reading. And second, people are attracted to articles with numbers in the title (e.g., "8 ways salespeople can spend less time traveling, more time at home").

As long as you fulfill the promise of the article title, don't worry that the story is too simple or basic. It may be old hat to you, but many potential customers do not have this information and can put it to good use. I have written short, basic how-to articles as well as longer, more complex ones, and I always get the greatest response from the short ones.

Do not be afraid that the reader knows it all and you have nothing new to contribute. People read for reinforcement as well as new knowledge. You can impress them not only by telling them something new, but also by confirming what they already know. If you make statements about the best way to perform a certain task, and the reader already knows and agrees with your points, he or she will think you are wise and will be more inclined to buy services or products from your company.

When the article is written, go through it several times to ensure accuracy, and have several people proofread it. Some editors are put off by a sloppy manuscript, and almost all editors at technical magazines are concerned about accuracy. Numbers and figures especially should be checked and rechecked.

Placing the article

Now that you have a topic and have started researching and outlining the article, you should think about where it should be published. Finding suitable publications for your article may not be as difficult as you think. Start with the trade or business publications you already read. Chances are that one or more of these covers your market and would be a suitable outlet for your article. Next, see what your customers are reading. Magazines and newsletters you find on the prospect's desk or in their reception area are ones they subscribe to and read, so you can try to place your article there. Third, check some directories. The one I use most often is *Bacon's Magazine Directory*.

Some editors offer guidelines for potential authors, and it's a good idea to look these over to make sure your story fits these guidelines before you submit it. Some magazines publish these guidelines in each issue; others offer them free if you request them. But the best way to evaluate whether your story fits in with the publication is to look through an issue of the magazine. Take a look at the types of articles published. If the magazine does not run case histories, and your article is a case history, chances are they will not publish it; you'd be better off going to a magazine that runs case histories.

Also check to see if the magazine runs stories contributed by vendors; some magazines do not. If all of the bylines are from the magazine's staff and professional freelance journalists and reporters, your contribution will probably not be welcome. Fortunately, you'll find many trade and business publications that run articles contributed by vendors, and these publications will be more interested in getting a manuscript from you.

.   How do you get free sample copies of magazines? If your company is a potential advertiser, just call the advertising department. Request that a free sample copy be sent along with a media kit. Say you are thinking of advertising in their magazine. Do *not* tell the display advertising manager or sales rep you are planning to write an article, or they will be less inclined to send the material to you.

Querying

To "query" means to contact the publication's editor to ask whether there is any interest in your article. Ideally, this is done before you have written the article. That way, if an editor shows interest but wants the article done a certain way, you haven't wasted time creating an article that will have to be rewritten.

While some editors are open to phone calls, the best way to query is with a query letter. This is a letter that outlines the article you want to write and asks the editor if he or she would be interested in reviewing a full manuscript for possible publication.

How to write a good query letter? The first step is to address it to a specific editor by name and title and make sure the name is spelled correctly. Send your letter to the managing editor; *Bacon's* gives the name of the managing editor for most of the magazines it lists. Before you mail your letter, you might call the magazine to verify the name; editors move around a lot, so PR directories get dated quickly.

Ideally, the lead of the letter is written like the lead to your article. This not only attracts the editor to your topic, but it also helps the editor see how the article will begin. In the rest of the letter you tell what the topic is, give a suggested title, describe the contents of the article, and then give your qualifications to write it. Close by asking the editor if he or she would like to see a completed manuscript.

Most query letters are one page long. If the outline for your article is complex or lengthy, you can go to a second page or attach a separate sheet containing the full outline, making reference to the attached outline in your cover letter. Always enclose a self-addressed, stamped #10 envelope with your query letter; many editors are flooded with unsolicited query letters, proposals, and manuscripts and will not return your material or reply if you do not supply your own return envelope with postage.

Figure 13-1 is a sample query containing a one-page letter and an attached one-page outline. The editor responded favorably, and the article was published.

Figure 13-1 Sample Query Letter

Mr. Kenneth J. McNaughton
Associate Editor
CHEMICAL ENGINEERING
McGraw-Hill Building
1221 Avenue of the Americas
New York, NY 10020

Dear Mr. McNaughton:

When a chemical engineer can't write a coherent report, the true value of his investigation or study may be distorted or unrecognized. His productivity vanishes. And his chances for career advancement diminish.

As an associate editor of CHEMICAL ENGINEERING, you know that many chemical engineers could use some help in improving their technical writing skills. I'd like to provide that help by writing an article that gives your readers "Ten Tips for Better Technical Writing."

An outline of the article is attached. This 1,500-word piece would provide 10 helpful tips—each less than 200 words—to help chemical engineers write better letters, reports, proposals, and articles.

Tip number 3, for example, instructs writers to be more concise. Too many engineers would write about an "accumulation of particulate matter about the peripheral interior surface of the vessel" when they're describing solids build-up. And how many managers would use the phrase "until such time as" when they simply mean "until"?

I am the author of a book on technical writing, The Elements of Technical Writing, published by Macmillan. While the book speaks to a wide range of technical disciplines, my article will draw its examples from the chemical engineering literature.

I hold a B.S. in chemical engineering from the University of Rochester and am a member of the American Institute of Chemical Engineers. I was formerly manager of communications for Koch Engineering, a manufacturer of chemical process equipment. Now I'm an independent copywriter handling several industrial accounts.

Ken, I'd like to write "Ten Tips for Better Technical Writing" for your "You and Your Job" section.

How does this sound?

Sincerely,

Bob Bly

Article outline

TEN TIPS FOR BETTER TECHNICAL WRITING
by Robert W. Bly

1. *Know your readers.*
Are you writing for engineers? managers? laypeople?

2. *Write in a clear, conversational style.*
Write to express—not to impress.

3. *Be concise.*
Avoid wordiness. Omit words that do not add to your meaning.

4. *Be consistent . . .*
. . . especially in the use of numbers, symbols, and abbreviations.

5. *Use jargon sparingly.*
Use technical terms only when there are no simpler words that can better communicate your thoughts.

6. *Avoid big words.*
Do not write "utilize" when "use" will do just as well.

7. *Prefer the specific to the general.*
Technical readers are interested in solid technical information, not in generalities. Be specific.

8. *Break the writing up into short sections.*
Short sections, paragraphs, and sentences are easier to read than long ones.

9. *Use visuals.*
Graphs, tables, photos, and drawings can help get your message across.

10. *Use the active voice.*
Write "John performed the experiment," not "The experiment was performed by John." The active voice adds vigor to writing.

Give the editor at least 4 to 6 weeks to respond to your query. If you hear nothing, send a follow-up letter or call to make sure the editor received it. If the editor likes your proposal, he or she will ask to see the completed article. You then write and submit the manuscript, following any guidelines, instructions, or direction provided by the editor. Assuming the article delivers on the promise of the query letter, is well written, informative rather than promotional, and accurate, chances are it will be published.

However, please be aware that there is no guarantee of publication, and editors asking for the full manuscript are merely expressing interest, not making any firm commitment or promise to you. You may spend countless hours writing and polishing your article, only to have it rejected for any reason or no reason. Perhaps the magazine has changed focus, or the editor has left and the new editor isn't interested in the topic. If this should happen, you can send out your query letter again and try to place the article with another publication, perhaps one similar to the original.

When you query, always send your query letter and outline along with a self-addressed stamped reply envelope. Do not send the full article, even if you have already written it. Send the query first. Editors want to see queries, outlines, and proposals, because these take less time to read and review than full-length article manuscripts. Unsolicited manuscripts are rarely given serious consideration for publication.

Never tell the editor in your query letter that you advertise or are thinking of advertising in the magazine. Although some magazines openly run articles and press releases to help promote their advertisers, many editors frown on this practice and consider it a breach of ethics. Saying you are an advertiser or potential advertiser is likely to offend the editor and gain your proposal a speedy rejection.

Resource boxes

The author's bio, as it usually appears with the article, is not of much use to you in a marketing sense. Such a bio typically reads, "Jack Johnson is a senior consultant with Acme Consultants, a management consulting firm." Why is this ineffective? First, it doesn't really explain what you can do for the reader. And second, it doesn't give the reader a clue about how to contact you for more information. That's why I recommend you run articles, whenever editors will allow, with a Resource Box instead of an author's bio.

The Resource Box (a term coined by Jeffrey Lant, a Cambridge, MA–based marketing consultant) is an expanded bio that helps turn your article from an ordinary trade journal feature into a powerful direct response ad for your product or service. The Resource Box tells the reader what your company does and what services or products it offers. Most important, it provides an address and phone number to facilitate direct contact between reader (prospect) and author (vendor). In addition, if space allows, it may also make a specific offer.

Here is a sample Resource Box:

> **Jack Johnson is a senior consultant with Acme Consultants, a management consulting firm that helps companies of all sizes increase productivity by improving the way employees work together as a team. For more information and a free special report on "The Teamwork Breakthrough," contact Jack Johnson, Acme Consultants, 100 Elm Street, Anytown, USA, phone (XXX) XXX-XXXX.**

The Resource Box is a "mini-ad" for your product or service, and when linked to your article, it's tremendously effective. The article positions you as an expert and gets the prospect interested in you, and the Resource Box tells the prospect precisely what you offer and how to get in touch with you to find out more. By adding a Resource Box, you can create articles that not only generate visibility but also produce direct sales leads. And from long experience, I can tell you this: Such an inquiry is *extremely* valuable. The person who contacts you as a result of reading an article you wrote is much more likely to become a customer than someone whom you contacted cold.

How do you get Resource Boxes published with your articles? When you query, don't bring up the issue of whether the editor will include a Resource Box with your article. Instead, when you submit the completed article, type a Resource Box at the end of your manuscript (titled "About the Author"; do not use the term Resource Box). Will all editors use it? No. Some magazines and newsletters are happy to run Resource Boxes and do it all the time. Others have a firm policy against it. Most have never given it much consideration either way.

When you supply a Resource Box at the end of your manuscript, you will find that many editors who would not have otherwise "promoted" you will automatically run the Resource Box pretty much as you have written it. This whole idea of Resource Boxes may seem mundane or even petty to you, but I assure you it's not. Getting feature articles published is fine, but by itself it has limited value in terms of generating immediate short-term business.

But when you add a Resource Box, that changes. Now your article becomes a direct response vehicle. People read your article, see your Resource Box, learn what you do, get in touch with you, and request more information. A certain percentage of those leads will translate directly into business—something that rarely happens when you place the standard article without the Resource Box.

Perhaps the greatest value of the Resource Box is that it supplies contact information—your address and phone number—at the time the prospect is most interested in talking with you (when they finish reading your article). Many people who read articles that don't contain Resource Boxes would like to contact the authors to buy their product or service, but they are too busy to spend time tracking them down. The Resource Box makes it easy to respond, and in direct response, that's the name of the game.

What if the editor refuses to run a Resource Box? One solution is to take an ad in the issue where your article will be published. Run the ad on a page where someone reading your article is most likely to see it; a good position is the page immediately following your article. Since the magazine is already publishing a lengthy article by you, you don't need a full-page ad; a small ad is all that's required to supply complete contact information.

If you don't want to run an ad, and the editor will not run a Resource Box, at least try to get *some* contact information in your author's bio, for example, "Steve Brown is a freelance graphic artist based in New York City." Although the editor won't let you include an address, you can often get at least the city in your bio without objection. The prospect can then locate you through the Yellow Pages or information operator.

One other point: If your article does not run with a Resource Box, add one when you reprint. Reprints get separated from other materials, and, as a rule, *every* marketing document you print should have complete contact information on it: company name, address, and phone number.

14

How to Generate Direct Response from Speeches, Presentations, and Seminars

A wasted promotional opportunity

Recently, the public relations director of a large manufacturer of data communications equipment asked me to prepare abstracts of papers to be presented by company engineers and managers at a major data communications convention. The convention manager in charge of presentations would select which companies and individuals would present papers based on these abstracts.

Fortunately for me, almost all of my client's abstracts were accepted. However, the whole effort was largely a waste for her and her company. Why?

1. The company did not invite its best customers and prospects to any of the presentations. So attendance was lower than hoped for.

2. The company did not capture the names and addresses of those who did come to hear the papers, so they were unable to do follow-up marketing to this group of people who had shown interest in the company's technology by attending.

3. The company did not distribute reprints of any of the papers to its customers or prospects, or use them as bait pieces in advertising or direct mail.

4. The company did not professionally record any of the presentations for possible use as promotional videos or audio cassettes.

5. The engineers made their presentations just at the one show; the company made no effort to recycle the material for use in other presentations, nor did it try to rework the material and get it published as feature articles.

This is not unusual behavior. Marketing communications managers at many companies pay little attention to the presentations, papers, and speeches given by their executives, managers, and technical professionals (except for those made by the CEO and other top-level executives), yet these presentations can be among the most powerful forms of direct-response marketing communications if they are worked properly.

This chapter explains what to do before, during, and after a speech, presentation, or other event to maximize its effectiveness. It also briefly discusses how to generate opportunities for speaking as a promotion if you are not already being invited to give such presentations.

The promotional speaking circuit

The world of public speaking falls into two categories: professional and promotional. Professional speakers give motivational or informational talks and seminars for a living, and are paid $2,000 or more for a one-hour keynote address or after-dinner speech. We are interested in the other category: promotional speaking. This involves going to a group and giving a talk or lecture for free. Why would someone speak for free when others are paid? You speak for free to promote your product, service, or company before a group of potential customers.

Chances are people in your company are already being asked to give such presentations. Let them know you are interested in helping them increase attendance, put together their talk, and give it wider distribution beyond the specific event it is being created for. They will appreciate your assistance, and you will gain a valuable marketing tool.

If your company is not being invited to speak, send letters to people who run local meetings, trade shows, national conventions, symposia, and similar events offering your people as presenters, along with suggested topics that you know would fit in well with their program.

Finding opportunities for presentations

Where is the best place to speak? If your business is local, regional meetings of clubs, groups, and professional societies whose members are potential customers are your best bet. Such groups usually have a speaker at their monthly dinner meeting and are always looking for speakers to fill slots.

If your business is national, you should target major industry events that feature vendors as speakers. In conjunction with the exhibit hall, most major trade shows have educational sessions, and these are ideal opportunities for presenting a paper on a topic related to your product or service. Big annual conferences sponsored by such groups as Executive Enterprises and the Institute of Management Accountants are another opportunity to address an audience of potential customers in a short format.

Turning the soft sell into a marketing tool

How do you turn this traditionally soft-sell activity of public speaking into a marketing tool without blatantly promoting your firm? There are basically four marketing opportunities surrounding each presentation. These occur:

1. Before the talk

2. During the talk

3. Immediately after the talk

4. In the days and weeks following the talk

Let's take a look at each and see how we can increase the marketing effectiveness of these programs.

Before the talk.

I remember a client who once spent more than $20,000 to develop an elaborate, 90-minute presentation for a major industry trade show. It was exciting, informative, and supported by a sophisticated multi-projector slide show. Just one problem: When he gave his $20,000 talk, there were only seven or eight people in the room to hear it!

Had this speaker's company done a selective mailing to his database of customers and prospects living within a 100-mile radius of the location of the trade show? No. If they had, there would have been more people in the audience, and he would be putting his company's message in front of a group already shown to have an interest in the product.

If you want to reach the maximum number of customers and prospects with your talk, mail invitations to your house list, selecting those who live within a two-hour drive or so of the site. The invitation should tell the location, speaker, time, date, and a little bit about the program and speaker. Be sure to add a closing paragraph that encourages people to call for more information or to register. If the speech is held in conjunction with a trade show or exposition, enclose a free pass to the event with your invitation.

During the seminar.

The goal here is twofold. First, you must deliver a good presentation so that the audience is impressed and not disappointed. If they don't like the presentation, they won't be inclined to learn more about your company and its products or services. If they're impressed with the talk, a certain percentage of the audience will seek the presenter out for private con-versation regarding what you do and how it might meet their needs.

As with the feature articles discussed in the previous chapter, the seminar or speech must be purely information, with no promotion. Sometimes vendors are so aggressive about promoting themselves that many seminar sponsors and trade show managers send notices to speakers stressing that they are not allowed to promote themselves or their company from the platform.

If you're tempted to do some selling during your talk, resist the temptation. The best salesperson for your product or service is an informative, useful talk. There is no need to do any selling at all in your speech. As you will soon see, the selling—and it's a soft sell rather than a hard sell—will take place following the presentation.

In addition to delivering a good presentation, your second goal should be to connect with as many potential customers as possible. Although not all attending your session will buy from you, a percentage will. While this percentage is usually small, just one or two sales or new accounts can make such an activity extremely worthwhile.

You can get many more leads and sales, however, with *follow-up* promotion to the people who came to the speech or lecture. The trick is to get their names, addresses, and phone numbers so you can do this follow-up marketing. But how? If you've sent out invitations and gotten RSVPs, then you already have many of the names and addresses. However, you get many walk-ins who have not registered in advance, especially at seminar sessions held in conjunction with trade shows or conventions. You want to get those names for your database as well.

Start by asking the sponsoring organization if they are keeping a list of those who attend; perhaps names are taken at the door. Ask if you can have the list so you can follow up with the attendees. Most convention and event managers won't object and will give you such a list if they keep it. The problem is, most keep a list of everyone who attended the convention but not a separate list of those who came to your session.

There are several ways to get attendees to give you their name and address for follow-up. The easiest and most successful is to hand out an evaluation form at the beginning of the talk, then stop five minutes early and ask them to complete and return the form to you. Leave a space for their name, company, address, and phone number. If you give a decent presentation and the evaluations are favorable, most attendees won't mind putting their name on the form. However, many people will not put their name on a negative evaluation.

A second way to get names and addresses is to collect business cards. Normally, only a small percentage of the audience will come up to the podium after the talk and give you a card. But you can get almost everyone in the room to give you their business card if you offer a valuable bait piece or premium related to your talk.

Tom Winninger, a professional speaker in the areas of sales and marketing, says that when he addressed a group of meeting planners and spoke on how they could put on better meetings, he closed by saying, "We have a booklet called '101 Ideas for Meeting Planners.' If you'd like a free copy, just give me your business card." Almost all of the meeting planners in the room gave Tom their card. Compare this with the typical two or three cards most speakers get after their talks.

It's also beneficial to make sure everyone in the room walks away with *your* name and phone number, so they can contact you once they return to their office. How to do this? You don't want to walk around the room pushing your business card at people. A better method is to create some simple hand-out or reprint for them to keep, and to put your contact information in a Resource Box on that material.

You can hand out the printed text of your talk or, if you use slides or overhead transparencies, copies of your visuals. Reprints of articles related to your topic also make a good hand-out. Do not put out sales brochures, as this sends the wrong message to the audience. Most people will take hand-outs if you leave them on chairs or at the registration desk. But this causes a problem: If they have your written material before you start talking, they'll read the material and ignore the speaker. It's best to make reprints available immediately after the presentation, or to offer to mail the material to anyone who gives you their business card.

In addition to getting people to take your hand-out, would you love it if they crowded around the speaker at the podium after the talk? To accomplish this, I use something I call the "green sheet" method. I bring a one- or two-page handout photocopied or printed on a single sheet of green paper (you can use any color other than white or off-white). The reprint contains material that relates to my talk but is too lengthy or complex to include in my presentation. It might be a list of recommended reading, a technical example of how to solve a problem, or elaboration on one of the points made in the talk.

Somewhere in the middle of the talk, I hold up a green sheet and say something like, "I don't have time to go into all the ways to do XYZ, so I've reprinted 16 techniques for doing XYZ on this green sheet. If you'd like a copy, I have them up here, so come to me at the end of the program and ask for a copy of the green sheet."

Virtually everybody will want to get the reprint; calling it a "green sheet" somehow adds an element of mystery that arouses curiosity. This technique is best used at programs where the close of your talk ends the session, and the room will be free before the next speaker arrives, such as in breakout education sessions at a trade show or convention. It is less effective at talks where additional business must be conducted and the group addressed by others after your talk; doing the green sheet in this case may disrupt the meeting and annoy the chairperson.

One other thing I recommend you do is professionally audiotape or videotape the speech. This enables you to capture the presentation and reproduce it in audio or video form to be used as an audiovisual brochure or bait piece. We'll talk more about how to use audiotapes and videotapes of presentations in a bit. For now, keep in mind that if you intend to reproduce the audio or visual portion of the seminar as a marketing tool, it must be professionally recorded. Hand-held video cameras and little portable cassette players won't do. Look under audiovisual services in the Yellow Pages to find studios or independent professionals who can do the taping for you.

Immediately after the seminar.

I said earlier you shouldn't mix in any selling with your presentation. But it's perfectly okay to give a 1- or 2-minute commercial immediately following your talk. After your conclusion and the applause that follows, you say, "One more thing: My company provides XYZ services, and if you'd like more information on what we do, just write 'TIK' (for Technical Information Kit) on your business card, give it to me, and I'll make sure the information is sent right away." This encourages people who are prospects and have some interest to give you their business cards and request a brochure.

Some presenters write out the closing commercial on an index card and ask the conference leader or meeting chairperson to read it for them. This further insulates the presenter from being perceived as a salesperson and comes across almost as an endorsement from the meeting sponsor.

Some presenters close by saying, "There is more information about what we do in the brochures on the table in the back of the room, and they're available if you're interested." This doesn't work too well. After a presentation, most people seem disoriented or in a hurry to get to the next session, and they will breeze by such a table without a second glance. You'll get better results using the "TIK" or green sheet methods I've described.

You might want to write out the introduction to your talk as well as the closing comments for the sponsor or chairperson to read. This is the one other place where a little soft sell is appropriate, if done in a low-key manner. Have the meeting chairperson read your bio, which you have written like a Resource Box. Instead of just saying where the presenter went to college or that he or she has a lovely family, give the job title, company, a short description of what the company does, and tell where it is located.

Follow-up after the talk is over and everyone has left.

Once the presenter returns to the office with a pile of business cards or evaluation forms, you should enter the names into your prospect database. Use a filter or key so you can target this list segment later separately from the rest of your prospect list, if you wish to. In the meantime, by putting their names in your prospect database, you ensure automatic repeat follow-up by whatever marketing methods you already have in place for selling to your database.

Send a personalized letter to attendees. Thank them for coming, and offer to answer any questions or send additional literature on your product or service. If you promised to send a reprint of your talk or some other information, enclose it with the letter. If you didn't offer such information during the talk, do so now, in your letter. Enclose a business reply card they can use to request the reprint, booklet, or whatever you are offering.

Another thing you can offer or even enclose (if the list is small) is an audiotape or videotape of your talk. This doesn't have to be a million-dollar production, but it should be professionally recorded and edited. Because of the lower recording, editing, and duplication costs, and also because most company presenters are not smooth on camera, I usually recommend making an audiotape of select talks rather than video. A video must be more polished and requires more production time.

If your subject is best communicated visually, you may need to use a videotape. A talk on mathematics or engineering design doesn't lend itself well to an audiotape presentation, because of the complex equations, mathematics, and graphs the speaker is showing or drawing on flip charts. If there is a live demonstration of a product, this may also require video to be meaningful when reproduced.

Using audiotapes of presentations as a marketing tool

Speaking from personal experience as a consultant and copywriter who sells his own services, I can tell you that audiotapes of speeches and talks I have given have been enormously effective as a marketing tool. I recommend audiotapes to clients frequently, and those who use them report good results.

Why are audiotapes such an effective promotion? One reason is that most of the marketing materials your prospects receive are paper—two-dimensional. An audiotape is three-dimensional, so it stands out in a crowded in-basket.

A second reason audiotapes work well is that more and more businesspeople own cassette players and regularly listen to spoken-word audio cassettes. More new cars than ever before are being equipped with audio cassette players, so your prospect can listen to your cassette during time spent driving to and from work.

A real case history: A prospect called me about doing some consulting work on a direct mail project. I sent him my literature and included an audio cassette recording of a seminar I gave on "How to Boost Your Direct Mail Response Rate." The prospect listened to it that night driving home and hired me the next day. He said, "I listened to the entire tape and after it was finished, I was sold."

Here are some ideas for making good use of audio cassette recordings of talks and seminars:

- Include an audio cassette in the inquiry fulfillment package you send to prospects who request more information on your product or service. It will make your package stand out, and they will get to it sooner.

- Offer a free copy of the audio cassette as a bait piece to people who respond to your direct mail or print ads.

- Enclose audio cassettes with outgoing "cold" mailings sent to rented lists of names. This is expensive, but it is an attention-getter and works with some audiences—especially those who are jaded and get a lot of mail.

- Send a letter to your customer and prospect database telling them about the recent presentation, and offer to send them the audio cassette recording of it at no charge.

15

How to Create a Winning Inquiry Fulfillment Package

The importance of inquiry fulfillment

When you think about how most companies do business-to-business direct marketing, it's amazing. They spend countless hours, and thousands of dollars, trying to come up with all sorts of promotions designed to do one thing: generate sales leads. These promotions are professionally produced, beautifully written, and carefully planned. The copy has been written by a pro, then checked and rechecked through the corporate approval process. Every *i* is dotted, every *t* crossed. Now, if the company has done things right, they are rewarded with the leads they are seeking. These leads are expensive—they might cost $10, $20, $30, or more per lead. Each one represents an opportunity to make a sale.

So what do they do next? They mail out literature with a photocopied, sloppily typed, hard to read cover letter that has no "sell" in it at all. Often, there is no reply element, and no instructions on what to do next. The result is that the brochure may be read or filed, but no action is taken by the prospect. The hot lead grows cold, and no sale is made.

I'm constantly amazed that companies spending huge amounts of money to generate leads spend very little time and effort in the follow-up of those leads. They mail a top-quality package to generate the lead, then send out a poorly conceived follow-up package.

Yet the inquiry fulfillment package is as important as the mailing that generated the lead, and maybe more so. A good inquiry fulfillment package can move the prospect to take action—the next step toward a purchase decision. A weak package can dampen initial interest or, at best, do nothing to further the prospect's interest. This chapter looks at the elements of a successful inquiry fulfillment package and also discusses the best way to follow up so that the maximum number of leads is converted to sales.

How quickly must you respond to inquiries?

The answer is: faster than ever. Modern innovations such as modems, the fax, electronic bulletin boards, and voice mail have made your prospect accustomed to instant gratification when it comes to getting information. Nowadays, when customers or clients want something done, they usually want it yesterday. The same holds true for many prospects requesting information on your product or service. I have seen this first-hand in my own business: The more serious the prospect and the more genuine their interest, the more likely they are to be in a hurry to get your material.

So how quickly should you respond to inquiries? The inquiry fulfill-ment package should be mailed first class to the prospect within 48 hours of your receipt of the sales lead. If you will be much slower than that, you might consider sending a postcard acknowledging receipt of their request and telling them that a package is on its way. The postcard should include a telephone number the prospect can call if the need is urgent.

In today's fast-paced world, however, even a 48-hour turnaround might not be fast enough. By the time the material is mailed, delivered by the post office, and routed through the mail room to the prospect's desk, four or five days may have passed. That's fine for routine inquiries. But if the prospect has indicated serious interest, you may want to respond faster.

One technique is to send some preliminary information to the pros-pect via fax, then follow up with a more complete literature package in the mail. Lou Weiss, of Specialty Steel in Leonia, is a pioneer in doing this. Lou had a standard two-sided sell sheet printed in four colors. He created a black-and-white version of this specifically to be sent via fax. Instead of photos, he used simpler line art so the material would fax clearer. Now he has set up his desktop computer system so that a personalized note from a salesperson to the prospect can be added to the sell sheet fax.

I do the same thing in my seminar business. I have a standard package for each of my seminars (one on direct mail, another one on copywriting, etc.). Each contains a fact sheet on the seminar, audiotape, article reprints, and other materials. I mail the package first class the day I receive an inquiry. But sometimes a prospect has to make a quick decision about booking me as a speaker and wants to get material quickly to show a committee. Each seminar fact sheet is set in large, legible type, so the fact sheets can be faxed immediately, with the other materials to follow in the mail.

If you sell a product or service needed on an urgent basis, or your prospects are typically in a hurry, consider making a one- or two-page sell sheet designed specifically as "fax fulfillment literature." There will be more and more demand from prospects and customers in the future for this type of instant response to requests for information. You should prepare for it now.

The elements of an inquiry fulfillment package

Although the contents vary widely, a classic inquiry fulfillment package usually includes the following: (1) outer envelope, (2) cover letter, (3) product brochure, (4) inserts, and (5) reply element. Let's look at each element in a bit more detail.

Outer envelope

Mail your material flat in a 9-by-12-inch outer envelope. If your package is bulky, consider using a padded envelope to protect the material. First impressions are important, and prospects are put off by brochures that are crinkled or ripped.

The outer envelope should be imprinted or rubber-stamped with either of the following teasers:

HERE IS THE INFORMATION YOU REQUESTED
or
HERE IS THE INFORMATION YOU ASKED US TO SEND YOU

Without this message, prospects might mistake your package, which they requested, for unsolicited direct mail. And, because prospects are more likely to open and read material they sent away for than a direct mail package they didn't ask for, you need this teaser to identify your package as fulfillment material.

One business owner told me he doesn't stamp the outer envelopes in his fulfillment kit because he thinks everyone uses "HERE IS THE INFOR-

MATION YOU REQUESTED," and people are tired of seeing it. It's true this is used widely, but I know of no substitute. And a blank envelope risks being mistaken for direct mail. So use this teaser.

Cover letter

Should you agonize over the cover letter and treat it as an important promotion? Or is it just routine correspondence that people throw away without a second glance, and therefore not deserving of much attention? Opinions are split. Many industrial manufacturers either don't use cover letters or else send out form letters that are written so badly they are meaningless.

Companies doing classic two-step direct marketing (generate the lead, convert to sale), on the other hand, will tell you that the cover letter is an extremely important part of the fulfillment package—perhaps the most important part. The cover letter, they say, is what determines whether the prospect will order or not. What about you? Do you need a great cover letter for your inquiry fulfillment package? Here are some guidelines:

- If you have a complete, clearly written sales brochure that tells the whole story persuasively and in an interesting fashion, you don't need an elaborate or hard-sell cover letter. Just a short note will do.

- If you do not follow up inquiries by telephone and instead rely on your fulfillment package to make the sale by mail, the cover letter is all-important and is the primary vehicle for communicating the sales message.

- If you have a generic brochure that doesn't speak to the prospect's particular application or market, a cover letter that addresses specific concerns of prospects running those applications or operating in those markets can help overcome the fact that the brochure does not target the prospect's needs and concerns.

- If you do not have a brochure, or if the brochure is mainly a visual piece without much information, you can use a longer cover letter to convey the missing information.

I think that an inquiry fulfillment letter enhances the selling power of all inquiry fulfillment pieces, and I do not recommend mailing your inquiry fulfillment materials without one. A brochure mailed "bare" in the mail somehow lacks warmth, appeal, and the human touch most of us look for in today's fast-paced, impersonal, high-tech business world.

Also, many prospects are so busy that *they do not remember requesting your literature even when you respond to their requests immediately.* The letter orients prospects, reminding them of who you are and why they requested your company's literature in the first place.

Most inquiry fulfillment letters are dull and lifeless, or so generic as to be meaningless. If yours put you to sleep, rewrite them so they are breezy, light, fun to read, and interesting—much like any good direct mail letter. Here are some guidelines for writing the inquiry fulfillment letter.

Thank the prospect.

In most cases it's best to begin by thanking the prospect for requesting your material. Examples:

"Many thanks for your inquiry, which we received today."

"Thanks for your interest in [name of product]. The information you asked us to send is enclosed."

The main purpose of such a beginning is not actually to thank your prospect (although that's always nice), but to remind them that this is *material they requested*—something they may not realize right away.

Focus on the prospect's need or problem.

Many inquiry fulfillment letters concentrate on talking about the company. Avoid this. The company is always of some interest to the potential buyer, but it is almost always of less interest than the product or service. And the product or service is of less interest than the problem or requirement the prospect has.

Avoid repeating the brochure.

Another mistake is to use the cover letter to repeat all the facts in the brochure or describe in detail the various brochures you are sending. The brochures, if done properly, should stand on their own, so there is no need to rewrite and repeat their contents in your letter, or explain to the prospect the contents of each brochure in the package.

Figure 15-1 shows a letter that commits this error, and you can see how deadly dull it is. (Don't you agree this is typical of many of the inquiry fulfillment letters you receive?) What's wrong with this letter? Here are some of the typical mistakes you see in this type of letter:

Figure 15-1 Typical Fulfillment Letter

Mr. Ron Brick
Chief Engineer
Chemtech Corp.
Anytown, USA

Dear Mr. Brick:

CHEMICAL PROCESSING magazine has informed us of your interest in the level detectors manufactured by our firm for use in the chemical processing industry. As you may perhaps know, we are one of the oldest and most well-respected manufacturers of such equipment, and our product line includes the following types of level detectors: Beam Breaker, Bubble Diaphragm, Capacitance, Conductive, Differential Pressure, Displacer, Float and Tape, Glass and Magnetic Gauge, Hydrostatic Pressure, Inductive, Infrared Microwave, Optic Sensor, Paddle, Pressure-Sensitive, R-F Admittance, Radiation, Sonic Echo, Strain Gauge, Thermal, Tilt, Vibration, and Weight and Cable Level detectors that are described in the enclosed technical sales literature.

Since you may also have requirements for our other types of process equipment, we are enclosing our All-Line Catalog and Data Sheets with the request that you fill in the Data Sheets for the consideration and recommendations of our engineering applications. Finally, as our Company is now in its fourth decade of continuous service to its many Customers in this Country and Abroad, we are sending along a reprint of our latest annual report, which will give you more information on our activities. We will await with interest your specific inquiries. Thank you once again for contacting us.

Very Truly Yours,

John N. Guterl, President

1. The paragraphs are too long. The whole letter looks dense and intimidating to read.

2. The language and style is antiquated and stuffy. ("As you may perhaps know . . . " "We will await with interest your specific inquiries.")

3. The listing of types of level detectors is boring and should be on a separate sheet (or at least the items should be separated by bullets for easier reading).

4. There is an offer ("fill in the Data Sheets"), but the prospect is not given a reason or benefit for doing so ("consideration and recommendations" is vague and has little appeal). The sentence also reads as if the writer is telling the reader to do work, something your prospect wants to avoid.

5. There is too much about the company and its reputation. It comes across as bragging.

Contrast this letter with Figure 15-2, which is not perfect, but is (in my opinion) far superior.

Figure 15-2 Improved Fulfillment Letter

Mr. L. Moore
Project Engineer
Spartan Co.
Anytown, USA

RE: Pelletizing Information

Dear Mr. Moore:

Thanks for your interest in our Pelletizers. Literature is enclosed that will give you a pretty good idea of the simplicity of our equipment and the rugged, trouble-free construction.

The key question, of course, is the cost for equipment to handle the volume required at your plant. Since the capacity of our Pelletizers will vary slightly with the particulates involved, we'll be glad to take a look at a random 5-gallon sample of your material. We'll evaluate it and get back to you with our equipment recommendations. If you will note with your sample the size pellets you prefer and the volume you wish to handle, we can give you an estimate of the cost involved.

From this point we can do an exploratory pelletizing test, a full day's test run, or we will rent you a production machine with an option to purchase. You can see for yourself how efficiently it works and how easy it is to use. Of course, the equipment can be purchased outright, too.

Thanks again for your interest. We'll be happy to answer any questions for you. Simply phone or write.

Very truly yours,

Robert G. Hinkle, Vice President, Sales

The best inquiry fulfillment letters talk about the prospect's need or problem and suggest definite steps the prospect can take to solve that problem. These steps also lead, of course, to evaluation and eventual purchase of the seller's product.

The letter in Figure 15-2 works because it outlines a specific step (testing the 5-gallon sample) that is relatively easy to do and makes a lot of sense. It also gives the prospect a choice of options for going further (exploratory test, full-day test run, rental, or purchase). The language is friendly, informal, and conversational, like one friend talking to another. This is what your letter should sound like. Short paragraphs and indenting each paragraph further add to the readability and appeal of this letter.

How long should the letter be? For most business-to-business and industrial offers, a single page should suffice. However, I have seen three- and four-page fulfillment letters that got read and were effective. So it depends on how much you have to tell and whether you can write a longer letter that will sustain a prospect's interest.

Product brochure

As Larry Whisenhant, advertising manager of Koch Engineering, observes, "The brochure—what they asked for—is the most important element in the inquiry fulfillment package." Virtually every business-to-business marketer needs a brochure describing their product or service; in today's market, it is virtually impossible to do business without one. The brochure is the accepted means of communicating product information to someone who makes an inquiry. Without one, you won't be taken seriously; people won't think you're a real company.

When I started in this business in 1979, I produced elaborate, expensive, four-color brochures for my employer, an electronics firm, with the typical brochure running 16 to 32 pages. The trend today is away from longer brochures. Most of the brochures I now write for clients are 4 pages; some are 6; and I occasionally do 8- and 12-pagers. But that's rarer and rarer.

The trend is also away from elaborately designed and expensively printed full-color pieces toward simpler, less elaborate, less costly two-color literature. With technology changing so rapidly, you risk having an expensive brochure go out of date even while it's being printed because your product specifications change. Less costly brochures, produced in smaller press runs, are used today because the smaller press run means you won't be throwing out quite as many old brochures when the piece is updated and a new version printed, which happens more and more frequently.

In fact, many companies are maintaining mechanicals of their brochures in electronic form on in-house desktop publishing systems and printing up extremely small quantities at a time. With the desktop system, changes to a data sheet can be made in the morning and the new sheets delivered by the printer in a few days.

How many different brochures you have is up to you. Some companies like to have one brochure that fits all occasions and do not tailor literature to the market. Other companies have separate brochures for each product line, for each product, and even for each application or market.

The trade-off is cost versus effectiveness. It costs more to do many literature pieces tailored to different markets and applications; on the other hand, such pieces speak more directly to the needs of different prospects and are therefore more effective. See Chapter 10 for additional tips on producing brochures.

Inserts

Inserts are any pieces of paper (or any objects, for that matter) that you put into an inquiry fulfillment package along with the brochure and reply element. Typical inserts include:

- Spec sheets and data sheets
- Product briefs
- Application notes
- Case histories/user stories
- Article reprints
- Press releases
- Reprints of letters from satisfied customers in the prospect's business or industry
- Fliers
- Photos
- Drawings and diagrams
- Product samples

The question is whether to have one standard inquiry fulfillment package that never varies or to customize each package by selecting and adding inserts appropriate to each prospect's requirements. The trade-off again is cost versus effectiveness.

Having a standard package saves time (and therefore money), because it does not require someone to sit down, think about which inserts are appropriate, pull them, and place them in the envelope. If you receive huge quantities of inquiries from a large market of people with pretty much the same level of interest and needs, you should probably use one standard package, as customization would be impractical and probably not beneficial.

On the other hand, using a customized package allows you to deliver to prospects an initial sales pitch that is much more relevant and therefore interesting to them. If you handle a modest quantity of inquiries, and your product or service is highly tailored to the individual needs of each customer, you should probably start building a file of inserts so each package can be tailored to the interests of that particular prospect.

You can determine what should be sent to each prospect either by reviewing their answers to questions you posed on the reply form they used to make their initial inquiry, or by making a brief follow-up call and asking a few pertinent questions before mailing your material.

I have used both types of packages for clients and myself. In my copywriting business I send out highly customized inquiry fulfillment kits, taking time to select article reprints and copywriting samples relevant to the prospect's needs. In my seminar business, however, I have standard fact sheets on each program, and these go out with the same demo tapes and background material to every prospect. The choice of whether to customize depends on your resources, your product or service, and the nature of the customers you serve.

Reply element

The inquiry fulfillment package should contain a reply element. This should lead the prospect to the next step in the buying process. Since you've already gotten an inquiry, the inquiry fulfillment reply form should be designed so that it brings back a stronger level of commitment than the initial mailing. You might ask the prospects to provide certain information about themselves and their requirements. Or you might actually ask for the order. Again, it depends on the sales cycle for your particular product.

The most common type of reply form used in inquiry fulfillment packages is an 8-1/2-by-11-inch sheet of paper designed as a questionnaire or fill-in spec sheet. It is printed on one or both sides. These days, the primary method for returning it is via fax, and you should encourage this. But also tell the prospects where to mail it, if they prefer mailing to faxing. Your phone number should also be highlighted in case they prefer to call; many do not want to fill out even simple forms and would rather go through the points in a phone call with you.

I recommend you print the reply form on blue, pink, yellow, gold, or other brightly colored stock, anything except white or off-white. This makes it stand out from the other elements in the package and draws attention to the fact that you have provided a mechanism the prospect should use to take the next step. You can also draw attention to the reply form by referring to it, by color, in your cover letter. For example, write "Just complete and mail the enclosed yellow Needs Assessment Form."

Give the form a title that creates the perception of importance. Instead of reply form, you can call it an audit, needs assessment, survey, questionnaire, specification sheet, or analysis sheet. If the prospect gets a free estimate for filling in and returning the form, call it a "Free Estimate Request Form." If the form is used by the prospect to communicate preliminary requirements, call it a "Preliminary Requirements Transmittal Form."

Do you need to include a reply envelope? No. The prospect will either fax the form back or give it to a secretary, who will mail it in a company envelope.

Folder

An optional element of the inquiry fulfillment kit is the pocket folder. The folder is usually printed on glossy stock, with the company name, logo, and possibly some artwork or graphic design on the front cover.

Inside there are one or two pockets for holding the various brochures and other inserts. Often one pocket is die-cut to hold a business card. The back is either blank or imprinted with the company logo or a continuation of the front cover graphic.

Such folders are optional, and I have no strong feeling about them one way or the other. They do add expense, so if the cost of inquiry fulfillment is an issue with you, you probably don't want to use a folder, and the package will likely be just as effective without it.

On the other hand, if conveying a professional, high-class quality image is important, and the extra 50 cents or $1 for the folder isn't a big factor, use pocket folders if you so desire. They're especially useful if your fulfillment kits have lots of different brochures and inserts that must be held together.

Conclusion

As I said in the beginning, no single book can completely cover all that can be said about business-to-business marketing, and this one is no exception. Instead of being comprehensive in my coverage, I've chosen to be selective. What you have here are the techniques I practice every day—utterly pragmatic, nuts-and-bolts advice I have found works well and does not require excessive expenditures.

These tips and techniques can increase your response rates, reduce your marketing costs, and get you the leads and sales you want. Please try the ones you feel are appropriate for your business, and let me know the result.

Appendix: Sources And Resources

There's plenty of good information available on direct marketing. What follows is a sampling of some of the resources I personally use and can recommend.

Publications

BUSINESS MARKETING MAGAZINE
740 North Rush Street
Chicago, IL 60611
(312) 649-5260

Monthly magazine devoted exclusively to business-to-business marketing.

DIRECT
Cowles Business Media
6 River Bend Center
P.O. Box 4949
Stamford, CT 06907-0949
(203) 358-9900

One of several monthly magazines covering the direct marketing industry. Free to those in the business. Mixes news, analysis, case histories, and how-to.

DIRECT MARKETING MAGAZINE
Hoke Communications
224 Seventh Street
Garden City, NY 11530
(516) 746-6700

A monthly magazine covering the direct marketing industry. Many how-to articles.

THE DIRECT RESPONSE SPECIALIST
Galen Stilson
Stilson & Stilson
P.O. Box 1075
Tarpon Springs, FL 34688
(813) 786-1411

Monthly newsletter on selling via direct-response advertising and direct mail. Good how-to's on the basics of direct marketing.

DM NEWS
Mill Hollow
19 W. 21st Street
New York, NY 10010
(212) 741-2095

Weekly newspaper covering the direct marketing industry. Free to those in the business.

JEFF DAVIDSON
Jeffrey P. Davidson, CMC
3713 S. George Mason Drive, #1216W
Falls Church, VA 22041
(800) 735-1994 or (703) 931-1984

Davidson is the author of 1,900 articles, 17 books, and numerous audio cassettes, many on marketing and sales topics and all of them excellent. Call or write for a catalog and order form.

THE LEVIN REPORT
Don Levin
Levin Public Relations
30 Glenn Street
White Plains, NY 10603-3213
(914) 993-0900

A newsletter presenting practical, proven public relations tips and techniques.

THE LIBEY LETTER
Donald R. Libey Consultancy Inc.
1308 Keswick Avenue
Haddon Heights, NJ 08035
(609) 573-9448

A highly informative monthly newsletter on the strategies, trends, and future direction of business-to-business direct marketing. Recommended.

THE MARKETING COMMUNICATIONS REPORT
Pete Silver
P.O. Box 570217
Miami, FL 33257-0217
(305) 252-7757

Short, concise, lively monthly newsletter providing marketing tips and ideas. Silver is expert in all phases of marketing communications, especially use of newsletters and toll-free 800 numbers as marketing tools.

SURE-FIRE BUSINESS SUCCESS CATALOG
Dr. Jeffrey Lant
JLA Publications
50 Follen Street, Suite 507
Cambridge, MA 02139
(617) 547-6372

Quarterly 16-page catalog containing more than 120 recommendations on small-business marketing and management. Call or write for free one-year subscription.

TARGET MARKETING MAGAZINE
North American Publishing Co.
401 N. Broad Street
Philadelphia, PA 19108
(215) 238-5300

Monthly magazine covering the direct marketing industry. Concise, quick-reading format. Free to those in the industry.

WHO'S MAILING WHAT? and THE DIRECT MARKETING ARCHIVE
Dennison Hatch
P.O. Box 8180
Stamford, CT 06905
(203) 329-2666

Unique monthly newsletter analyzing winning direct mail packages (mostly large-volume consumer mailings). Subscribers gain free access to the Direct Marketing Archive, a large collection of sample direct mail packages organized by category.

Mailing list brokers/consultants

EDITH ROMAN ASSOCIATES
Steve or Wayne Roberts
875 Avenue of the Americas
New York, NY 10001
(800) 223-2194

Good mailing list broker for business-to-business mailing lists.

IRV BRECHNER
P.O. Box 5125
Ridgewood, NJ 07451
(201) 445-7196

One of the best mailing list brokers for computers and high-tech.

MORRIS DIRECT MARKETING
Ken Morris
1376 Midland Avenue, Suite 104
Bronxville, NY 10708
(914) 776-1777

A top mailing list consultant and broker specializing in financial, computer, and high-tech lists.

Letter shops

FALA DIRECT MARKETING
Mitch Hisiger
70 Marcus Drive
Melville, NY 11747
(516) 694-1919

Good full-service letter shop, especially for personalized mailings. Send for free booklet, "Should I Personalize?"

JERRY LAKE MAILING SERVICE, INC.
Jerry Lake
15 Bland Street
Emerson, NJ 07630
(201) 967-5644

Good full-service letter shop. Reasonable prices, especially for smaller-volume mailings.

Graphic artists

STAN GREENFIELD
39 W. 37th Street, 14th Floor
New York, NY 10018
(212) 889-0762 or (201) 902-9773

First-rate freelance graphic artist specializing in direct mail.

RUTLEDGE & BROWN COMPANY
Steve Brown
25 West 39th Street, Suite 1101
New York, NY 10018
(212) 730-7959

Freelance graphic artist specializing in brochures and collateral; also does excellent work in direct mail. Lots of business-to-business experience.

Desktop publishing

MARTIN UNLIMITED
David Martin
2 Marine View Plaza
Hoboken, NJ 07030
(201) 798-0298

Quality Macintosh desktop publishing at reasonable prices.

Books on business-to-business marketing

Tracy Emerick and Bernie Goldberg, *Business-to-Business Direct Marketing* (North Hampton, N.H.: Direct Marketing Publishers). Hardcover, $69.96.

Solid information on business-to-business direct marketing. Especially strong on planning, strategy, databases, catalogs, and telemarketing.

Roy G. Ljungren, *The Business-to-Business Direct Marketing Handbook* (New York: AMACOM, 1989). Hardcover, 456 pp., $65.

A thorough and comprehensive book on all aspects of business-to-business direct marketing.

Howard G. Sawyer, *Business-to-Business Advertising: How to Compete for a $1-Trillion-Plus Market* (Chicago, Ill.: Crain Books, 1989).

A lively collection of articles on business-to-business advertising. Out of print.

George C. McNutt, *Business/Industrial Marketing and Communications: Key to More Productive Selling* (Chicago, Ill.: Crain Books, 1978).

A nuts-and-bolts treatment of how to manage a business-to-business marketing communications program. Out of print.

Profiting from Industrial Advertising Sales Leads (Cleveland, Ohio: New Equipment Digest Magazine, 1984). Hardcover, 138 pp., $15.95.

A practical and valuable book on how to generate more sales leads from industrial advertising. Not generally available in bookstores. Contact the publisher, (216) 696-7000.

Organizations

BUSINESS/PROFESSIONAL ADVERTISING ASSOCIATION
901 North Washington Street, Suite 206
Alexandria, VA 22314
(703) 683-2722

The only national association for professionals involved in business-to-business marketing communications. I have been a member since 1981 and recommend it highly.

DMA
Direct Marketing Association, Inc.
11 West 42nd Street
New York, NY 10036-8096
(212) 768-7277

A national association for direct marketers, the DMA has a separate council that focuses on business-to-business.

NOTE: In addition to memership in DMA, you might consider joining one or more of the many local or regional direct marketing clubs. To find out whether there is such a group in your area, ask colleagues, consult the DMA, or check meeting announcements in *Direct Marketing* magazine.

Conferences

BUSINESS-TO-BUSINESS DIRECT MARKETING CONFERENCE
Box 4232
Stamford, CT 06907-0232
(203) 358-9900, Conference Department

Annual conference on business-to-business direct marketing co-sponsored by the Direct Marketing Association and *Direct* magazine. Usually held in April or May.

DMB
Direct Marketing to Business
Target Conference Corporation
90 Grove Street
Ridgefield, CT 06877
(203) 438-6602

Annual conference on business-to-business direct marketing. I've attended and recommend it highly. Usually held in April or May.

For more information on books, tapes, and other publications by Bob Bly, write for a free "Business-to-Business Marketing Resource Guide":

Bob Bly
174 Holland Avenue
New Milford, NJ 07646.

ALSO BY ROBERT W. BLY

Secrets of a Freelance Writer

The Copywriter's Handbook

How to Promote Your Own Business

Creative Careers: Real Jobs in
    Glamour Fields

Dream Jobs: A Guide to Tomorrow's
    Top Careers

Direct Mail Profits

Ads That Sell

The Elements of Business Writing

Create the Perfect Sales Piece

Selling your Services

Technical Writing: Structure, Standards,
    and Style

Index

About The Author

Robert W. Bly is an independent copywriter, consultant, and seminar leader specializing in business-to-business, industrial, high-tech, and direct response marketing.

He has written ads, brochures, sales letters, direct mail packages, feature articles, newsletters, PR, and marketing programs for more than a hundred clients including PSE & G, Convergent Solutions, Associated Air Freight, CoreStates Financial Corporation, DBM Publishing, Yourdon Inc., Grumman, Sony, Timeplex, EBI Medical Systems, American Medical Collection Agency, Howard Lanin Productions, Fala Direct Marketing, Edith Roman Associates, Value Rent-A-Car, M&T Chemicals, Chemical Bank, On-Line Software, and ITT.

Mr. Bly is the author of 20 books including *Create the Perfect Sales Piece* (John Wiley & Sons) and *The Copywriter's Handbook: A Step-by-Step to Writing Copy That Sells* (Henry Holt & Co.). His articles have appeared in *Direct, Direct Marketing, Business Marketing, Amtrak Express, Writer's Digest, Computer Decisions, Cosmopolitan,* and *New Jersey Monthly.*

A frequent speaker, Mr. Bly has presented seminars on direct mail and other sales and marketing topics to numerous groups including the Publicity Club of New York, American Marketing Association, Business/Professional Advertising Association, Women's Direct Response Group, Direct Marketing Creative Guild, American Chemical Society, Women in Communications, Self-Employed Writer's and Artist's Network, and Financial Advertising and Marketing Association.

He has taught advertising copywriting at New York University and is a member of the Business/Professional Advertising Association. He currently teaches the popular on-site seminar, "How to Use Direct Mail to Generate More Leads and Sales," for corporate clients nationwide.

Questions and comments on *Business-to-Business Direct Marketing* may be sent to:

Bob Bly
174 Holland Avenue
New Milford, NJ 07646
(201) 385-1220